The Screenplay's the Thing

The Screenplay's the Thing

Movie Criticism 1986–1990

BRUCE BAWER

Archon Books 1992

Published 1992 as an Archon Book,
an imprint of The Shoe String Press, Inc.
Hamden, Connecticut 06514

Printed in the United States of America

The paper used in this publication meets the minimum requirements of American National Standard for Information Sciences—Permanence of Paper for Printed Library Materials, ANSI Z39.48–1984 ∞

Library of Congress Cataloging-in-Publication Data

Bawer, Bruce, 1956–
The screenplay's the thing : movie criticism 1986–1990, / Bruce Bawer.
p. cm.
1. Motion pictures—Reviews. I. Title
PN1995.B323 1992 92-7219 791.43'75'09048—dc20
ISBN 0-208-02332-1

Dedicated to the memory of
Josephine Bawer, *née* Józefa Maria Zawadska

Contents

Preface

In 1986 I was invited by Wladyslaw Pleszczynski, managing editor of the Washington-based conservative monthly *The American Spectator,* to serve as the magazine's movie reviewer. It was a post that I happily filled for four years. The job was ideal for a literary critic, providing a needed monthly change of pace from the pieces on Coleridge, Emily Dickinson, Ezra Pound, and the like on which I spent most of my working hours. What helped make it ideal was that Wlady gave me great leeway: his only instructions were to keep the length down (to about 2,000 words per piece) and not to write about too many esoteric or foreign films (as was, alas, my preference). Otherwise I was pretty much free to do as I liked: I could devote my space to one film or several, or could even, on occasion, forget about reviewing entirely and instead address some movie-related topic. Nobody at the magazine expected me—or, at least, made me feel as if they expected me—to write about movies from a political perspective, to take a "conservative" line. Having discovered (in connection with an assignment to review an E. L. Doctorow book for *The Nation*) how unsporting editors of political magazines could be when confronted with opinions of which they didn't approve, I was impressed, during the first few months of my tenure, by my editors' willingness to print, among other things, my criticism of *Top Gun*'s vapid militarism and my praise of the gay love story in *My Beautiful Laundrette.* Yet this gratifying state of affairs didn't last forever: when I submitted my review for August 1990, Wlady said that the editors wouldn't run it unless I omitted a certain passage; as their reasons were, in my view, both political and morally objectionable, I quit. *C'est la vie.*

Since most of my critical writing is about literature, perhaps a few words are in order here about the differences between reviewing books and reviewing movies. I am a serious literary critic, and when I began writing film criticism I considered myself a serious film critic. Yet I soon discovered that, as John Simon has observed,

> the serious film critic finds himself in a uniquely unhealthy situation. A book reviewer is not expected to read all the

> bestsellers and ephemera that come out, yet even the most fastidious film critic, unless he wants to sit around idly for weeks on end, is compelled to review schlock. Can you imagine Lionel Trilling reviewing Rod McKuen, or Edmund Wilson having to write a critique of Jacqueline Susann? Yet that is what a film critic must do.

To be sure, I was not as bad off as some. Reviewers for daily newspapers have to take on every bad picture that comes along; I had the luxury of being able to avoid obvious junk. And I did seek out those movies that seemed to promise at least a degree of aesthetic interest; though I ended up writing a lot of negative reviews, I did everything I could to find good films to write about. Nor did I review them as if they were poetry or literary fiction: to hold most movies up to the highest standards of art would be as pointless as comparing every new Harlequin romance to *Wuthering Heights*. Since these movies were designed, for the most part, as lowbrow-to-middlebrow entertainment, I reviewed them as such, measuring action-adventure thrillers against the best action-adventure thrillers, romantic melodramas against the best romantic melodramas, and so on. I also adopted a more informal tone in my movie reviews that I'd been using in my literary criticism: one simply couldn't talk about *Uncle Buck* in the same way one talked about T. S. Eliot or I. A. Richards. By the same token, however, I had no interest in being a pop-culture consumer guide, giving thumbs-up and thumbs-down verdicts and churning out blurby encomia tailor-made for newspaper ads. (There are, I might add here, two kinds of reviewers: those who go out of their way to pen catchy phrases that cry out to be reproduced by publicists in twenty-point type—e.g., "a sure-fire Oscar contender," "Michael J. Fox has never been more brilliant," "Move over, Meryl Streep"—and those who go out of their way to remove from their reviews every sentence that seems remotely capable of being found suitable for such purposes.)

Literature and movies have little in common. I can never watch a film crew in action without marveling at how many months, how many dozens of people, and how many millions of dollars it can take to put together a very bad movie, when one man can sit in a quiet room with a few pads of paper and a box of pencils and write a masterpiece. Literature demands that a reader be active, engaged, able to concentrate and to envision; movies invite the viewer to be passive and voyeuristic, to relax and soak in sounds and pictures. A novel is created word by word, a movie image by image; a novelist constructs his invented world like a man putting together a car, while filmmakers are presented with a car and must decide where to drive it. Words badly put together add up to nothing, as a car poorly constructed will not run; but a film badly put together may still contain some arresting images and produce a powerful visceral *frisson,* as a drive along country roads without a map or destination may offer spectacular scenery. It is this unique virtue of film that Pauline Kael and her many protégés tend to celebrate. They ridicule movies that try to be too cerebral, too literary, dismissing those with stylistic polish and formal precision as "contrived" and "synthetic" while celebrating for their "vigor" and "authenticity" those that are crude and slapdash. It is as if the principles of art were irrelevant to celluloid. Such critics seem not to understand that the built-in peril of film lies precisely in the ease with which it can be made to gratify those in search of mindless pleasures or documentary-style renderings of reality, and that the ultimate challenge every filmmaker faces is to bring some degree of intellectual sophistication, human complexity, and aesthetic structure to a medium that resists these things at every turn.

And resist it does. Very few great novels have become first-rate movies; some of the best movies, conversely, derive from works that are decidedly not of the first literary rank. *Brief Encounter* was adapted from a short story by Noel Coward, *The African Queen* from a novel by C. S. Forester. Much better films have been made from books by Daphne DuMaurier than from books by Flaubert or Tolstoy or F. Scott Fitzgerald; perhaps no serious writer has been the source of more fine movies than Graham Greene, whose "entertainments" (a term he employed to distinguish his lighter novels from his weightier ones) seem to be scaled just right for film. In the case of many a classic author, there seems almost to be an inverse relationship between the proportions of a given work and the merit of the movie based on it: perhaps the best Henry James film is *The Heiress,* based on the relatively modest *Washington Square;* likewise, the screen version of Melville's story "Billy Budd" works better than that of his magnum opus, *Moby Dick.* The problem with many a film adaptation of a great novel is typified by the Greta Garbo version of *Anna Karenina,* directed by Clarence Brown from a script by Clemence Dane and Salka Viertel. It is a fine film, but one can never stop feeling that the characters of Anna and Vronsky exist on a different scale than the movie itself, the arcs of their personalities transcending the narrow bounds of the film; one is constantly aware that there are levels of thought and action and resonance, worked out in some artistic dimension larger than that of the film, toward which the film itself can only point. A movie like *Ninotchka,* by comparison, seems to be all there: one never feels as if the picture has been cut, as it were, to fit the frame.

As there are differences between literature and films, so there are differences between New York publishers and Hollywood filmmakers—differences which tend to redound to the credit of the former. Though an assortment of non-literary criteria figure nowadays in the acceptance of many a book manuscript, and though good novels are frequently passed over by editorial boards in favor of those that are less deserving, one nonetheless feels relatively confident that many people in publishing care deeply about literature and that most of the age's best writers will thus sooner or later break into print and be appreciated. Perhaps they won't be paid as much money, published in as big an edition, or appreciated as soon and as widely as they should be, but their books will be printed and will eventually find their way to readers who will recognize their worth.

With movies it's different. Unquestionably there are people among us who have it in them to write and direct great films; but does anyone in a position of power care? Of the countless people who aspire to write or direct in Hollywood, the chances of any given individual ever receiving an opportunity to do so depends less on his talent than on his luck, push, perseverence, business savvy, family connections, and ability and willingness to cater to the insipid tastes of the under-21 audience. A responsible movie reviewer is constantly aware that the criteria by which scripts are selected, directors assigned, and production decisions taken are radically different from his own critical criteria, and that the script for a typical studio release these days is likely to be no better or worse than a thousand other scripts that are, at any given moment, languishing in the furnished garden apartments of ten thousand Los Angeles-area waiters and lifeguards and gas station attendants. Indeed, anecdotes about outstanding unproduced scripts are almost as familiar in Hollywood as anecdotes about incompetent nincompoops being signed to write or direct multimillion-dollar productions.

As American movies have declined, so has Hollywood's appreciation for the craft of screenwriting. Since its introduction in the 1960s, the auteur theory—the notion that the director should be regarded as the "author" of his film—has been embraced at all levels. Television entertainment reporters routinely mention a movie's director while neglecting to name its writer; the movie listings in such publications as *The New York Times, The New Yorker,* and Leonard Maltin's widely consulted *TV Movies and Video Guide* invariably cite directors, but only occasionally identify the authors of screenplays. (The late Leslie Halliwell's superior *Film Guide* gives the names of both.) To be sure, a film *can* be too "literary," in the sense that the novel or play or story from which it was adapted has defeated the filmmakers' attempts to assimilate it, resulting in a stiff, lifelessly reverential translation; but a movie can't be too literary in the sense of being too well written or artfully shaped. As I argue in the title piece of this collection, moviemakers seem to have lost sight of the fact that it is not the director but the scenarist who establishes the tone and scope and texture of a film, who pitches the material to the proper scale; it is for the director either to follow through intelligently upon the intentions of the scenarist or to screw up. (There are, to be sure, those instances—*The World According to Garp* reportedly was one—in which the director has such a strong hand in the shaping of a screenplay that he is, in effect, head writer.)

One more thing. The artistic aridity of most American films, in this age of Spike Lee and Jean-Claude Van Damme and Chris Columbus, too often goes hand in hand with an ethical vacuity, a saturation in what one might call Universal City values—in, that is to say, a combination of vulgar materialism and modish liberalism. If films are not engaged in a hyper-Rousseauvian exaltation of childhood ignorance, they're offering viewers an opportunity to celebrate their sensitivity and political correctness. Set in a world without history—a world in which nearly every place on earth (apart from midtown Manhattan) is a variation on Southern California—one film after another betrays a distressing lack of regard for manners and morals, for life's richness and complexity, and for human dignity. The young people that go to today's movies appear to be less interested in the drama (or the comedy) of interpersonal relations than in special-effects spectaculars or two-hour gagfests, in films that are as crowded with tenuously connected jokes or gore or sex or the latest wizardry from International Light and Magic as they are emotionally uninvolving and morally barren. Moviegoers seem not to care—or even notice?—that the heroes they're cheering on are cookie-cutter stereotypes of a sort that give one a new appreciation for the wit and nuance and humanity of even the most familiar thirties and forties clichés: the wisecracking Eve Arden sidekick, the high-toned Lucile Watson matron. But of course to be witty or high-toned in an American movie nowadays is to have walked onto the wrong set. Toniness is Richard Gere playing a corporate raider; wit is Arnold Schwarzenegger saying "Hasta la vista, baby," as he blows away the bad guy; humanity is a slickly cold-blooded surgeon (William Hurt) or lawyer (Harrison Ford) enduring a ritual of suffering and thereby learning to become slickly warm and sensitive. What's especially sad is that many moviegoers, the young as well as the not-so-young, are so accustomed to the plastic versions of themselves that they see onscreen that they often don't even appreciate the rare film—such as *Mr. and Mrs. Bridge* (a first-rate adaptation, incidentally, of two first-rate novels)—that actually captures and illuminates something of the texture and ambiguity of real life.

Reading books is a very private affair; going to the movies is a social event. I attended most of these movies with various friends, at screenings and multiplexes, mainly in New York but also in other cities—from Washington, D.C., to Los Angeles, from Charlotte, North Carolina, to Cannes—and many of these reviews owe a good deal to the conversations that began in the lobby during the closing credits. I want to thank Chris Davenport, Tom DePietro, Jon Kushner, Michael Kwart, Sanford Operowsky, Chip Teply, Sarah Wenk, and Judy White, each of whom has, at some time or other, made the post-film parley at least as diverting and illuminating as the movie itself. And I want to thank my contacts in The Business (a.k.a. The Industry)—namely, my sister, Carol Bawer, and my mother, Nell Bawer—for their comments, advice, and enthusiasm.

SHOOTING BLANKS

Top Gun

Every so often, while watching the current hit *Top Gun*, I found myself fondly remembering *An Officer and a Gentleman*. Now, as movies about the military go, *Officer and a Gentleman* was no *Grand Illusion*, but it accomplished quite well what it set out to do. You believed in Richard Gere's motivation for entering Officer Training School (he wanted, you'll remember, to be a finer specimen of a man than his dissolute father), in the depth of his friendship with his best buddy, in his love for Debra Winger, and in the relationship—at first hostile, and finally mutually respectful—between Gere and sergeant/father figure Louis Gossett. Of course, the film was a compendium of clichés, but it managed to make them feel fresh. It had sensitivity, humor, and chemistry; at times it even seemed to be earnestly—if not very deeply—engaged with genuine moral questions.

Top Gun covers much the same territory, but with nowhere near as much skill or conviction, and with a thoroughgoing lack of moral sense. Teen heartthrob Tom Cruise plays Lieutenant Pete "Maverick" Mitchell, an ace U.S. navy pilot who has been sent for a course in Air Combat Maneuvering (ACM) to the Navy's Fighter Weapons School (nicknamed "Top Gun") in Miramar, California (nicknamed "Fightertown, USA"). Only the top one percent of all Navy pilots are sent to the school, and the top pilot in each graduating class, as we learn during the orientation sequence, gets his name added to a rather tacky-looking plaque on the classroom wall. Maverick makes it his goal to get his name on that plaque.

"Maverick" is an appropriate nickname for Pete. He's Movie Hero Cliché #4A—the guy who keeps driving people in charge crazy because he refuses to play by the rules, and who would have been shown the door years ago except for the fact that, damn it, he's the best at what he does; nobody can touch him. And Maverick is (we keep hearing) the best. He flies, as they say, by the seat of his pants. He's all instinct: "You don't have time to think up there," he says, arguing with an instructor at Top Gun. "If you think, you're dead." (Coincidentally, this also seems to be Cruise's theory of acting.)

But he's also an arrogant showoff. He's been busted from the rank of squadron leader three times for his "showboating," of which we get a prime sample during the opening sequence: In the course of maneuvers over the Indian Ocean, Maverick meets a Soviet MIG-28 and pulls a Blue Angels-type stunt, buzzing the Russkie, upside down, at a distance of about two (yes, two) meters, while his backseat partner, "Goose" (Anthony Edwards), takes a Polaroid of the astonished enemy. (Maverick thus becomes the only American pilot ever to engage a MIG.) Later, on their first day at Top Gun, Maverick and Goose buzz the tower, causing an officer to spill coffee on himself (this becomes a running gag); Maverick is reprimanded for breaking "a major rule of engagement" by going below 10,000 feet. "I don't like you because you're dangerous," says his principal competition at Top Gun, the by-the-book Kazansky, nicknamed "Iceman" (Val Kilmer), whose every aeronautical move is a "perfect example of a textbook maneuver."

Maverick, the film is at pains to convince us, is also a wild man in the sack. He's a notorious ladykiller whose past victims (the lovable rogue!) include an admiral's daughter. When, soon after his arrival at Top Gun, he spots a hot-looking chick at a crowded bar, he makes a public spectacle of his interest in her, grabbing a microphone and crooning "You've Lost That Loving Feeling" at her. The hot chick, naturally, turns out to be Charlie (Kelly McGillis), his new civilian instructor who's just arrived from Washington, D.C. She's not in the habit of romancing her students, but Maverick's boisterous charm soon wins her over. It's love.

Or, at least, so we are supposed to believe. But we don't. We don't, in fact, believe in much of anything in this film. We don't believe in the great brotherly affection that is apparently supposed to exist between Maverick and Goose. We don't believe in the tension that is meant to exist between Maverick and Iceman, or in their requisite end-of-movie conciliation, or in the father-and-son-type bond between Maverick and the top instructor at Top Gun (Tom Skerritt) who, we learn, used to fly with Maverick's old man. It's a stunningly inert, uninvolving film—so much so that we don't even feel anything when Goose perishes in a plane accident.

A great part of the problem, naturally, is that the script (by Jim Cash and Jack Epps, Jr.) is mediocre and the direction (by Tony Scott) superficial. But the weakest link in the chain is without question the vaingloriously vapid Tom Cruise. His performance as Maverick is downright ludicrous. He stalks through the movie with a board up his back and a macho snarl frozen on his face. The point of the snarl, apparently, is to make him look more like a man than a boy, but it backfires: He looks more than ever like an adolescent playing a grownup in a junior high school show—an adolescent, I might add, who has absolutely no star quality, no charisma, no presence whatsoever, but whose every move demonstrates that he himself believes quite the opposite to be the case.

Nor, alas, is he a very convincing ladykiller. Here's the funniest line in the movie—it's Charlie speaking solemnly to Maverick after Goose's death has shattered his self-confidence (a development which we have to take entirely on faith, because Maverick's snarl doesn't waver): "When I first met you, you were larger than life." And she's serious! Likewise, just before they get down to business in the obligatory coition sequence (performed to the hard-driving rhythms of Harold Faltermeyer's banal score), she purrs, "Maverick, you big stud," and it's unclear whether the line is supposed to be a joke, and, if so, whether anybody connected with the film realizes just how big a joke it is.

What is clear, however, is that this is meant to be an intensely sensuous film. We're supposed to be stirred by both the sex and the Air Combat Maneuvering; predictably, the script keeps drawing parallels between the two. When Maverick and Goose walk into a bar full of women, for instance, Maverick says, "This is what I call a target-rich environment"; over drinks, Goose's wife tells Charlie that Maverick once "went ballistic" with a gal named Penny Benjamin; while discussing fighter-plane engagement Maverick shoots Charlie a significant glance and tells her, "When I see something I want, I go after it." The film pointedly cuts from an intimate encounter between

Maverick and Charlie to an F-14 takeoff. "This gives me a hard-on," says a pilot while viewing training films of F-14s in action, and the joke resurfaces during the final air-battle sequence, when some F-14 pilots over the Indian Ocean, Maverick among them, are keeping an eye out for Russian MIGs: "Must be close," says a pilot, "I'm getting a hard-on."

The implicit message throughout appears to be that cruising chicks is more or less like going on a search-and-destroy mission and that war is sexy—that gunning for MIGs, to put it baldly, is a thrilling and manly way of sublimating homoerotic drives. If we take this to be the film's underlying "logic," it may well help to explain why Scott shows us relatively little of McGillis's body while, during a number of seemingly gratuitous locker-room and volleyball-game sequences, he unstintingly exposes the rippling flesh of Cruise and his fellow pilots (several of whom seem, *à la* Stallone, to have undergone extensive muscle-building workouts in preparation for the film). Patently, this is a film that does not shrink from attempting to exploit the most ignorant, infantile, and ignoble attitudes toward both personal and international relations. Yet it is outrageously unsuccessful even at achieving this unworthy objective: for all the fierce fondling and the fancy flying, it is one of the most remarkably dull movies in recent memory.

And one of the most formulaic, too. Like many recent service pictures, *Top Gun* trades on the typical adolescent male moviegoer's conflicting feelings about his father. In *An Officer and a Gentleman* Richard Gere strove to prove himself a better man than his dad; in a film (which I haven't seen) released earlier this year the boy hero stole an Air Force jet and flew to his father's rescue. In *Top Gun* we are told that Maverick is the son of the late Duke Mitchell, a top-notch seat-of-his-pants Navy pilot who mysteriously disappeared in an F-4 in Nam in 1965. The legend (which Maverick refuses to accept but can't disprove because the relevant documents are classified by the Pentagon) is that Duke Mitchell "screwed up" somehow; because he "screwed up," we are to believe, Maverick was unable to get into the Naval Academy. This, the film suggests, is why Maverick is so driven, so cocky, and so damn good. He's out (a) to erase the blot on the family escutcheon, and (b) to be an even better pilot than his dad. "It's like every time we go up there you're flying against a ghost," Goose says to him. This conflict is resolved so clumsily and half-heartedly that you get the feeling even Cash and Epps couldn't get themselves to take it seriously.

What *Top Gun* does take altogether too seriously, however, is the increasingly familiar Hollywood philosophy (nowadays often equated, in filmland, with the American dream) that if you ain't the best, you ain't nothing. Every few minutes somebody or other in this movie speaks of belonging to "the elite" or being "the best of the best" or observes that "There are no points for second place" or that (and here's the moral of the whole shebang) "To be the best of the best you've got to make mistakes and then go on." In the end, of course, Maverick gets a chance to regain the self-confidence he lost after Goose's death. At his class's graduation exercises, news comes of a "crisis situation" in the Indian Ocean: A disabled U.S. Navy ship has drifted into enemy waters (for the purposes of this movie, the less geography you know, the better) and some F-14s are needed to provide air cover while the ship is rescued. Naturally, both Maverick and Iceman are called into action, and when they come up against a couple of Soviet MIGs it is Maverick who mows them down handily, thus proving the superiority of his "instinctive" fighter piloting to Iceman's by-the-book approach. Why this episode doesn't escalate into World War III is anybody's guess.

Given this state of affairs, it is almost a shame that *Top Gun* is so well photographed. The cinematographer, Jeffrey Kimball, has done a masterly job, especially with the breathtaking aerial sequences. But though the film is crowded with lovely light, fog, smoke, and cloud effects, and features a number of arrestingly photographed surfaces, the exquisite camerawork only serves to point up the fact that there's nothing beneath those surfaces. This is, indeed, a "designer film" in the tradition of *Flashdance*; it's a movie in which the magnificently lit and shot beads of water, for example, on the just-showered faces and shoulders of Maverick and his cohorts leave a more lasting impression than their dialogue or the expressions on their faces. And this, ultimately, is the most disturbing thing about *Top Gun*—that such deliberate mindlessness, such calculated vacuity, is brought to bear upon a theme whose implications are of the most solemn consequence. This film lionizes ignorance, venerates immaturity, reveres raw, primitive instinct; it strives aggressively—and, alas, manages completely—not to contradict a single inane illusion of the type cherished by the most horrible sort of teenage boy. Certainly the good old USA deserves better.

LUV STORIES

Letter to Brezhnev
My Beautiful Laundrette

At the beginning of *Letter to Brezhnev* two young Soviet sailors stand expectantly at the railing of a ship entering port, like Frank Sinatra and Gene Kelly in *On the Town*. "Liverpool!" one of them exclaims; "Beatles!" the other replies, demonstrating, apparently, that Soviet sailors are like young people everywhere. We cut to a seedy working-class neighborhood of Liverpool, where young Elaine (Alexandra Pigg) and Teresa (Margi Clarke) decide to forget their troubles and get happy for an evening. And do they have troubles: sexy, streetwise Teresa holds down a dismal factory job stuffing chickens; sweet, stolid Elaine is unemployed, a victim of Britain's crumbling economy.

Though they can't afford it, the girls take a taxi downtown, sharing a joint with the driver; Teresa's original plan is to stiff him, but she ends up paying the fare (plus tip) because "he's one of us." Which is more than can be said for the pair of well-heeled gents who, in the first pub the girls step into, crudely offer to rent them for the night. Teresa takes revenge for this insult by lifting the bigger one's wallet—thus proving herself a proud, clever, and gutsy foot soldier in the British class war (not to mention providing the motivation for a brief chase scene).

But the story doesn't really get underway till our young ladies hit a flashy dance club. There Elaine and Peter (played by the pallid Peter

Firth), one of those two Soviet sailors, lock eyes across a crowded room and fall in love. They meet, they dance, they wander the grimy streets and neck, they gaze up at the stars and deliver some astoundingly corny dialogue. And they have a conversation whose purpose is patently to suggest that the girls' negative image of Soviet life is wholly the result of ignorance and insidious Western propaganda. When Peter, for example, announces that he's from a warm, sunny resort town on the Black Sea, the girls protest: Isn't Russia *cold*? Not all of it, Peter informs them; it has many different climates, "not like here." When they ask about Soviet food shortages, Peter explains patiently that there *are* no shortages; if there are long lines at the stores, it's because the men in charge of distribution are idiots. (Peter, for his part, is surprised by Elaine's unemployment; he observes that in the Soviet Union, if you don't work, you don't eat. Elaine, who's on the dole, replies that "it works that way here too.")

The four end up at a hotel. Teresa and the bearlike Sergei (Alfred Molina), who speaks no English and whom Teresa calls "Eye-gor," have a lusty time of it; but Elaine and her bright, sensitive Peter (who seems to understand the Liverpudlian brogue much better than I do) spend the night jawing about life and stuff. By the time the next evening rolls around—and the men have to rejoin their ship and head back out to sea—Elaine and Peter have cornily declared their mutual ardor. (Peter: "We will be together again." Elaine: "When, Peter, when?" Peter: "I'll always love you, you know.") Screenwriter Frank Clarke doesn't miss a cliché.

During the weeks after Peter's departure Elaine tries to forget him. She attends a party, but the crude English lads there want only one thing from her; she realizes that all she wants is to escape from this dismal, loveless corner of the world and marry Peter. When her letters to the proper authorities don't result in permission to do so, she does what we are apparently meant to see as a gutsy thing: she pens an obsequious plea to the late Uncle Leonid.

The missive does the trick. The Kremlin bosses permit the marriage and invite Elaine to Mother Russia. Elaine becomes a local celebrity. But everybody in town (except Teresa) is against the marriage: her classic foul-mouthed English working-class movie witch of a mother, her horrible Commie-hating friends, a grotesquely cruel reporter who harasses her about being a Red, and an improbably slimy Foreign Office chap who tries to convince her that Peter already has a wife. They all keep yammering at her that if she goes to Russia she'll be sacrificing her freedom. You've got to be prepared, the Foreign Office chap tells her, "to give up *everything*." Her reply:: "I haven't got anything to give up." Elaine, you see, is savvy enough to recognize this "freedom" jazz for what it is: a dastardly fiction designed to keep nice English girls and nice Soviet boys from getting to know and trust and love each other.

For all the message-mongering, of course, *Letter to Brezhnev* is really nothing more than an old-fashioned fourth-rate love story with a twist—girl meets Red, girl loses Red, girl wins Red. Directed by Chris Bernard, it's packed with not only verbal but visual clichés: a newspaper headline spinning into focus, lovers gazing up at a phony-looking skyful of stars. And it's got more than its share of dubious plot developments. Would a British girl really have so much trouble trying to get into the Soviet Union to marry a sailor? Would the Liverpool papers carry it on the front page, if at all? Would a Foreign Office chap actually try to convince her that the young man was already married—considering that the Soviets, presumably aware of the boy's marital status, had already permitted the wedding?

Probably not; but then this is not a realistic film (the graphic *mise en scène* not withstanding) but a romance. And it's a romance in more ways than one. For it's yet another document in the history of the Western left's long-distance romance with the Soviet Union—or, rather, with some vaguely and rosily conceived *idea* of the Soviet Union. If the love story in this film recalls countless banal tearjerkers of the thirties, its view of Russia is astonishingly reminiscent of the blinkered perceptions of American and British Communists during that same decade.

My Beautiful Laundrette is also set in the English slums—London this time—and is likewise concerned with England's faltering economy, with the moral crisis of her working classes, and with a love affair between two young people who are supposed to hate each other. Like *Brezhnev,* it has a grainy, inexpensive look (were both originally shot in 16mm?) and is heavy on grim urban atmosphere. But that's where the similarities end. For *Laundrette* is far more imaginative and sensible, more honestly and delicately felt, than *Brezhnev*. The author (Hanif Kureishi) and director (Stephen Frears) are out not to present a simpleminded argument upon a theme they know little or nothing about, but rather to explore perceptively and dispassionately a milieu they obviously know very well.

The film's protagonist is Omar (Gordon Warnecke), a sweet and gentle young second-generation Anglo-Pakistani who lives in a gloomy flat with his poor, ill journalist father. The old man, who has strong (mostly socialist) opinions, wants Omar to go to college and become a journalist, a leader of his people. Omar, however, chooses instead to work for his wealthy wheeler-dealer of an uncle (Saeed Jaffrey), and soon develops into a canny small-time entrepreneur, graduating from a job washing cars in the uncle's underground parking garage to the managership of his rundown laundrette.

At the same time Omar renews a childhood friendship with a tough Anglo punk named Johnny (Daniel Day Lewis), from whom he has been estranged for years because his father once glimpsed Johnny at an anti-Pakistani rally. Before long the young men are not only friends but lovers, a development that the film treats matter-of-factly. (Interestingly, though there isn't a line of "romantic" dialogue between them, their love is a good deal more convincing than the soppily proclaimed *amour* of Elaine and Peter in *Brezhnev*.) They also become business partners, and together the two of them turn the laundrette into an elegantly hip, almost surrealistically glitzy establishment.

Laundrette has many virtues: wit, intelligence, perceptiveness, an exquisite tone, a well-paced narrative, a gallery of vivid and variegated characters, an excellent ensemble of players. But perhaps the movie's greatest strength lies in its unpolemical yet *engagé* approach to virtually everything it touches. It is plainly the product of a sophisticated moral sensibility, of a mind (or a pair of compatible minds) too fine to be easily violated by a mere idea. The film thus refrains from drawing facile comparisons of value between Omar's homosexuality and his uncle's heterosexuality, between his father's stubborn socialism and his uncle's fanatical capitalism, between Omar's devotion to the Western way of life and his aunt's obstinate loyalty to Pakistani folkways, or between the conflicting claims and grievances of the Anglo-Pakistanis and the lower-class natives. The film's goal, remarkably, is not to score points for this or that side but to understand and illuminate the human condition in all its motley manifestations, and to discover the pathos and humor—and humanity—that proliferate on every front. The only side it takes, indeed, is that of family and friendship—and, most of all, love, of whatever variety—against hatred and factionalism and violence.

This is not to suggest that Kureishi and Frears shrink from an honest examination of working-class despair and racial tension in contemporary England. They don't. But neither do they wallow in nihilism or depict Britain (à la *Brezhnev*) as a place fit only to escape from. On the contrary, they have made a life-affirming film that touchingly and persuasively proclaims the potency of affection, kindness, and hope, a film that celebrates the modest triumphs which bring meaning and even a sort of magic to ordinary lives. The film begins with an image of death—an elevated train rattling past the apartment where Omar and his father live, and where Omar's mother, we learn, recently committed suicide by throwing herself on the tracks—and concludes with an image of life: Omar and Johnny playfully splashing water on each other, cleansing bloody wounds. It's a lovely image, the perfect ending to a wondrously original and affecting film.

EAST MEETS WEST

A Great Wall

As its title suggests, *A Great Wall* is a study in barriers—specifically, the cultural barriers between two branches of a family. One branch consists of a highly successful San Francisco computer exec, Leo Fang (played by the film's director and co-writer, Peter Wang), his wife Grace (Sharon Iwai), and their college-age son Paul (Kelvin Han Yee); the other consists of Leo's sister (Shen Guanglan) in Peking, her husband Chao (Hu Xiaoguang), a retired government official, and their teenage daughter Lili (Li Qinqin). The episodic story concerns a summer vacation during which the Fangs visit the Chaos in Peking (where most of the film was actually shot, with real Red Chinese actors playing the natives). During their time together, the two families observe, bewilder, amuse, and learn from each other, and eventually part to resume their separate (but somewhat altered) lives in their different worlds.

In a way, the film's title is misleading; for to compare the cultural barriers between the Fangs and Chaos to the Great Wall of China is, I think, to prepare the viewer for a somewhat more pessimistic film than Wang (along with co-screenwriter Shirley Sun) has created. This is, indeed, a film not of prodigious divisions or colossal confrontations between cultures but of fine distinctions between two families' attitudes, customs, and standards of living. To be sure, there is the occasional mild animadversion. When Leo tells his sister, for example, that he has quit his position after a disagreement with his boss (he believes he was refused a promotion because he's a "Chinaman"), the sister insists he has acted unwisely: "Never disagree with your leader." Paul's high-fashion American togs likewise provoke reproach from his Chinese kin: the boy's Calvin Klein trousers look to Chao like "work pants," his expensive jacket like a piece of "burlap sacking with patches."

Politics are never explicitly mentioned. That the Chao family is living under Communism is not so much of an issue here as one might expect, and in fact we are reminded of this circumstance only occasionally, and with Oriental indirectness. For example, when Lili bicycles past the Great Hall of the People, we briefly see the portraits of Marx, Lenin, Stalin, and Mao; when Leo and his sister visit their father's shabby grave, Mrs. Chao refers obliquely to the Cultural Revolution: "Father passed away the year the chaos began. We couldn't give him a proper burial." And when a handsome boy named Liu (charismatically played by one Wang Xio) falls for Lili, he attempts (in one of the film's more charming sequences) to woo her by reciting the Gettysburg Address in a fractured but exuberant English.

The latter sort of sequence—a simple, realistic vignette that is plainly and lovingly observed—is the sort at which Wang excels. The film's strength, accordingly, resides largely in its convincing glimpses of the Chinese way of life. Wang takes us into a variety of settings: Lili's English class; a public bathhouse and a school for fashion models, both of which Liu visits in search of work; a gym where children, ranged in military rows, practice their ping-pong serves; a community center where old folks and youngsters alike sit glued to a TV screen, watching an opera performance; a small auditorium where a woman warbles a traditional Chinese melody about the Han Dynasty. Interesting touches abound. There is a view of the Chinese class system in operation—the principal obstacle to the romance between Lili (daughter of a retired Party man) and Liu (who lives in a "junkyard" with his scholar father) seems to be that they are from different social levels. And Wang devotes plenty of attention to the Chinese young people's preoccupation with things Western, especially American: They sing American popular songs and Italian arias; they drink Coke, though the taste makes them grimace; and they attend nightclubs where the dance music consists of extremely lame disco versions of "Oh Susannah" and "The Merry Widow Waltz." Some of the young Chinese even behave like Americans. When, near the beginning of the movie, Liu and his friend Yu greet Lili and her friend Jan in the street, Lili is surprised at Jan's encouragement of their fresh advances. "Why are you saying hi to strangers?" she berates Jan. "You're no American."

Despite this rebuke, however, it is Lili, more than anyone else, whose head is turned by her American relatives. Under the influence of her cousin Paul, she chides her mother for opening her mail, arguing that it's an invasion of her "privacy." (Lili uses the English word because, according to the film, there is no Chinese equivalent.) So fascinated is Lili by Paul that she begins to neglect not only her new admirer, Liu, but her studies ("Since your brother came," Mr. Chao complains to his wife, "I haven't seen Lili open a book") and instead dances around the house in American T-shirts, listening to tapes of rock music. She is supposed to be preparing for the all-important college entrance exam—as in Japan, only the very highest scorers will enter college—but Paul's genial indifference to such matters has infected her.

It should be mentioned here that, in a manifest attempt to contrast studious Chinese and frivolous American youth, Wang gives us, in Paul, an almost unbelievably pinheaded California rich kid—a stereotype of the party-all-the-time West Coast mentality. Paul is aggressively American; in the San Francisco sequence near the beginning of the film, he refuses to attend his Chinese I class and, when Leo scolds him for thus "deny[ing] his cultural background" (as well as for having a Caucasian girl friend), Paul counters that "all Chinese [i.e., Chinese-American] parents are racists. . . . Why do we have to do everything the Chinese way? It doesn't get you anywhere." On arriving in Peking, this spoiled boy is amazed to discover that his aunt's house has squat toilets and no shower bath, and he spends most of the remainder of his on-screen time doing typically American things that astonish his Chinese relatives (e.g., he affectionately smacks his father in the head) and reacting with naive amusement to Chinese mores. Sometimes, to be sure, his reactions are entertaining, but more often than not they make him seem more vacuous than is humanly possible. One cannot help but think that the film would have been more interesting and believable—and the contrast between him and his Chinese counterparts just as effective—had Wang given us a Paul who was intelligent and ambitious but who had made a career choice (to be a jazz musician, say) that for a student in Peking would be all but unthinkable.

Unsurprisingly, it is Paul who is at the center of the film's most dubious subplot. When Lili tells him that she plays table tennis, he boasts, "Hey, that's my sport," and our expectation is that she is going to beat the pants off him. But in fact Paul does very well, not only against her but against the best players the city has to offer—so well, in fact, that by the end of the summer (and the film) he makes it to the finals of the Beijing International Youth Ping Pong Tournament, where, before a large, anxious crowd, he vies for the championship with—who else?—Liu, his rival for Lili's attentions. The *Karate Kid*-type sequence is not only logically inexplicable (what is Paul Fang, who came to China with his folks for vacation, suddenly doing in an international sports competition?) but tonally inconsistent with the rest of the movie; it's precisely the sort of thing that gifted directors stick into their films in order to appease fatuous studio executives.

A Great Wall is, then, uneven. Aside from the ping pong tournament, there is a medical emergency sequence that seems gratuitous. And certain characters—Grace Fang for example—never do develop as fully as one might like. Yet on the whole this is an admirable piece of work—modest, sensitive, and perceptive. Rather than indulge (as one might have expected, given the current state of the celluloid marketplace) in facile, grandiose, and politically modish statements about the Walls Between Societies, Wang has quite remarkably created a film about *people,* a film lovingly attentive to its characters' every gesture, mood, peccadillo, and habit—a film, in short, vibrant with humanity.

DECEPTIONS

Mona Lisa Men

In *Mona Lisa,* the English writer-director Neil Jordan takes a conventional romantic-thriller formula and "classes it up"—spices the car chases with apocalyptic visions, hints at numerous layers of meaning beneath the absurd plot twists. The film (whose distinctive "look" consists of a cross between naturalistic grittiness and "Miami Vice"-style glitz) manifestly wishes to be regarded not only as an absorbing entertainment—which it is—but as a serious contemplation of love, loneliness, and the ubiquity of evil. In particular, like many another ambitious English film of this decade, *Mona Lisa* purports to probe the economic and moral decay of today's Britain, and apparently hopes that we will recognize in its pathetic but good-hearted protagonist—a middle-aged man named George, as in St. George the dragon killer—a symbol of the capacity for valor and virtue that postwar Britain has largely left behind.

When the film begins, George has just spent seven years in a mental institution and is trying to put his life back together. His wife having slammed the door in his face when he tried to return home, he seeks out Denny Mortwell (Michael Caine), an underworld kingpin who is his former employer (and who is apparently responsible, in some way, for his seven-year hiatus). Denny puts him to work as chauffeur for a high-priced call girl named Simone (Cathy Tyson). At first the two don't get along. George, who for all his seedy employment history looks down on prostitution, makes it clear to the exotic Simone that he resents having to work for a "tall thin black tart"; she, for her part, doesn't disguise her disdain for this vulgarian who drives a limo in a brown vinyl jacket, loud Hawaiian shirt, and olive polyester pants. When she tries to buy him some elegant togs, he is insulted, enraged—then touched; she's the first person who's done something nice for him in a long while. The hostility between them begins to evaporate; she shows him her unprepossessing little flat, opens up to him about her past ("I used to work that street," she confesses after an unnerving drive down a chippie-filled block); he asks questions: Do her customers ever fall for her? Her reply: "Sometimes they fall for what they think I am."

Soon she is turning to him for help. She asks him to find Cathy, a young friend of hers who's somewhere out on those raunchy streets. So George begins to haunt the peep shows and whorehouses. The grubbiness disturbs, obsesses him; in a porn-video store, he buys a tape of an X-rated film starring Simone and watches it at his friend Thomas's place. Thomas (Robbie Coltrane) is perplexed. "You used to be my hero, George," he says. "What's happened?" What's happened is that Simone and her fellow prostitutes have gotten to him; estranged from his wife, forced to meet his teenaged daughter covertly, and thrust into this world of adolescent girls who sell their bodies, he is—one gathers—simultaneously overcome with sexual excitement, moral revultion, a tender, instinctive feeling of paternal protectiveness ("Father George," a young hooker calls him), and love for Simone.

Eventually it becomes clear to George that this sleazy turf is not as foreign to him as he had thought; as one false identity after another is stripped away, one hidden connection after another exposed, it develops that he, Simone, and Cathy are all pieces of a Kafkaesque puzzle, functionaries in a Pychonesque empire run by Denny Mortwell. (Or so, at least, Mr. Jordan would have it; actually, these climactic reversals are more silly than surreal.) Ultimately, George acts heroically, virtuously, taking on a monstrous dragon, as it were, to save a beautiful princess; there is mounting tension, violence, death; and yet in the end it becomes clear that, far from striking a blow for innocence, he has, in all ignorance, been crusading on behalf of one sort of sleaziness against another. He has, we are to understand, made the mistake of falling not for Simone but for what he thought she was.

Which is, of course, where the film's title comes in. It's a rather-clumsy one, referring both to the Da Vinci painting and to the Nat King Cole tune (which, in turn, also refers to the painting). Like the subject of the painting, Simone is a woman of mystery, a creature with an enigmatic smile; like the lady in the song, she may be either warm and real or (like the painting) unfeeling and artificial. (Both painting and song, by the way, are worked into the film.) In the manner of many a romantic thriller, then (*Charade, Blindfold, Vertigo,* and *Obsession* come to mind), *Mona Lisa* is about false appearances, about deception.

Yet—the title to the contrary—it is not the deceiver but the deceived, in this film, who is really at the center of our interest. Though Cathy Tyson manages to make Simone convincingly ambiguous, she is hardly as mesmerizing or mysterious as Jordan seems to think she is. Yet if we are more interested in George than in Simone it is less because of Tyson's deficiencies (it would, after all, take a Garbo to give this part everything it calls for) than because of Bob Hoskins's depth and intensity: he's simply so good an actor, so good at making credible both the violence and sweetness submerged beneath George's banal surface, that Tyson seems bland and one-dimensional by comparison. Robbie Coltrane, for his part, manages in his handful of scenes to turn his *ficelle* of a character into someone funny and touching, while Michael Caine is wasted as Denny—he isn't on screen very much, and his character is a shallow piece of business, the usual slimily elegant underworld bigshot. Indeed—despite its taut and witty script, its excellent pacing, and Hoskins's powerful acting—*Mona Lisa* is itself, in reality, a shallow piece of business; and Jordan's attempt to pass it off as something more is the film's ultimate deception.

Doris Dörrie's *Men* (Männer) is an uncommon treat. It's not only a German film comedy—a genre only a bit less obscure than the Mongolian Western—but a wonderfully funny one. Its protagonist is thirty-eight-year-old Julius Armbrust (Heiner Lauterbach), the smugly prosperous creative director of a packaging company, who, on the morning of his twelfth anniversary, is devastated to discover that his wife, Paula, has for the past three weeks been having an affair with a long-haired bohemian "artist." "Is he better than me in bed?" Julius asks desperately. He's had affairs too, but to him this is different: he can't help but feel that Paula's betrayal represents a judgment that he's failed as a man. Deciding to spend the summer away from home and job—and discovering that Paula's lover, Stefan Lachner (Uwe Ochsenknecht), is in the market for a roommate—Julius (under the pseudonym of Daniel) applies for the vacancy. So it is that he casts aside suit and tie, dons T-shirt and jeans, and becomes the tenement roommate of his wife's lover—who, it turns out, is not really an "artist" but a freelance illustrator of brassiere ads and a counterman at a fast-food place called "Heiss and Gut" (Hot and Good).

At first Julius is barely able to conceal his hostility toward Stefan; when, during a morning job, he begins to flag and Stefan says, "Come on, can't you take it anymore?" Julius throws him to the ground and starts strangling him. "You're dangerous! Deranged! A real killer!" cries Stefan after fighting him off. But instead of dividing them, this incident brings them closer; for Stefan thinks that "Daniel" (who, according to Julius's fiction, has just been divorced, quit a lucrative job, and changed life-styles) is suffering a crisis of adjustment, and—being a very understanding sort—he sympathizes. They proceed to develop a tense but genuine friendship, their conversation consisting almost entirely of putdowns—and the more they criticize each other the closer they get. Stefan calls "Daniel" a moralist, accuses him of believing only in "money and power," and makes snide remarks about his credit cards; Julius, for his part, calls Stefan a "sponger," an "overgrown kid . . . lifeless, weak, boring, a failure. You live like you're fifteen years younger than you are. . . . You're proud of being a loser." When Stefan speaks of his love for Paula, Julius says, "Why did you fall for her? Because she lives in a world you'd like to belong to"; when Stefan confides that, in her heart, Paula still "clings to her husband," Julius explains that women like her "dream of glamorous adventure but with no risk. You know what that means? Money. What's it going to be tomorrow? Your toy car [Stefan plays with one] or her husband's Maserati?"

Gradually, "Daniel" persuades Stefan that the only way to get Paula to leave her husband for him is to find a job that pays as well as her husband's. Arranging an interview for Stefan with a friend's firm, Julius helps him select a suit, cuts his hair, teaches him how to behave on a job interview, edits his portfolio, and forces him to really *work* for the first time in his life. "I'll end up looking like her husband," Stefan objects—and that of course is precisely what Julius, a master of packaging psychology, wants.

Like *Mona Lisa, Men* is, in its own humorous way, concerned with deception—not only with Julius's deception of Stefan but, in a larger sense, with the roles men assume, the disguises they wear, to conceal their fear and pain (which explains the gorilla mask that figures prominently in the plot). "I wonder what your disguise is," Stefan says while they're doing laundry together, "the suit or the jeans." Julius replies, "Both." And indeed, for all their differences, deep down both men are essentially the same—they are, in Julius's words, "overgrown kids" whose childish jealousy, criticism, and betrayal of one another should not be taken too seriously. Stefan, for instance, continually sports a puerile pout and plays with his toy car (and, when he gets the big job, buys a real car identical to the toy); Julius (near the beginning of the film) trails Stefan on his kid's bike. They're antagonists, true enough; yet for all their antagonism, they're closer to each other than they could be to any woman, because they *understand* each other. At bottom, they're not rivals at all but allies in the battle of the sexes.

In its preoccupation with the theme of "male bonding," and its view of men as overgrown boys, *Men* seems very American; and Lauterbach and Ochsenknecht, in their characters' mutual devotion, distrust, and derision (as well as their exceptional chemistry), recall a host of American film teams: Abbott and Costello, Hope and Crosby, Martin and Lewis, Newman and Redford, Matthau and Lemmon in *The Odd Couple,* Curtis and Lemmon in *Some Like It Hot.* This American influence should not come as a surprise, for the thirty-one-year-old Dörrie spent several years in the United States, and claims to have found her sense of humor here. ("What I realized when I came back [to Germany]," she told *New York Times* reporter James Markham in a recent interview, "is that we Germans don't have a real feel for humor—or any sense of humor at all.") Yet the filmmakers who have most obviously influenced *Men,* interestingly, are not just Americans but German- and Austrian-Americans—Ernst Lubitsch, Billy Wilder.

On the whole, what makes *Men* stand out among contemporary German films is not just its humor but its apolitical humanity—it's not a feminist or Marxist treatise, not (thank God!) a critique of The System. From beginning to end, the film is fresh, acutely observant, and structurally elegant, building to its hilarious conclusion with a precision reminiscent, again, of *Some Like It Hot* or, more recently, *Tootsie.* Dörrie's touch is always light and sportive, her attitude toward Julius and Stefan consistently affectionate and empathetic. She does not jest at men in order to elevate women; on the contrary, if anybody in the film comes across less than sympathetically, it is Paula—partly because by the end of the movie she seems fickle and phony and easily manipulated, and partly because we simply spend less time with her than with her two men. In this, as in many other ways, *Men* is a surprising—and refreshing—departure from the current norm.

WEIRDOS

Blue Velvet
Down by Law
Tough Guys

When I look back now, it seems to me that I spent countless hours at college in the mid-seventies sitting in a dormitory room and listening to my friends extol the virtues of a movie called *Eraserhead*. Written and directed by one David Lynch, it seemed always to be playing somewhere on campus. "It's so *weird*," my friends would tell me—*weird*, naturally, being a term of exalted, unqualified praise—"and it's even weirder when you're high." Alas, as one who wasn't interested either in "weird" or in getting high, I never did go to see *Eraserhead*. Nor did I catch Lynch's subsequent films, *Dune* and *The Elephant Man*. (Lynch served only as director on these films; the scripts were the work of other, apparently far less weird, individuals.) So it is that I came to Lynch's new film, *Blue Velvet,* which he both wrote and directed, knowing nothing about this notorious filmmaker except what I had heard.

As far as *Blue Velvet* is concerned, of course, what I had heard—and what most of North America has also doubtless heard by now—is that the film is not only weird by extremely disturbing. It is certainly not a movie for children and—what with the obscenity, the profanity, and the graphic rape, violence, sadomasochism, and multilation—it may not be a movie for many adults, either. What makes it so disturbing to this viewer, however, is not so much any of these things in and of themselves—which are, in any event, less shocking than the reviews and the scuttlebutt would lead one to expect—as the fact that Lynch manages, in this film, to communicate quite powerfully a moral vision that is utterly despicable.

The film is set in the real-life town of Lumberton, North Carolina, but from the beginning it doesn't *feel* quite like Lumberton, North Carolina (or, for that matter, like Wilmington, North Carolina, where the picture was actually shot). The major characters' accents are wrong, and the atmosphere is wrong too: Lumberton, as Lynch renders it, feels more like a medium-sized Midwestern city than a small Southern burg. The film is supposedly set in the 1980s, but it feels and looks and sounds more like the fifties; the only significant contemporary touch—and significant it unquestionably is, considering that the plot revolves around a severed human ear—is the hero's earring. Everything is just a bit off—and creepily, insidiously so, in a manner reminiscent of the ominous, synthetic American-home-town-on-Mars in Ray Bradbury's *The Martian Chronicles*.

In the film's opening sequence, Lynch presents Lumberton as a caricature of pure, wholesome, hardworking small-town America. He makes a running surrealistic joke out of the town's name: the call letters of the radio station are W-O-O-D, and lumber trucks keep roaring past in the background while the radio announcer delivers a cheery, hi-ho-hi-ho-it's-off-to-a-day-of-tree-chopping-we-go aubade. This town, clearly, is meant to be perceived as America in microcosm, a place from which, day after day, the Children of Light religiously set forth to tame the dark wilderness. The film's hero, a high-school boy named Jeffrey Beaumont (Kyle MacLachlan), lives with his folks in a nice white frame house with a big green lawn and a garden containing big red and yellow flowers under a solid blue sky. This world of primary colors is photographed in bright, even, and shadowless light, with the objects very sharply defined, and the result is that the well-tended flowers and grass are not beautiful but laughable, grotesque, even a bit chilling, as if to indicate that the sort of wholesome, innocent life suggested by this Disneyish setting is nothing but a banal lie, an impossibility; indeed, the perfectly real flowers and grass look positively phony, like the illustrations in a Dick and Jane book.

Significantly, it is not on that excellently maintained, sunshiny lawn but in the shady wild grass outside of Lumberton that Jeffrey—whose father has just suffered a heart attack while watering the lawn—finds a severed human ear. While he holds it in his hand, the camera closes in on it, as if to enter through it (as through a black hole) an alternate universe; and alas, after Jeffrey delivers the ear to a police detective (George Dickerson), it's as if he *has* entered another world, as if *Mary Poppins* had suddenly given way to *Un chien andalu*. He discovers, from the cop's blonde daughter, Sandy (Laura Dern), that a singer named Dorothy Vallens (Isabella Rossellini), who sings "Blue Velvet" in a local night spot, is somehow implicated in the case. With Sandy's help, Jeffrey does a little snooping, and finds himself drawn to—and, before long, inextricably involved in—Dorothy's smarmy world. That world, which is symbolized by Dorothy's gloomy brown apartment, is the antithesis of his own; it is as starkly real (though the only sign of nature in Dorothy's flat is a phallically long-stemmed potted plant) as the grounds of Jeffrey's home are fake-looking. Likewise, Dorothy herself, a woman of strongly earthy passions, is the opposite of the other young woman in Jeffrey's life, the vapid, antiseptic Sandy. (Incidentally, Dorothy's accent is vaguely European, which seems to suggest that Lynch intends for the two young women to represent a contrast between European experience and American innocence.)

Jeffrey learns that Dorothy is being forced to have sex with a repulsive vulgarian named Frank (Dennis Hopper), who has kidnapped her husband and child. (The ear, apparently, was the husband's.) Taking Dorothy violently on her living room floor, Frank calls her "Mommy" and forces her to call him "Daddy"; he hurts her and she, for her part, manifestly wants to be hurt. Jeffrey, in watching this sadomasochistic encounter from a nearby closet, is effectively witnessing a sort of post-adolescent primal scene; he's an infant all over again, a babe being introduced to a whole new level of sexual awareness. What's most disturbing of all, though, about Frank is that, compared to Jeffrey's unbelievably nice-nice world, this sadistic sicko and his grubby team of conspirators have, for the viewer, an uncomfortable *realness* about them—and it is only a small step from realness to naturalness, from naturalness to rightness. Dorothy, at one point in the film, says, "I know the difference between right and wrong," but the whole purpose of *Blue Velvet* is to confound our sense of right and wrong, to suggest that such distinctions are simpleminded, that what's thought of as "right" can be inhumanly dull and spiritless, and that what's "wrong" can be passionate, vibrant with life. In the logic of this film, indeed, love and evil, passion and violence are essentially one; to feel deeply is to hurt (and to be hurt) deeply; to love is to be obsessed as Frank is obsessed (and as Jeffrey comes to be obsessed) with Dorothy. "You're just like me," Frank tells Jeffrey, and Lynch's implication plainly is that, under the skin, anybody with a capacity for deep emotion is just like Frank; only the bland and affectless, like Sandy—to whom love is a superficial, cheerleaderish entity, lightly bestowed, easily transferred, and powerless to inflict deep or lasting pain—can truly lead productive, orderly, and responsible lives.

Sometimes—for example, when Frank drags Jeffrey, at gunpoint, to a cheap dive where a bizarre little man lip-synchs a pop tune and three fat, garish women stand around watching—the film seems to descend into a broadly campy mode suggestive of John Waters; one has the feeling, at such moments, that Lynch takes nothing seriously, that he is just playing with clichés of black comedy and surrealism and experimenting with pseudo-Felliniesque notions of casting. But on the whole the film succeeds at what is wants to do—which is to say that it is repulsive on a profound level. The conclusion, moreover, is disquietingly ambiguous: when Sandy's father bursts into Dorothy's blood-spattered apartment, gun in hand, and says, "It's all over now," it's hard to tell whether the ensuing happy ending is supposed to represent what really happens or whether it depicts what goes on in Jeffrey's head in the instant before he dies of a bullet from the cop's gun.

The film brings to mind several of Blake's proverbs of Hell: "The road of excess leads to the palace of wisdom." "He who desires but acts not, breeds pestilence." "Sooner murder an infant in its cradle than nurse unacted desires." It also recalls *Heart of Darkness,* with its suggestion that we are all capable of doing unspeakable things to one another, that beneath the tame exterior of civilized modern man lurks a primitive beast. But, unlike Conrad's novel, Lynch's film ultimately leaves us not with a highly moral lesson in the possibilities of evil but with a vision of life that is, in fact, morally reprehensible. *Blue Velvet* may be thought of as posing a question: namely, which is more desirable, to settle for a civilized life of vacuous, superficial cheer, or to allow oneself to sink into the pit of cruel, destructive sadomasochistic passion? Lynch leaves the impression that life presents us with only these two alternatives, and that one would have to be less than human not to choose the latter. The catch, needless to say, is that there *are* other alternatives. But the film's awful effectiveness lies in its ability to make us forget that—for the duration, at any rate.

Visually, *Blue Velvet* would make an interesting double bill with Jim Jarmusch's *Down by Law*. Jarmusch's film is in stark black and white; its first third is set in the lower-class precincts of New Orleans, its second third in a prison, its last third in the Louisiana wilderness. (Hell, purgatory, heaven?) Both the urban and rural settings are shot in deep focus, with high-contrast dramatic lighting, so that nearly every frame, whether it depicts a slum apartment or the Mississippi delta, looks like an artsy documentary photograph.

Played against this naturalistic background, the film's surreal action seems even more surreal than it might otherwise. Jarmusch's two dense, hapless protagonists are essentially mirror images of one another; Zach (Tom Waits) is a down-on-his-luck DJ, Jack (John Lurie) is a small-time pimp. Both of these lowlifes are lone wolves, too dumb to get anything out of a human relationship; we laugh at their morose self-dramatization, at their tacky ambitions, at the way they let themselves get set up. It is not until they are both thrown in prison for crimes they didn't commit that they meet one another—and a goofy Italian named Roberto (Roberto Benigni) whose relentless cheer and chumminess contrast sharply with their wary, glum demeanor. Yet the three cellmates are compelled to become friends, after a fashion. Though Jarmusch (characteristically) never shows us how they manage it, they break out of prison together and, during their flight through the wilderness, learn to care about each other.

Jack and Zach, however, learn nothing from their experience. While Roberto, in a most unlikely way, stumbles upon love and happiness in the middle of the woods, his two companions, eager to shake one another off, part company and head down identical empty roads to identically barren futures—one on the West Coast, one on the East. Jarmusch (who manages to work Robert Frost's poem "The Road Not Taken" into the film—in Italian, yet) wants to make a cyncial point about the illusion of choice, wants to tell us that we don't have any real say in our destinies, that Emerson's self-reliance and Whitman's Open Road are myths, that our only buffer against the random and abusrd cruelties of fate is the attachments that we can form with those whom fate thows in our path. Like Lynch, in short, Jarmusch is out to score a few points against the American dream. But, though the odd tone and the striking photography make *Down by Law* consistently interesting to watch, this stylized, pervasively ironic film leaves the viewer strangely unmoved; it lingers on the mind as an eccentric curiosity, a series of arresting but mute images.

Tough Guys gives us a very different pair of jailbirds. Harry Doyle (Burt Lancaster), 72, and Archie Long (Kirk Douglas), 67, two big-time train robbers, are set free on the streets of L.A. after thirty years in the can. "We ain't changed," Archie says as they leave the Big House in their 1950s-vintage outfits. "The best things never do," Harry replies. But life on the outside *has* changed, and the movie derives most of its humor from our heroes' reactions to new-wave fashion, the fitness craze, gay bars, black street gangs, and the like. It is, in other words, a one-joke movie.

This would not be so bad except for the fact that director Jeff Kanew and writers James Orr and Jim Cruickshank don't keep the joke consistent—sometimes we end up laughing with the tough guys, sometimes at them. It's dishonest: Kanew and company pretend to be making a case for senior citizens' right to self-respect and self-determination, but at the same time they're shamelessly willing to sacrifice their protagonists' dignity for a cheap laugh. You get the feeling, after a certain point in this film, that you care more about the characters than the director and writers do.

As for Lancaster and Douglas, they're the film's strongest assets by far. Even at their least inspired, they have a presence, a magnetism, a way with a line that most of today's young supericons of the screen could never hope to match. Of the two, however, Lancaster creates the more believable character this time out. Douglas's problem seems to be that he is too embarrassed by his role to throw himself into it entirely. His performance has a self-conscious, noblesse-oblige quality about it; it's the sort of acting job you might imagine him giving in a slapped-together, tongue-in-cheek skit at the Friars Club. He does everything but wink into the camera and say, "Hey, I'm not this pathetic has-been, I'm Kirk Douglas, a big Hollywood wheel, still on the 'A' list after all these years. This is just a picture." Physically, he is in excellent shape, though his face looks a bit strange, as if he's had one too many face-lifts; come to think of it, he looks like somebody wearing a Kirk Douglas mask. At any rate, he certainly doesn't look like a man who's spent the last thirty years in prison.

But then, there are a lot of hard-to-believe things in this movie. For instance, since Harry and Archie, who were sentenced to thirty years, have served their full term (which in itself strains one's credulity), what are they doing with a parole officer? Why is Harry, who's been placed in a retirement home, forbidden to have a sexual relationship? And why would any parole officer, even a callow twenty-eight-year-old like Richie (Dana Carvey), involve himself in a hopeless, madcap stunt like the one that ends this film? In a certain sort of way-out farce, needless to say, the lack of logic and credible motivation would be part of the joke; but this is not that sort of film.

What's most disturbing about *Tough Guys* is that when the guys get sick of the straight life and recidivate, we are expected to stand up and cheer for them—which is exactly what Harry's retirement home friends do when they hear on the television news about the guys' return to crime. ("Give 'em hell, Harry!" his lady friend, played by the ever-lovely Alexis Smith, screams at the TV.) Crime, we are meant to recognize, is what Harry and Archie do best; it is what makes them feel important; it is their *raison d'être.* For Harry to sit around a retirement home, and Archie to try to hold down a job washing dishes, is undignified; crime makes them feel young and tough and most of all *important,* and is therefore okay. The movie's moral logic is pure 1980s Hollywood: it honors its heroes for striving, not after truth or beauty or goodness, but after notoriety—and for being willing to do almost anything to attain it.

To say all this is not to deny that *Tough Guys* is intermittently very amusing, even (at least in its opening sequences) rather charming. Nor is it to overlook the fine supporting performances by Charles Durning as an aging cop, Eli Wallach as an aging hit man, and Miss Smith as an aging showgirl. But the fact is that without the talents of Lancaster and Douglas—and, equally important, without our affectionate memories of the two actors' past performances, which cause us to feel an instant empathy for Harry and Archie that the script does little to stimulate—this film would be a feeble offering indeed.

PAST AND PRESENT

Something Wild
Peggy Sue Got Married
Caravaggio

Something Wild is a contemptible film, and the obtuse reviewers who have hailed it unequivocally as a delightfully wacky comedy—a "wonderful offbeat movie," as one of them put it—are contemptible too. Our would-be hero is Charlie Driggs (Jeff Daniels), a Yuppie nerd who, in the film's opening sequence, establishes his sterling character by pocketing his check in a SoHo coffee shop and sneaking out without paying—just for kicks, you understand; our would-be heroine is Lulu (Melanie Griffith), a zanily dressed counterculture cutie who, intrigued by Charlie's crime, follows him out of the coffee shop. "You're a closet rebel, aren't you?" she coos admiringly, clearly recognizing that the two of them are soulmates. Offering him a lift to his Manhattan office, Lulu drives him instead to New Jersey, guzzling scotch all the way, throwing his beeper out the car window, and stopping in a liquor store to rifle the cash register.

At first Charlie protests Lulu's high-handedness. He's got to get back to work, he tells her; he's just been promoted to v.p. But before long he's swilling scotch with her as they speed down the New Jersey Turnpike and admitting that, by golly, he *is* a rebel ("but I channel it into the mainstream"). And before you know it they're in a roadside motel having a lusty bit of afternoon delight—complete with handcuffs and black stockings and (to Charlie's horror) a phone call to his boss *in medias res*. That done, they leave Lulu's car behind (it's hot, naturally), buy another, and hie it to Pennsylvania, picking up along the way a carful of hitchhikers—a poor black family, a hippie type with a guitar, et al. Why the hitchhikers? The idea here is plainly that Lulu (who defends her crimes by speaking of "equal distribution of assets") is introducing Charlie, the naive corporate lackey, to The People—and to The Open Road, as well. (One is reminded that the film's director, Jonathan Demme, is also responsible for *Melvin and Howard*, another quirky picture about a have and a have-not together on the American road.)

In Pennsylvania, Lulu (whose real name, it turns out, is Audrey) takes Charlie home to her gentle, harpsichord-playing mother, and introduces him as her husband; when he carries the act off with aplomb (though her weirdly serene mother, Peaches, is not deceived), she's impressed: "You're a pretty good liar when you wanna be, Charlie." (It is good to be a good liar.) She then puts on a sweet little white dress and takes Charlie, still posing as her spouse, to her high-school reunion.

It is at the reunion—where they run into her psychotic ex-con husband, Ray Sinclair (Ray Liotta)—that the film radically shifts gears. Suddenly Audrey's and Charlie's adorable, harmless crimes give way to Ray's violent ones. He takes them to a convenience store where he knocks the counterman unconscious and empties the cash register. He then forces Audrey to accompany him to Virginia; Charlie (who, we are supposed to believe, has come to care for Audrey) trails them covertly and steals her back. Next thing you know they are all back in New York, where, after a few minutes of grisly violence, Ray is killed and Charlie—having "seen the other half" of himself and decided to throw over his "boring but very safe life"—quits his job. And just as one expected, the denouement takes place in the SoHo coffee shop where it all began.

Something Wild is a screwball comedy, but it is also clearly trying to be something else, to make some kind of statement about Yuppies and rebels. This is not an impossible task; a couple of years ago, after all, Martin Scorcese took the same basic premise—Yuppie boy meets counterculture girl—and came up with *After Hours*, a witty, perceptive, gorgeously constructed Kafkaesque comedy that had something truly original and thought-provoking to say about life in the age of condos, computers, and Commie chic. In his cheap and puerile way, Demme too wants to make a serious statement along these lines while being funny at the same time. Near the end of the film, accordingly,

Charlie makes a remark that sounds an awful lot as if it is meant to be taken as the film's moral (it appears earlier in the film, too): "It's better to be a live dog than a dead lion."

What are we to make of this? Does "lion" mean rebel and "dog" mean wage slave? Is Ray thus the "dead lion"—which, at least compared to a "dog," sounds rather heroic and romantic? Does the film mean to suggest, therefore, that Ray is some kind of tragic hero, a guy with the right idea who maybe went a little too far? Perhaps. But perhaps not: it's my genuine impression that Demme and his screenwriter, E. Max Frye, are not absolutely certain *what* they mean to suggest. Their principal purpose seems to be to establish their political correctness (i.e., leftism).

This would explain why, in one scene, Demme puts a book about Winnie Mandela in Audrey's hands. Whatever one thinks of Winnie Mandela, there's something very offensive about this sort of facile political gesturing, this distribution of Consciousness McNuggets. Besides, as a statement of political solidarity with the Mandelas, putting that book in Audrey's hands hardly makes sense: would an intelligent pro-Mandela filmmaker want even to *hint* at an equation between the Mandelas and the reckless, selfish pair of "rebels" in this movie? That this is a screwball comedy by no means excuses such frivolous and muddleheaded moral logic. (Demme and Frye don't seem to realize that in a screwball comedy, it's just the *characters* who should be screwballs, not the writer and director too.)

Patently, Demme and Frye idealize rebellion. But rebellion, to them, has no moral dimension, has nothing to do with self-sacrifice or commitment to a principle, with the right challenging the power of the wrong. Their sensibilities are so fundamentally immature and solipsistic that the only conception that they have of their theme is as follows: Being a rebel is fun. Being a rebel means not going to work, means stiffing a coffee shop on a check, means getting a free ride. The definition, needless to say, has its corollaries: Stealing and lying and drinking behind the wheel are really neat (so long as you don't physically hurt anybody); the road to happiness is paved with irresponsibility; the worst thing you can do with your life is to hold down a job, especially a *good* job. It disturbs me profoundly to think of the number of children and teenagers who will be exposed to this movie, and of the number of reviewers who have blithely praised its madcap comedy while managing thoroughly to ignore its moral scuzziness.

A class reunion and an estranged husband also figure prominently in *Peggy Sue Got Married.* The title character, played charmingly by Kathleen Turner, is so nostalgic for her high school days, when she was homecoming queen and life was full of promise, that she attends her Class of '60 reunion in her prom dress. There she sees Charlie (Nicholas Cage), her failure of a hubby, once the class hotshot, with his new lady friend, and Richard, the onetime class nerd who is now a big success. Clearly, Peggy Sue is under great tension—and the tension becomes so acute, when she and Richard are called onstage to be named queen and king of the reunion, that she passes out. And when she awakens, she's back in high school. It's 1960 again, and everything is as it was—except she's got the mind and the memories of a forty-something-year-old woman who's already lived through the sixties, seventies, and half of the eighties. The ensuing scenes are both funny and touching: she laughs hysterically when her proud father shows the family his new car—and Edsel—and is moved to tears when she finds herself speaking on the phone with her grandmother, who died before 1986.

But the movie proves to be something other than the sentimental journey into the past that its first few minutes might suggest. As the story develops, director Francis Ford Coppola initiates potentially affecting sequences only to slice through the sentiment, time and again, with some pointed piece of absurdity. Why? Because the idea of time travel—specifically, the idea of being able to go back and do it *right* this time around, which is what Peggy Sue proclaims her intention of doing—is itself absurd. You get to where you are, the film is saying, not by waking up and finding yourself there, but by living your way there, day by day. Back in 1960, when Peggy Sue describes to Richard the glorious technological triumphs of the next quarter-century, he replies, "The future is so exciting!" But the film's message is that "the future," as such, doesn't really exist; when it arrives it will be the present, and will not be "exciting" in any simple way, but will be, rather, an ambiguous mixture of pleasures and disappointments and regrets, for which technological triumphs and such will merely provide a context.

Just as it seeks to demystify the future, the film deromanticizes the past. One of the things that Peggy Sue comes to learn is that she was mistaken to think that life, back in high school, had offered her an infinite number of choices. It didn't, according to the guiding philosophy of this film, for life has brought Peggy Sue to where she is now, and was never going to take her anywhere else. The film echoes *It's a Wonderful Life* in a couple of respects (for example, the inscribed book at the end), but the message that Peggy Sue—and all of us—are meant to receive is not that our lives are necessarily wonderful, but that, whatever our lives have been, they couldn't have happened any other way, simply because they *didn't* happen any other way.

The film, in short, takes on the theme of fate vs. free will and comes down strongly on the side of fate. But it's not darkly or nihilistically fatalistic, as one might expect from Coppola. On the contrary, it's a film in which the heroine learns to live in the present, not in the past or the future; learns the proper relation between the person she was and the person she is now. She learns, in short, to accept her life because it is, simply enough, all hers; she has created it; character is fate. To be sure, the film has its weak points. For one thing, it's hard to understand Peggy Sue's attraction to the nauseating Charlie (if only Coppola would stop hiring relatives!); for another, a deliberately absurd sequence that takes place at Peggy Sue's grandfather's lodge is so bizarre that it all but throws the picture off kilter. On the whole, however, this is an extremely admirable piece of work—not the major artistic accomplishment that many might expect from Coppola, but clever and thoughtful nonetheless.

If you like Caravaggio, you'll hate *Caravaggio*. Derek Jarman both wrote and directed this British film, which purports to be about the life of the Italian painter Michelangelo Amerighi da Caravaggio (1573–1610). The film has received considerable acclaim for its profusion of deliberate anachronisms, the number of which increases exponentially as the film proceeds. Caravaggio the boy (a tough, unlovable urchin) enjoins someone to speak "in plain English"; Vatican officials use pocket calculators and Royal typewriters and read the art magazine *FMR*; by film's end virtually everyone has traded period garb for twentieth-century shirts and trousers. Caravaggio and most of his lowlife cronies speak in pronounced Cockney accents, and their grubby communal way of life suggests not Rome during the Renaissance but the East End of London in 1986.

Why all the anachronisms? An article in *Art News*, based in part upon interviews with Jarman, tells us that he meant, by them, to give us all an idea of how radical Caravaggio's paintings would have seemed to his contemporaries. But the anachronisms hardly have this effect—

after all, Caravaggio isn't the only one in the film with whom they are associated. My own impression, while watching the film, was that Jarman was playing with the popular image of "Caravaggio our contemporary." As James Gardner put it in the June 1985 *Commentary*, "To a degree unparalleled in the Old Master tradition, Caravaggio would appear to have preserved through four centuries the power to awaken in us the kind of interest that we can ordinarily summon only in respect to our contemporaries. To some he would even seem an emissary of our times sent back into the benighted years of Counter-Reformation Europe. . . ."

But, far from making it easier to identify with Caravaggio, Jarman's anachronistic touches keep the real Caravaggio perpetually at a distance. They come across as pretentious and self-indulgent, even flippant: one approaches this film wanting to become immersed in Caravaggio's life and art and time, but Jarman keeps shoving a string of electric light bulbs or a motorcycle or truck in the way. This mindless, Peter Sellars-type nonsense is so frustrating—and, ultimately, so predictable and boring—that before long one finds oneself eyeing the exit, glancing at one's watch, and echoing the exasperated words of Rex Harrison's Pope Julius II to Charlton Heston's Michelangelo Buonnaroti, as he labored on the Sistine ceiling in *The Agony and the Ecstasy*: "When will you make an *end* of it?"

Clearly, Jarman's major aim in *Caravaggio* was to avoid making a film like *The Agony and the Ecstasy*—that is, a conventional movie biography with a plot, some sign of an attempt at period authenticity, and a deferential tone toward its subject. Rejecting convention is fine if you've come up with something better—but Jarman hasn't. He doesn't seem to understand that the main reason we are interested in the life of a great artist is that we want to know how this particular person, in this particular time and place, came to create these particular immortal works. What forces shaped him? How did he discover his Muse? Jarman gives no indication of having the slightest interest in such questions. He doesn't even seem to be especially interested in Caravaggio's art.

What Jarman *is* interested in, however, is sex. If *The Agony and the Ecstasy* skirted Michelangelo Buonnaroti's homosexuality, Jarman seems to have chosen to take on the life of Michelangelo Caravaggio (who is widely thought to have been, like his namesake, a homosexual) because it offered him the opportunity to invent a story of two men's sadomasochistic passion for one another. Caravaggio (Nigel

Terry) is one of the men; the other is a handsome tough named Ranuccio (Sean Bean). The film, for the most part, is concerned with chronicling the development of, and the complications that arise from, their violent mutual attraction (which, by the way, is more convincingly acted by Terry than by Bean).

And it tells this unpretty story with less and less clarity: while the inane anachronisms multiply, the plot spirals off into almost complete incoherence. Twice near the end, groups of characters fall into dramatically lit Caravaggio-type poses, in what comes off as a joke at Caravaggio's expense, an implicit suggestion that his work is artificial, that art—of Caravaggio's old-fashioned type, at least—can't really hope to capture reality. (Which, I suppose, is why Jarman, the film artist, doesn't consider it worth his trouble to try to comprehend the sensibility of the age in which Caravaggio lived—though I suspect that we are meant to feel that *Caravaggio*, with its graphic bloodspilling and overt sexuality, brings us closer to "reality" than does Caravaggio.) As Jarman's Caravaggio says, "All art is against lived experience. How can you compare flesh and blood with oil, ground pigment?"

Of course, he's right. Capturing life perfectly *is* impossible. The obligation of every artist, however, is to attempt nonetheless to capture it as richly and accurately as he can—not to make a joke out of everything, not to abandon the rigor and self-discipline that are necessary to any sort of artistic success. In this regard, Derek Jarman's *Caravaggio* fails miserably.

LIFE WITH FATHER

The Mosquito Coast

The new film *The Mosquito Coast,* which is based upon the best-selling 1982 novel by Paul Theroux, tells the strange, captivating, and ultimately horrific story of a fanatical visionary named Allie Fox (Harrison Ford), an inventor and Harvard dropout who, disgusted with America, uproots his wife and four children from their rural Massachusetts home and moves them to a remote river settlement in the Mosquitia district of Honduras.

Allie's litany of grievances against the U.S. is a hodgepodge of familiar left- and right-wing gripes, and he continually lectures everyone around him—especially his sensitive, level-headed thirteen-year-old son, Charlie (River Phoenix), the narrator—to the effect that America has become a nation of mindless consumers, that the dollar is worth only twenty cents, that American kids are all drug addicts and murderers, that we're selling our country out by buying foreign-made products, that TV is numbing our minds, junk food is rotting our bodies, and aerosol cheese spread is destroying the ozone layer. "I'm the last man!" Allie proclaims, and his obsessive determination to create a new life for his family in the tropical wilderness away from Holiday Inns, Fudgesicles, Twinkies, and Duraflame logs makes him at once funny and frightening.

Paradoxically, it also makes him a grotesque parody of the traditional foursquare American individualist—an arrogant, self-reliant, jeremiad-happy New Man obnoxiously proud of his "know-how" and his New England thrift, devoted to the invention of labor-saving gadgets, eager to construct a City on a Hill, cockily certain that all problems can be fixed, all burdens lifted. At bottom, indeed, Allie's real gripe against America is that its civilization is already in place; there's no wilderness to conquer, no way for him to build a New World of his own.

So it is that Allie drags his clan to the village of Jeronimo in the Honduran jungle, a place as primitive as Plymouth Rock must have been when William Bradford first climbed off the boat, and begins to transform it. But because he is reckless and headstrong and absolutely incapable of compromise—and mostly because, as soon becomes apparent, he is out-and-out insane—Allie leads his family into disaster. The novel's nightmarish vision of their fate recalled Joseph Conrad; its strengths—aside from its memorable portrait of Allie Fox—were a richly detailed depiction of the Central American milieu, an excellently paced and suspenseful narrative (which gradually assumed an almost mythic power), and a touching delineation of Charlie's feelings—of love and hate, resentment and worship—for his tyrannical, godlike father. As a matter of fact, the novel was most effective not as a tragic fable about the futility of challenging God's power or the folly of visionary excess, or (as some reviewers vigorously maintained) as a cautionary tale about the consequences of unrestrained American individualism, meliorism, or colonialism (after all, Allie's most ruinous escapades are the consequence not simply of too much American-style zeal and determination but of *madness*). Rather, the novel succeeded most decidedly as an allegory about fathers and sons—about the way fathers dominate their young sons with threats, promises, lies, and the construction of personal mystiques, and about the way sons yearn for their fathers' approval, secretly and guiltily long for their fathers' death, and, upon learning ultimately that their fathers are not all-knowing and omnipotent gods, feel the world opening up to them, and become more able to understand, to forgive, and to love.

On the whole, the film—which was directed by the Australian Peter Weir (*The Last Wave, The Year of Living Dangerously, Witness*) and written by Paul Schrader (*Taxi Driver, Raging Bull*)—is extremely faithful to the novel, achieves much the same effects, and shares its main weaknesses. John Seale's cinematography excellently captures the primitive lushness of the jungle (the film was shot entirely on location in the U.S. and Belize), and Thom Noble's editing accentuates the frenetic pace of Charlie's life with father. The actors in the principal roles, moreover, are strikingly good. Harrison Ford captures to perfection Allie Fox's energy, wit, and charisma, and the increasing rashness and illogic with which he tyrannizes his family; River Phoenix, as the quietly decent, loyal, and brave Charlie, turns in a performance of extraordinary sensitivity and intelligence. (One is particularly impressed by his handling of the voice-over narration, with which a less gifted young actor could singlehandedly have wrecked the film.) Though her character, as in the novel, remains largely undefined, Helen Mirren, as Mother, has a very strong presence, which, alas, only makes one wonder all the more why this seemingly sensible woman permits Allie to torment and endanger her children.

Yet there are differences in tone and emphasis between Theroux's *Mosquito Coast* and Weir's. In the film, for example, Charlie plays a somewhat less active part than in the novel; among other things, Weir drastically de-emphasizes Charlie's role in saving his family during the destruction of Jeronimo, and has eliminated entirely Allie's fierce resentment of the boy afterwards. And where the novel drew a sharp contrast between Allie's compulsion to change Jeronimo and the real harmony with nature enjoyed by Charlie and his native playmates (who, while Allie remade Jeronimo in the image of an American town, gamboled half-naked in a jungle clearing they called "The Acre"), the film fails to point up this contrast; in the film, the sequence concerning the Acre is brief and confused, and the intended antithesis doesn't come off.

In the film, furthermore, the initial humor and humanity of Allie's personality are brought to the forefront; the script eliminates instances of his thoughtless cruelty to Charlie but carefully retains episodes that present Allie's funnier, more sympathetic side. When the family leaves Baltimore harbor, for example, Allie, one of whose gripes is the phony friendliness of store clerks, shouts sarcastically, "Goodbye, America—and have a nice day!" And when the Reverend Spellgood (Andre Gregory)—a missionary who is the local representative of Allie's chief rival, God, and is therefore Allie's principal antagonist in Honduras—tries to win this maverick over to the Lord with a copy of the "Blue Jeans Bible," Allie (who is extremely well versed in Scripture) holds up the dungaree-bound Good Book and says, "Look, kids, just what I've been warning you about!" Allie despises missionaries because, as he explains, they teach the natives to tolerate poverty and to bear their burdens stoically; he believes, on the contrary, that everything can be changed for the better, that—at least with him at the helm—the poor natives can markedly improve upon the miserable circumstances that an inefficient and uncooperative Maker has forced upon them.

For a while, anyhow, Allie seems marvelously successful in his attempt to improve upon God's handiwork. He turns the shabby little clearing of Jeronimo into a pretty town with sanitary huts, productive and mosquito-free gardens, and a happy, hard-working native population. (And even air conditioning.) The perverse symbol of his audacious challenge to God is a huge, fire-powered ice machine called Fatboy, which towers over the huts of Jeronimo and looks rather like a church. "Ice is civilization," says Allie; he is determined to bring ice not only to the town's natives but (when they begin to take it for granted) to a tribe of "pure people" in the mountains who have supposedly never seen a white man *or* ice and who he hopes will, as Charlies tells us in his narration, "see his ice as a jewel and be amazed."

Yet by the time Allie and Charlie and their companions reach the mountain settlement with their block of ice, it has melted away; and this event marks the turning point in Allie's fortunes. Soon Jeronimo is invaded by three evil-looking gunmen, and the town is destroyed by fire, the river polluted with ammonium hydroxide from Fatboy, the native population fled into the arms of the Reverend Spellgood downriver. As the town burns, Allie howls in horror, and one is reminded of the scream at the climax of *Heart of Darkness*. But he is not demoralized for long. "I'm happy," he says. "We're free."

The fact is that Allie can't tolerate a stable, prosperous society of the sort that Jeronimo was fast becoming. Like many American protagonists before him—Natty Bumppo, Huck Finn, Sal Paradise—he is forever restless; he wants to tame a primitive landscape and create a civilization, but he doesn't want to *live* there. So, abandoning the ruins of Jeronimo and disregarding the warning of the family's native friend, Mr. Haddy (Conrad Roberts), that the rainy season will do them in, Allie takes his family to the coast and—all their money and supplies having been lost in the destruction of Jeronimo—eagerly improvises clothes and a dwelling from the rubbage scattered on the beach.

His children, who don't like their sub-native standard of living, want to return to America, but Allie lies to them, saying that they can't go back "because it's not there anymore—cataclysm—millions of Americans burned to a crisp!" In his mind, he's magnified the disaster of Jeronimo into a nuclear holocaust. And he refuses to put into any port, for that would be admitting defeat: "If it's on a map I can't use it." His failure with Jeronimo has only made him more fanatical, more a megalomaniacal visionary; he seems to see himself now not as a seventeenth-century Pilgrim, bringing civilization to a wilderness, but as a new Adam whose goal is to recapture Eden on Earth. He tells his family, "Living in harmony with nature—that's my vision. And anybody without vision has no place here." But he is incapable of living in harmony with nature, because he is unwilling to learn anything from the natives who have been living in harmony with nature for generations.

To be sure, as Mr. Haddy predicted, the rains come and almost wash the Foxes out to sea; fortunately, however, their makeshift log-and-tarp house floats (its "hull" is marked with the Conradian word Victory) and they manage to get it back on the river and to go upstream. The family is filthy and ragged by this point, and there's no food ("I don't know when we'll eat next," Allie says with a demented smile), but it is not till he dives into the river and fails to surface for a minute or so that Mother finally breaks down and screams, "I can't stand this!"

The film's politics are somewhat contradictory, to say the least. While ridiculing the folly of which self-declared visionaries and idealists are capable, it patently intends to present Allie as an emblem of a pushy, parochial America—one that seeks to impose its values and technology upon the Third World, one that talks, talks, talks but refuses ever to listen, learn, or understand. But Allie is too erratic and inane a figure to bear convincingly the weight of such inconsistent (and, frankly, silly) political symbology. Consequently, it is all to the good that the emphasis at the close of the film is not upon political thematics or even upon the tragedy (if tragedy it be) of Allie Fox, but upon the archetypal relationship between Allie and Charlie—who, like Nick Carraway at the end of *The Great Gatsby,* emerges from the shadows of a strange, obsessive self-exile to become the real hero of the piece. Despite its paradoxical politics, then, *The Mosquito Coast* works marvelously as an allegory about the paradoxical bonds between fathers and sons.

POLTROON

Platoon

The parking lot outside the Wadsworth Theater was filled with Jaguars, Mercedes-Benzes, and BMWs. "Gee," I said, "Beverly Hills must be empty tonight." "A lot of rich folks come to these things," my sister replied. "A lot of people in The Industry."

We were in Westwood, city of Los Angeles. We had driven over the Santa Monica Mountains from the San Fernando Valley to this theater in the Veterans Administration complex, where my sister attends weekly screenings of about-to-be-released films as part of an extension course she takes at UCLA. (Actually, the screenings *are* the course.) The films are introduced by the course's "professor," film critic Stephen Farber; afterwards, Farber appears onstage in the company of someone connected with the film, and the "students" ask questions. This week there was a "bonus screening," which meant that the students could bring guests; since I was in town, my sister had invited me.

Tonight's treat was a Vietnam war movie called *Platoon,* and the evening's guest was its writer and director, Oliver Stone. Prior to *Platoon,* Stone had written or co-written *Scarface, The Year of the Dragon, Midnight Express,* and *Conan the Barbarian,* and had written and directed *Salvador.* Farber prepared us for Stone's newest effort by explaining that Stone had himself been a soldier in Vietnam, that Stone was a "left-of-center" director whose intention in all of his films was to "*épater le bourgeoisie,*" and that tonight's flick—which, as Stone would later affirm, was highly autobiographical—would be "abrasive," "disquieting," and "disturbing."

And so it was, right from the git-go. *Platoon* opens with an epigraph from Ecclesiastes which is obviously intended to carry bitter irony: "Rejoice O young man in thy youth." It's September of 1967 and we are on an airstrip in Vietnam; as body bags containing the remains of American soldiers lie waiting on the tarmac to be loaded onto a plane, a number of young men who have come to take their place—including our hero, Chris Taylor (played by Charlie Sheen, son of Martin)—step down for the first time onto Asian soil. Chris, who narrates the movie in a series of voice-over excerpts from successive letters to his grandmother, is a rich white boy who has dropped out of college and, against his parents' wishes, has volunteered for the infantry. (The record shows that Stone himself, born in New York City, attended Yale for a year before going to Nam—first as a teacher, then as a soldier.)

Chris has volunteered for several reasons. He wants to serve his country, wants to learn something about Life, and wants to be "anonymous." For Chris, in other words, going to war is in large part a rich boy's way of rebelling against Daddy and of escaping—only temporarily, of course—from the oppression of wealth. (Presumably the Peace Corps was full.) Besides, as Chris explains to a black member of his platoon named King (Keith David), the poor always do most of the fighting in wars; Chris thinks the rich should do their part, too. (King isn't impressed by this talk: "Shit, you gotta be rich in the first place to think like that.") Chris's early communications to Grandma are almost impossibly starry-eyed and idealistic: he's thrilled to be serving alongside the "poor" and "unwanted"; they're "the best I've ever seen, Grandma—the heart and soul." (Almost like real people!)

Yet even before Chris has seen any combat action, his illusions have begun to be shattered. "I think I made a big mistake coming here, Grandma," he writes, his tone that of a Yalie who has foolishly chosen to spend his junior year abroad in London rather than Paris. His expectations of Vietnam have been sharply contradicted by reality, but exactly what those expectations were and how he came by them are never explained. (Oliver Stone, in a revealing article that appears in the January/February issue of *American Film,* remembers himself as a "solitary, wide-eyed youth standing under those raggedy Asiatic clouds, looking out at the sea with . . . fantasies of Lord Jim and Julie Christie . . .") All that is clear is that Chris had no idea war was so *icky*. (Apparently you don't have to read *All Quiet on the Western Front* or the poetry of Wilfred Owen to get into Yale.) What makes this callow boy's point of view so problematical is that it is also the film's point of view: King's sardonic remark notwithstanding, Stone does not regard either Chris's initial rich-boy illusions about war, or his subsequent facile moralizing about it, with the slightest hint of objectivity.

To say this is not to deny that the film, which follows the fortunes of Chris and his platoon over a period of several months, is extremely effective in many ways. Thanks largely to Robert Richardson's fine cinematography, Claire Simpson's editing, and Yves De Bono's special effects, *Platoon*—which was shot on location in the Philippines—is a genuine triumph of atmosphere. Stone does a magnificent job of re-creating the experience of the typical foot soldier in the Vietnam bush: the jungles, swamps, mud, and rain, the leeches, insects, and snakes, the pounding music and mind-altering drugs, the friction between blacks and whites, the contrast between the wholesome, inexperienced, college-boy lieutenant and the tough, haunted-looking "grunts." Most powerfully of all, the film evokes the terrible suspensefulness of a progress through the jungle, the suddenness with which a few clumps of leaves can turn out to be a horde of armed and camouflaged Vietcong, the utter chaos of the ensuing combat, and the apparent randomness with which bullets in the night find their marks, booby traps find their victims, the Angel of Death finds his prey.

But if the harrowing *mise en scène* of *Platoon* strikes one as astonishingly realistic, the plotting too often seems romantic, even melodramatic, and at least a couple of the characters are absurdly one-dimensional. Chris, we are led to understand, has turned his back on his real father—an Establishment type, apparently, who wanted him to stay in college—but in his platoon he finds two antithetical father figures, both of whom strain credibility. Sergeant Barnes (his face disfigured by a gruesome wound) is unspeakably evil, a human exterminator whose dedication to destroying the enemy knows no bounds. (Barnes, as enacted by an almost unrecognizable Tom Berenger, rather reminds one of the sick foulmouth played by Dennis Hopper in *Blue Velvet*—the difference, of course, being that Hooper *meant* to be excessive to the point of self-parody.) Sergeant Elias

(Willem Dafoe), whose years in Vietnam have left him disillusioned, is almost saintly; the film seeks to identify him with Christ. When Elias speaks, we are meant to take his word as gospel—and this is where one's problems with the movie really begin. "We're gonna lose this war," Elias tells Chris. "We been kickin' other people's asses for so long [whose? the Nazis'?] it's about time we got ours kicked." After Barnes and a protégé named Bunny (played by Matt Dillon's kid brother Kevin) bloodthirstily waste a couple of peasants during a search for VC in a remote village, and Elias forcibly prevents them from committing further atrocities, the platoon begins to break into pro-Barnes and pro-Elias camps. Chris—who, out of sheer exhaustion, tension, and fear, has come close himself to committing an atrocity or two—writes Grandma that he's losing his strength, his sanity, his sense of right and wrong.

And this is only the beginning. By the end of the film we've seen not only atrocities but more than one incident of "fragging" (the deliberate killing of one American soldier by another), the attempted rape of a little girl, and an unnerving nocturnal battle in which so many men are killed that, in the morning, a bulldozer must be used to scoop their bodies into a ditch. At movie's end, as Chris—twice wounded, like Oliver Stone, and therefore free to return home—ascends from the scene of carnage in a helicopter, he tells us in a heavily didactic voice-over that "We did not fight the enemy. We fought ourselves. The enemy was in us." Apropos of Barnes and Elias, he says that since the war, there have been times when "I felt like a child of those two fathers." And he concludes by saying that it has been his aim, since the war, to try "to find a goodness and meaning to this life."

Though Stone's political position is not as explicit here as in his previous film, *Salvador*—a "fictionalized" story about an American photojournalist in 1980 El Salvador—*Platoon* and its predecessor have much in common. Both films are symphonies of death, full of graphically depicted corpses, many of them mutilated, many of them children's. Both are relatively plotless and are filmed in a brilliantly effective *faux*-documentary style. Both show American (or American-supported) soldiers killing peasants for being "Communists"—in parts of the world where, according to Stone's way of thinking, words like *democracy* and *Communism* don't really mean anything. Though Stone does take pains to portray intelligent, well-meaning Americans who feel otherwise, the ultimate message in both films is that America's military presence in places like Vietnam and Central America serves only to make the lives of the local peasantry more miserable and tragic—it's the powerful rich destroying the lives of the helpless poor. (Plainly, Stone is going to spend his life trying to atone for being born rich.) Just as Stone romanticizes Sergeant Elias in *Platoon,* so in *Salvador* he romanticizes a leader of the rebel army who, standing in his tent before a portrait of Marx and Lenin, tells a group of journalists that "the will of the people and the march of history cannot be changed—not even by the *norteamericanos!*" Outside, members of his happy and noble peasant army sing "*el futuro será nuestro*" ("the future will be ours").

When *Platoon* ended, the Westwood crowd applauded enthusiastically, and it applauded again when Stephen Farber brought Oliver Stone onstage. Stone—whose attitude throughout the ensuing half hour or so would best be described as smug—offered some inside dope: he said that he had written the film in 1976, had been unable to interest an American studio in making it, and had finally secured financing from an English company. He informed us that all the members of Chris's platoon were based on people with whom he had served in Vietnam, and explained that he had helped his actors to capture the sound, the bearing, even the look of real jungle-weary soldiers—which they *had* captured, remarkably so, down to that chilling, half-mad look in the eyes—by making them dig their own foxholes, making them sleep in those foxholes, and allowing them only two or three hours of sleep each night during the weeks of filming. Disconcertingly, Stone spoke of the hardships he imposed upon his actors with an almost sadistic glee, so that one had the feeling that, his anti-war rhetoric notwithstanding, there was a part of him that positively reveled in the role of drill sergeant, in the idea of putting a cast of pampered young actors through some tough paces—a part that reveled, indeed, in war itself.

Then the audience began putting in its two cents. There were one or two folks who had complaints. A man with a cane, who politely identified himself (to the immediate derision of the crowd) as a conservative, asked whether it bothered Stone that *Platoon* might persuade young American men that their country wasn't worth serving, and whether he thought such a film could be made in the Soviet Union about, say, the Soviet war in Afghanistan. Stone replied that he considered himself a patriotic American, and quoted Gore Vidal on the real meaning of patriotism. (Hearty applause from the audience.) Then he added that he was confident that the "liberal thaw" presently underway in the USSR would result in a spate of films by Soviet filmmakers critical of the Soviet role in Afghanistan. (More applause.) A young lady then offered the opinion that the end of the picture was too didactic; Stone replied, "I like it that way." (More applause and warm laughter.) In reply to another audience member's question, Stone compared *Platoon* to two other Vietnam war films, Francis Ford Coppola's *Apocalypse Now* and Michael Cimino's *The Deer Hunter*. The Coppola and Cimino films, he said, were symbolic in their approach; his film was "realistic."

Stone suggested that many viewers, especially in places like Georgia, would consider *Platoon* anti-American. "*I* didn't think it was anti-American," declared a middle-aged man who sounded as if he was ready to take on the entire state of Georgia, and Alabama too. Stone grinned. "Well, you're obviously a *liberal,*" he said, and the man beamed proudly. Most of the other "students" laughed affectionately and applauded, congratulating themselves on being liberals (and on not being from Georgia). Somebody asked Stone what his next project was. "I'm probably gonna do something about Wall Street," he replied, to the crowd's delighted whoop of laughter and applause. Clearly, the great majority of the audience was in love with both Stone and his movie. One after another, the Beverly Hills types stepped up to the microphones at the front of the auditorium to tell Stone how *powerful* his film was ("I feel as if I was there," said a slim, bearded gent who looked disturbingly like *New York* magazine's John Leonard; "I feel as if I should get a Purple Heart"), how *drained* they felt, how *eye-opening* it was, how much it had *taught* them, how much better they *understood* things now.

To be sure, the film did have stunning immediacy, perhaps unparalleled in any other war movie. But what, I reflected, could *Platoon* really have "taught" anybody about war in general or Vietnam in particular? Only that war is hell—which these presumably well-educated adults should already have known. *Platoon*'s logic was much the same as that used by anti-nuke propagandists in connection with the television film "The Day After": just as "The Day After" presented an uncompromisingly realistic picture of the possible consequences of nuclear war, so *Platoon* assaults its audience with a ground soldier's view of Vietnam. Just as "The Day After" was used to support arguments in favor of unilateral nuclear disarmament, so *Platoon* is meant in part as an argument against American involvement in Vietnam—and, by extension, an argument against our involvement in Central America. But what does either of these films really prove? Not a thing. Both of them pretend to be contributing to intellectual discourse upon a significant issue, when all that they actually have to offer is a searing visceral experience that sheds no light on anything. For all its sheer cinematic effectiveness, then, *Platoon,* considered as a serious statement on Vietnam, amounts to nothing more than a high-priced piece of faulty logic.

Yet why were these affluent folks in the Westwood auditorium so struck by the film? Largely, I think, because the protagonist was one of them. Chris Taylor might well have been their own spoiled Ivy League brat, off on an ill-advised idealistic tear. Patently, it made these affluent people feel virtuous to applaud Stone's indictment of America, and of the American rich, in particular, for sending poor boys to do their fighting for them—and yet they felt comfortable applauding these sentiments because they were voiced by a rich boy who himself (if we take the liberty of identifying Chris with Oliver Stone) returned home, after the war, to be the big success that his parents wanted him to be. Indeed, that rich boy was not only the film's protagonist but its moral conscience; one even had the feeling, at times, that though it assailed capitalism and wealth, *Platoon* was informed by the perhaps unconscious assumption that a rich white boy's moral sense is likely to be superior to that of the average poor black boy.

In short, the hypocrisy of *Platoon* was breathtaking; and the Westwood audience—possessed of an irresponsible, self-congratulatory variety of pacifism that was barely distinguishable from est or TM or any of a dozen other self-indulgent, quasi-religious, feel-good-about-yourself California movements—loved every minute of it. This was one movie that had found its audience in record time.

THESPIANS AND SPECIMENS

Outrageous Fortune
Sherman's March

Outrageous Fortune (as in "slings and arrows of . . .") combines several familiar motifs. It is a clash-of-two-incongruous-characters movie (like *The Odd Couple*) that turns into an innocents-caught-up-in-international-intrigue adventure comedy (like *Silver Streak*), and, somewhere along the way, also becomes a buddy picture (like *Butch Cassidy*). Refreshingly, the opposites-turned-buddies in this case are both women—actresses, in fact, though of very different kinds. Lauren (Shelley Long), a stuck-up rich girl, is an aspiring classical thespian who wants to play Hamlet; Sandy (Bette Midler) is a crude and raucous porno diva. The two of them, classmates in a Manhattan acting class taught by a great Russian acting teacher (Robert Prosky), can't stand each other, but when their mutual boyfriend, Michael (Peter Coyote), mysteriously disappears, they team up to search for him. Before they know it, they're on their way to New Mexico, with both CIA and KGB operatives nipping at their heels.

The pairing of Long and Midler sounds like a promising idea, but before their first sequence together is over you realize you've seen it all before: what this is, really, is *Cheers: The Movie* with Long playing a variation on her Diane Chambers character, Midler (in yet another rerun of her tacky-bimbo act) taking the place of Carla the waitress as Diane's loud, vulgar foil, and Peter Coyote replacing Ted Danson as the primary object of their rivalry. This is not to write the film off entirely: Midler, after all, is always good for a few laughs, no matter what happens to be in the script or who happens to be behind the camera, and there are sequences in which she and Long play off each other to truly amusing effect.

Nor is it to say that Leslie Dixon's screenplay is worthlessly derivative: indeed, there are some very funny lines here—or, rather lines that *would* have been very funny, if only they'd been directed properly. But the film's director, Arthur Hiller—who is, I think, most responsible for *Outrageous Fortune*'s weaknesses—just throws them away. This is Hiller's forte. Whereas some directors can take complicated pieces of material and turn them into lucid, coherent, effortless-looking films, Hiller (whose previous films include *Making Love* and *Silver Streak*) specializes in taking a relatively straightforward script and turning it into a confused, cluttered mess in which the tone wobbles, the characters never come into focus, and the jokes get lost in the shuffle. Likewise, whereas some directors rise above the clichés inherent in their material, Hiller manages—indeed, one cannot help feeling, at times, that he tries his damnedest—to make everything in his films seem as pallid and contrived as possible. Thus Hiller fails to make us believe in either Sandy or Lauren's affection for Michael, or to make the evolution of the ladies' relationship from mutual loathing to loyal friendship seem anything more than the cliché that it is.

One looks in vain, in a Hiller film, for a sense of style, of drama, of character, of humor, of pace—let alone visual interest or imagination or *joie de vivre*. He directs with a light head and a heavy hand. Alas, the only tried-and-true way to entertain oneself while watching a Hiller film is to tote up the missed opportunities—the failures, on Hiller's part, to exploit promising possibilities in the script. Dixon plainly meant *Outrageous Fortune*, for instance, to be in large part a meditation on acting; he simultaneously makes fun of the solemn pretenses of Lauren and her acting teacher, celebrates the sheer magic of dramatic illusions, and smiles at the outlandishness of his own plot (as well as its distance from Shakespeare, who is invoked at the film's beginning and end, and whose plays are, of course, themselves rich with meditations on reality, illusion, and the actor's art). But—though it's all there in the script—this thematic subtext fails to take shape, to take flight, in the actual film. To watch this flimsy farce is to have nightmares about what *Tootsie* would have been like with Arthur Hiller at the helm.

Several years ago, Ross McElwee, an independent North Carolina-born filmmaker residing in Boston, received a $9,000 grant to make a documentary about General William Tecumseh Sherman's march to the sea and its lasting effects upon American society. But when he went South to begin work on the film, McElwee, who had just been abandoned by his girlfriend, found himself using his newly bought film stock to record the conversations and activities of his family and friends—and, in particular, of the series of unattached young women into whose company he insinuated himself and his camera over the ensuing year. The film that resulted is a hilarious piece of *cinéma vérité* about contemporary Southern women and the frustrations of romance. It is also, of course, about Ross McElwee, who claims to be enamored of each of these young women, but who apparently never puts his camera down, even when they're gently explaining why they don't love him, even when they're packing to leave, even when they're backing out of the driveway and driving out of his life.

In all, unless I lost count, there are seven of these young ladies: (1) a none-too-bright aspiring actress and model who thinks that if only she can meet Burt Reynolds, he will fall in love with her and put her in a movie; (2) an interior designer who matter-of-factly converses about Revelations and the imminent Apocalypse, and who introduces McElwee to a community of survivalists; (3) a wholesome folk singer who, after spending a few weeks being courted by McElwee, confesses that she is a Mormon and wants to marry a man of God; (4) a lice-ridden linguist who lives alone, in primitive, hermitlike fashion, on one of Georgia's Sea Islands; (5) a rock-and-roll performer; (6) an ex-girlfriend of McElwee's who is a lawyer; and (7) another ex-girlfriend who is an elementary-school teacher and a left-wing activist.

Make no mistake: McElwee is a highly eccentric gent, and the ladies who allow him to enter their lives, camera poised constantly upon his shoulder while they calmly discuss the most intimate details of their lives, form a colorful gallery of grotesques who bear more resemblance to the bizarrest characters in Thomas Wolfe, Flannery O'Conner, Eudora Welty, and the early Capote than to the ordinary run of Southerners. One wonders frequently, during the film, whether he has sincerely chosen these women on the basis of their romantic appeal to him (they run the gamut from homely to mildly attractive), or whether he has deliberately sought out the most offbeat available specimens of Dixie womanhood.

But *Sherman's March* is not only about McElwee's romantic misadventures. It is also, in a sometimes subtle way, about—yes—Sherman's march. McElwee is fascinated by the paradox of Sherman's character: as he reminds us more than once, the general—whom Southerners to this day despise for his merciless destruction of farms and cities—was in private life a good and humble citizen who "loved the South." In this regard, McElwee seems to regard Sherman as something of a touchstone for our own time, in which a country made up of essentially good and humble people has at its command an arsenal of weapons capable of destroying the world. Throughout the film, the enigmatic, emblematic figure of Sherman hovers in the background. We are constantly aware of the role that his depredations played in shaping the insular, tragic postbellum South that is symbolized (however grotesquely) by the Georgians and Carolinians whom we meet in the film; and we are aware, too, that it was Sherman's use of modern weapons and his policy of total warfare against a civilian population that, in a way, marked the beginning of our present era—an era in which nobody, man or woman, civilian or soldier, can feel himself to be out of harm's way.

To be sure, the folks in McElwee's film seem unusually preoccupied with matters nuclear. At least two of his women, for example, are doomsday fanatics who keep provisions stored in their home in preparation for a nuclear conflict; another (the elementary-school teacher) spends her spare time organizing no-nuke protests. (Sometimes one wonders whether McElwee finds obsession with nuclear war aphrodisiacal.) A running "joke" throughout the film concerns McElwee's own recurrent nightmares about a nuclear holocaust and his childhood memory of an H-bomb test off the coast of Hawaii.

Indeed, Sherman and the Bomb aside, the subject to which the film keeps returning is McElwee himself—his thoughts, dreams, memories, desires, and chronic insomnia. At first one sympathizes with the graceless and unattractive filmmaker, who presents himself as a sincere young man in search of a good woman to love; if anything, he seems too nice, too laidback, too willing to let himself be dumped on. His sister (in between grisly descriptions of her recent plastic surgery) complains to McElwee that he is too dull and unkempt to attract a really nice girl; his ex-teacher (an outspoken Shelley Winters type who is the highlight of the film) gripes that he's a stick-in-the-mud who needs to learn how to sweep a woman off her feet, needs to stop using his camera to distance himself from real life. And McElwee sits there politely taking all this criticism—a sweet, sane man, apparently, in a nest of crazies, a sensible guy surrounded by ridiculous folks who don't seem to have the slightest inkling of how ridiculous they are.

But by the end of the film one realizes that both women have a point. There is something smug and self-satisfied, even arrogant, about the persona McElwee projects in this film; though he trains his camera relentlessly upon those around him, mercilessly exposing their foibles and foolishness, he seems perfectly content with himself just as he is. At times, to be sure, he does set his camera on automatic, sit himself in front of it, and speak from his heart—but he's hardly the guinea pig that his friends and lovers are. It is always McElwee who is in control, always McElwee and his romantic quest that form the chief topics of conversation. *Sherman's March* is, in short, a shameless exercise in solipsism. As such, however, it is an undeniable *tour de force*—quirky, funny, and almost continuously engaging throughout its epic two and a half hours.

SENTIMENTAL JOURNEYS

My Sweet Little Village *Radio Days*

My Sweet Little Village is a sweet little movie, a Capra-esque tribute to village life and virtues courtesy of the Czechoslovakian director Jiri Menzel (*Closely Watched Trains*) and screenwriter Zdenek Sverak. The hero of the film—which is said to be based partly on life in the village where Menzel himself grew up—is the corpulent, middle-aged Pavek (Marian Labuda), who drives a truck for the Mir (Peace) Cooperative Farm in the village of Koutna; his working mate of five years is the village idiot—a winsome young beanpole named Otik Rekosnik (Janos Ban). Together they're a regular Iron-Curtain Laurel and Hardy, with Otik's dimwitted maneuvers constantly landing the exasperated Pavek in hot water or exposing him to his comrades' ridicule. The last straw comes when Pavek—following Otik's directions—backs their truck into a post outside the fancy home of Mr. Rumlena, the village's affluent "Prague weekender." For days Pavek is the butt of local jokes; supremely embarrassed, he insists that after the harvest Otik be teamed with someone else—even though that someone will probably be the cruel Turek, who would make Otik's life hell.

But soon it looks as if the problem has been taken out of local hands: a higher-up in Prague requests Otik's transfer to Metalwood, a factory in the capital. Plainly someone of importance—or with connections—wants Otik out of Koutna. But who? Pavek? Or perhaps

Otik's friend Vaclav—an engineer, transplanted urbanite, and boyfriend of Turek's lovely young wife—who has been using Otik's house for romantic assignations and may be attempting to gain title to it? Whatever the case may be, the villagers are worried about Otik's moving to Prague, because they know that he could not survive there. The city, we are meant to understand, is decadent, indifferent, and amoral, whereas the village is a place where people care about each other. The film ridicules a strident song, "Prague's Calling You," which boasts inanely of the capital's noise and bustle, and contrasts it with the lyrical poems in praise of the countryside that the village doctor (Rudolf Hruninsky) recites while driving along in his car. That the doctor—whose wry, humane point of view is essentially equivalent to that of the filmmakers—keeps having car trouble is not just a running gag but a symbol: to a man of his solid, old-fashioned virtues, automobiles will always be alien and uncooperative.

To an extent, the film associates modern decadence not only with the city but with the West. When it turns out that Otik is being called to Prague because the director of Metalwood wants his house for a weekend place, an itinerant artist who has become Otik's roommate derides the director's city-slicker taste for Western accoutrements—for "imported plastic thatching from West Germany" and "an English lawn." Likewise, after Otik reports to Metalwood and shakes the director's hand vigorously, the director tells his secretary, "Bad habit, handshaking. They've given it up in the West." And Menzel mercilessly parodies American movies (one of which Pavek's family eagerly gathers around the TV set to watch), depicting them as absurdly violent and depraved, crammed with murders and explosions, populated by characters whose only thoughts are of money and sex and drugs. By contrast, positive human values are associated not only with the village but with the cooperative farm—and indeed the film closes on a shot of the farm's main gate, with a large red star looming over it.

But it must be added that *My Sweet Little Village* also pokes fun at its own viewpoint—at the doctor's paeans to the countryside, for example, and at the corny homespun music programs on Czech TV. It also criticizes the use of the word *comrade*. When the itinerate artist, just arrived in the village, addresses an old woman as "aunty," she tells him not to call her by that old-fashioned honorific, or to call her "comrade" either, she prefers "ma'am."

The film is full of small, interesting touches. Pavek's son Jarda, for instance—whose adolescent crush on his sister's teacher forms one of the movie's slighter subplots—wears a University of Utah sweatshirt in one scene. (Curiously, the same shirt appears on another village kid later in the film, causing one to wonder: do the locals pass this prized shirt around, or did the cooperative farm receive an entire shipment of them as a reward for fulfilling production quotas?) And then there is the fact that Pavek's family lives next door to a graveyard—which is not only a *memento mori,* but a suggestion, I think, that villagers are more conscious of, and more comfortable with, their mortality than city dwellers, and consequently less likely to succumb to a distorted set of values, less likely to forget that people are more important than posessions. Lazarus figures abound: the doctor feels miraculously better soon after his car rolls over him; Turek backs over a fellow worker with his truck, but the man hardly has a scratch on him; a truck driver unwittingly dumps a load of earth onto a sleeping Otik, but Otik emerges unscatched. Just as these villagers survive their encounters with cars and trucks—those dreaded modern phenomena—so the village of Koutna and its values ultimately triumph over the big city.

To be sure, *My Sweet Little Village* is rather slight, its denouement is extremely predictable, and its plot is based on a dubious premise (would a director of a major Prague business concern really have to go to such lengths to secure a country house?). But the film is redeemed by its affectionate and funny depiction of village life, and by the very fine performances of several of the actors, particularly Hrusinsky, who is strikingly reminiscent of Denholm Elliott.

Like *My Sweet Little Village,* Woody Allen's *Radio Days* is small, sweet, and sentimental—a relatively minor film by a major director, set (in large part) in the lowly precincts of his youth. It is also an *hommage.* Allen, of course, goes in for *hommages* in a big way: *Stardust Memories* was an hommage to Fellini, *Interiors* to Bergman, *Love and Death* to the Russian novel, *Broadway Danny Rose* to the New York show-biz world, *Annie Hall* to Diane Keaton, *Manhattan* to Manhattan, *The Purple Rose of Cairo* to the movies. So it should come as no surprise that Allen, who grew up in the radio era, should make a nostalgic film called *Radio Days* set in New York in the early 1940s. Though it is more plotless by far, *Radio Days* resembles *Annie Hall* insofar as it is an anthology of episodes, loosely tied to a theme, which Allen (who serves here as narrator, but never appears on camera) encourages us to view as autobiographical. He expects us to think of the eleven-year-old redheaded Jewish kid Joe (Seth Green) as young Allen Steward Konigsberg, to regard the kid's Rockaway Beach family as his own (though he grew up, as the whole world knows, in Brooklyn), and to believe that at least some of the things that happen to them—the less outrageous, more sentimentally depicted things—really happened.

For the movie *is* sentimental, and unabashedly so. In *Annie Hall* Allen portrayed his hero's folks as uncouth, ignorant, and argumentative; in *Stardust Memories* his protagonist's sister remembers their parents as "always fighting, always screaming at each other." In *Radio Days* there is some fighting and screaming, but the picture of childhood is mostly rosy. Take Joe's first visit to Radio City Music Hall. It's a shamelessly romantic sequence; while Frank Sinatra sings "If You Are But a Dream," the camera—equipped with a wide-angle lens and shooting up at everything from a small boy's height—moves slowly through the majestic lobby, up the grand staircase, and into the dark auditorium, where on the huge screen, James Stewart is kissing Katharine Hepburn in *The Philadelphia Story*. (Was it then that Allen first decided he wanted to be rich and date *shiksas*?) The sequence has nothing to do with radio, but it captures the child's sense of wonder very touchingly, and one does not doubt for a moment that it is based upon a real childhood memory of Allen's.

The sequence brings to mind other romantic epiphanies in Allen movies: the Central Park carriage ride with Mariel Hemingway in *Manhattan;* the moment in *Stardust Memories* when Allen's character (in a point-of-view shot) looks up on a Sunday morning in his apartment to see Charlotte Rampling smiling up at him from her newspaper; the hour of happiness at a Marx Brothers movie in *Hannah and Her Sisters*. To Allen, life is mostly meaningless and miserable, but it is redeemed, at least to some extent, by occasional blissful moments of this sort, most of them made possible either by romantic relationships or by some form of art or entertainment. (Remember his eccentric list of things, near the end of *Manhattan,* that make life worthwhile: Louis Armstrong's recording of "Potato Head Blues," Flaubert's *A Sentimental Education,* the Marx Brothers, "Tracy's smile.") His pre-*Annie Hall* movies were designed to provide such moments of joy; *Annie Hall* and its successors, on the contrary, have been intended largely as mediations upon the evanescence and transcendence of these moments.

About half of *Radio Days* consists of unconnected episodes—mostly radio-related—in the life of Joe's Rockaway Beach family. In one sequence, for instance, Joe—whose idol is a radio-serial hero called the Masked Avenger—purchases a Masked Avenger ring with the money he has helped collect for the establishment of a state in Palestine; when the rabbi angrily upbraids him for this, the radio-obsessed boy replies, "You speak the truth, my faithful Indian companion." In other sequences, Orson Welles's *War of the Worlds* broadcast scares the hell out of a boyfriend of Joe's aunt (Dianne Wiest), and a love song played over the radio causes another boyfriend of hers (Robert Joy) to break down in tears and confess that his previous beloved was a man. The other half of *Radio Days* consists of briefly glimpsed episodes in the lives of radio personalities whom one member or another of Joe's family particularly admires. The most prominent of these in the film is Sally White (Mia Farrow), a dumb Brooklyn blonde with a squeaky voice who—thanks to the help of a mobster (Danny Aiello) who at first intends to rub her out—becomes a celebrated gossip reporter. There are also Roger and Irene, a pair of high-toned first-nighters who chat wittily about their glamorous life every morning on "Breakfast with Roger and Irene"; though they give an impression of marital bliss, they are both manically unfaithful to each other (forming a nice contrast, by the way, with the surface discontent and deep affection and loyalty of Joe's parents).

But even Roger and Irene are human; indeed, the surprise about *Radio Days* is how *nice* almost everybody is—even that mobster, even the crooks who break into a Rockaway Beach house (and win its owners hundreds of dollars' worth of appliances when a radio quizmaster telephones during their burglary). But then, to Allen, radio itself is nice—a force for niceness. Significantly, the last line of *Radio Days* is "Beware evildoers, wherever you are," spoken by the Masked Avenger (Wallace Shawn) just before he descends from the roof over the ballroom where he and several other radio personalities are celebrating New Year's Day, 1944. Earlier in the film, when we get our first glimpse of the Masked Avenger—short and bald and nerdy, not at all the super-hero type that his young fans image him to be—we laugh; but by the final scene we don't find him ridiculous at all. He has come to symbolize radio itself, which (regarded in retrospect from the Age of Television) seems small and harmless, and which is truly a "masked avenger" because its faceless entertainers and announcers wreak vengeance upon the evils of everyday life—its banality, its disappointments, its alienation (just as the movies did for Mia Farrow in *The Purple Rose of Cairo).* Radio not only entertains Joe's family, but also—when it brings them war news, for example, or up-to-the minute reports on the fate of a little Pennsylvania girl, who fell into a well—binds them together with the rest of the country. (In a derivative, most un-Allen-like sequence, the film cuts from Joe's family huddled around the radio, to other families, bar patrons, and soda shoppe customers who are huddled around other radios and listening to the same reports.) The film's cozy, friendly feel is enhanced by the presence in the cast of several familiar faces from the Allen repertory company—some of them, to be sure, seen very fleetingly. Aside from Farrow, Shawn, Wiest, and Aiello, there are Jeff Daniels (reprising his Biff Baxter role from *Purple Rose*), Diane Keaton (who, in the role of a radio chanteuse, serves up "You'd Be So Nice to Come Home To"), and Tony Roberts (as a radio quiz-show host).

Critics have carped that the two halves of *Radio Days* don't fit together. While it's true that there is no dramatic connection between them—and, for that matter, precious little dramatic connection within them—this isn't as significant a weakness as one might expect. For *Radio Days* is not a story but a rambling personal essay; the anecdotes of which it consists are designed not to advance a plot but to communicate what the word *radio* means to Woody Allen. For the most part, they do so with considerable charm and wit.

RAISING COEN

Raising Arizona

H. I. "Hi" McDunnough (Nicolas Cage), the goofball protagonist of the hilarious offbeat comedy *Raising Arizona,* is not only a crook: he's a hapless, pathetic small-time crook, a crook with no imagination at all who keeps getting caught for holding up convenience stores—and who keeps getting paroled, after a few months in the slammer, because he never uses live ammo. About his recidivism, Hi (who narrates the first ten minutes or so of the film) tells us, "I tried to stand up and fly right, but it wasn't easy with that sumbitch Reagan in the White House. I don't know, he seems like a nice man. Maybe he has bad advisors."

This refusal to take responsibility for his own actions is characteristic not only of Hi but of everyone around him. The world of this film—which was produced by Ethan Coen, directed by Joel Coen, and written by both of the celebrated young brothers, who were previously responsible for the stunning *Blood Simple*—is a world whose denizens, amoral, selfish, stupid, and tacky though they be, are nonetheless highly conversant with the current clichés and jargon of pop politics, pop psychology, and pop sociology; they've been educated not to behave virtuously but to transfer blame, to get in touch with their feelings, to "like themselves." At the Tempe, Arizona, "maximum security facility" to which he keeps returning, for instance, Hi is part of an encounter group at which a huge, evil-looking con articulates his feeling that he is a woman trapped inside a man's body. So it goes.

The third and last time that he gets paroled, Hi married Edwina, a.k.a. Ed (Holly Hunter), a corrections officer, and they move into a "starter home in suburban Tempe"—i.e., a mobile home in the middle of the desert. Hi takes a factory job drilling holes in metal. "These were the happy days," Hi tells us, while we watch him and Ed eat dinner from TV trays in an awful little paneled room filled with black velvet paintings, "the salad days, as they say." But one horrible circumstance threatens their perfect bliss. They want a baby, but Ed is barren, and the adoption agencies won't give them a child because of Hi's prison record. (As Hi puts it, "Biology and the prejudices of others conspired to make us childless.") A despondent Ed loses "all interest in both criminal justice and housekeeping."

It is about this time that Nathan Arizona (Trey Wilson), the smarmy owner of Unpainted Arizona, a heavily advertised store that sells unpainted furniture, becomes the father of five babies—the "Arizona quints," Harry, Barry, Garry, Larry, and Nathan, Jr. Hi, watching the news reports of the infants' birth, decides that it's unfair for Nathan Arizona to have five babies when he and Ed cannot even have one, so, urged on by Ed, who has quit her corrections job, he sneaks into the nursery of the Arizona house and purloins Nathan, Jr. (though neither he nor the baby's father is ever really certain that this one *is* Nathan, Jr.). They take the baby back to their mobile home, where Hi has strung up a banner reading WELCOME HOME SON, and Hi sets up a camera to take a portrait of his new family (or, as he puts it, "family unit").

But the kidnapping of Nathan, Jr.—whom both Hi and Ed, characteristically, continue to refer to by that name—doesn't restore their bliss. On the contrary, Hi is racked with guilt, troubled by nightmares of a vengeful, monstrous, death-dealing "Lone Biker of the Apocalypse." Moreover, complications ensue almost immediately in the form of the arrival, at Hi and Ed's home, of two pals of Hi's, Gale and Neville, who have escaped from the Tempe prison and want shelter—and who are puzzled as to why Ed isn't breast-feeding her baby. ("Ma'am," Gale explains gently, "if you don't breast-feed him he'll hate you for it. That's why we ended up in prison.") Then there's Hi's awful Polish-joke-telling boss, Glenn, who recognizes Hi and Ed's baby from the TV news and threatens to turn them in unless they give the baby to him and his wife, Dot, who have been wanting another youngster (they already have half a dozen or so). And finally there's that death-dealing biker, who turns out not to be a figment of Hi's guilty imagination after all, but rather a professional manhunter named Leonard Smalls, who's out to find Nathan, Jr., and sell him to the highest bigger. Though all of these characters eventually find out, then, that Hi and Ed are kidnappers, it never occurs to any of them to do the right thing and return the baby to his parents. Everybody's got an angle, and before the film is over, Nathan, Jr., has been kidnapped and re-kidnapped five times over.

Though *Blood Simple* was a murder drama and *Raising Arizona* is a farce, the two films have a great deal in common. Both are set in the Southwest, whose dry climate and open spaces reflect the moral aridity and intellectual vacuity of the films' characters. Both films are about people matter-of-factly committing outrageous crimes (in *Blood Simple,* a man hires someone to murder his wife in cold blood); in both films, criminals betray each other, and violence begets violence. Both films, indeed, are gruesomely, grotesquely violent, violent to the point of hilarity, like a Monty Python movie. (The most memorable sequence in *Blood Simple*—in which a man has to reach out of one window and into another, in the next room, to remove a knife that has been plunged through the wall and into his hand—has a very similar counterpart in *Raising Arizona.*) Like some of the Python movies, moreover, the films of the Coen brothers, for all their absurdity, nevertheless reflect an acute and pained awareness of the evil of which human beings are capable.

But to go on too long about such matters would be to suggest that the film is more serious than it is. In the main, *Raising Arizona* is a top-notch screwball comedy. Perhaps the funniest sequence is one that begins when Hi and Ed drop by a convenience store to buy some Huggies for Nathan, Jr., and Hi, unable to resist the temptation, holds up the joint. The ensuing chase—complete with police cars, a vicious watch dog, and a pimple-faced counterboy who turns out to be far more bloodthirsty than Hi ever was—builds wonderfully, has a terrific pace, and is as elegantly choreographed as a Balanchine ballet. (Nicolas Cage, it should be said, is far more effective here than in his uncle Francis's *Peggy Sue Got Married;* one is almost tempted to say that Cage was born to play Hi McDunnough—a frightening thought.) Another particularly funny sequence is the one in which Gale and Neville, having found out Nathan, Jr.'s true identity, tie up Hi and make off with the baby, determined to hold him for ransom. Yet they're not completely evil: when they stop to rob a bank, they're conscientious enough not to leave the baby alone in the car for five minutes—so they drag him, car seat and all, into the bank with them. Soon afterwards, when they just miss losing Nathan, Jr., due to a foolish mishap, Gale and Neville weep tears of relief and Gale decides that they'll never give him up: "He's our little Gale, Jr., now."

One of the things that separate this movie from the typical witless and pallid contemporary film comedy is its plethora of wacky, weird details: the vulgar five-baby wooden crib, for instance, in the Arizona nursery, on which the boys' names are printed over their respective heads; the sign reading FARM SUBSIDY CHECKS CASHED HERE in the rural bank that Gale and Neville rob; the Mondale-Ferraro sticker on Gale and Neville's car. Another delightful aspect of the film is that the Coen brothers make fun not only of contemporary American manners and morals but of contemporary American film: *Raising Arizona* is full of camera moves and angles that parody the visual clichés of *Friday the Thirteenth* and *Halloween* type movies, as well as of Steven Spielberg. *Raising Arizona* is not a work of genius, by any means, but it is inspired and inventive throughout—and this alone places it head and shoulders above most of the comedy films of the day.

TOUGH GUYS

The Untouchables
River's Edge
Prick Up Your Ears

About halfway through *The Untouchables,* equable T-man Eliot Ness (Kevin Costner), who's involved in a sanguinary war with the bootlegging empire of Al Capone (Robert De Niro), erupts in unaccustomed anger when a thug refused to drop his piece and Ness is forced to blow him away. "What is this?" Ness cries. "A game?"

Precisely—or so, at least, the film's director, Brian De Palma, and writer, David Mamet, want us to believe. For at the end of the film, the risks, sacrifices, and deaths (Ness loses two members of his three-man squad of "untouchables" to Capone's gunmen) are made to seem meaningless. Yes, Capone's finally headed for the Big House. But so what? The Windy City's still crawling with corrupt characters—including the judge, jurors, and cops who, but for Ness's heroic efforts, would've gotten Capone off. As Ness's pal Malone (Sean Connery) observes, the only man Ness can really trust is Ness—and even *he's* not perfectly virtuous, and he knows it. He even goes so far as to claim that he's become just like the people he's been stalking; in the judge's chambers during Capone's trial he admits, "I've broken every law I've sworn to uphold." What's more, the law that he's dedicated himself to enforcing—the Volstead Act—is one in which he doesn't seem to believe; as he tells a roomful of police recruits, having a drink now and then may not be a bad thing—what's important is not right vs. wrong but legal vs. illegal. In the penultimate line of the movie, a reporter says to Ness, "They're going to repeal prohibition. What will you do then?" Ness's reply: "I think I'll have a drink." And he strides away from the camera, like the conventional Western hero riding off into the sunset. But De Palma and Mamet want our admiration for him to be mixed with a sense that all of his heroic efforts have come to very little, that his heroism is tinged with absurdity.

Indeed, as he is portrayed in this film, Ness *is* a bit absurd—ingenuously dedicated to law and order and unquestioningly patriotic. He's not unlike Ed Harris's John Glenn in *The Right Stuff*—a clean-cut, gee-whiz, all-American square. He has a wife, but all we really know about her is that she is pleasant, loyal, and antiseptically attractive, and that she and Ness love each other very much; her part in his life consists mostly of looking concerned when he is in trouble, of leaving town in police custody (with their young daughter) when Ness decides that her life is in danger, and of beaming proudly from her seat on the aisle when he triumphs over Capone in the courtroom. "Are you married?" Ness asks a cop during a stakeout, and when the cop replies that he is, Ness says—in an incredibly wholesome tone—"It's good to be married, isn't it?" Later in the film, virtually the same line comes out of the mouth of Malone, a bachelor.

But *why* is it good to be married? We're not going to find out from this film; the important interaction here is not between male and female, but between male and male. (Significantly, though *he* is married, Ness wants all of his "untouchables" to be bachelors.) It might be said, in fact, that on one level *The Untouchables* is a study in the way men relate to each other. Although Ness and his wife are hardly seen touching in the film, there are scenes aplenty which find Ness in a tight, riveting, almost erotically intense eye-to-eye two-shot with some other man. The film develops largely through a series of confrontations between men. When Ness first meets Malone they argue; when the two of them first meet Stone (another "untouchable"), Malone tries to provoke Stone's anger with ethnic slurs. Yet beneath the surface of each of these encounters one senses a strong personal attraction—these men are not simply confronting one another, they're sizing each other up, engaged in a sort of male version of a mating ritual. Even Ness and Capone—who come face to face twice, very dramatically—have between them a provocatively ambiguous chemistry. (There are, furthermore, some sequences—for example, the one in which Capone fondles a baseball bat while speechifying at a dozen or so of his tuxedoed cronies—that one can hardly avoid reading as homoerotic.)

Since *The Untouchables* is a Brian De Palma film, it is not only about Eliot Ness and Al Capone but about movies and moviemaking; like previous De Palma films it's set not in the real world—or to be specific, in the director's version thereof, where real-world values apply—but in a *movie* world, a deliberate never-never land of De Palma's imagination where style is nearly everything and moral questions are largely irrelevant. From the very first scene—an overhead shot of Capone in a barber's chair (cf. *Scarface*) being interviewed by reporters—the camera angles call attention to themselves. And they're *supposed* to: De Palma doesn't want us to forget for a second that this is a movie. This is why his camera never seems to sit still: he wants us to be aware constantly that there *is* a camera.

At one point, for instance, De Palma trains his camera upon a circular table at which the "untouchables" are seated, and then sends the camera spinning completely around the table, panning from face to face as it does so. The purpose of this shot may be defensible—De Palma may mean to point up these men's isolation from the world and their devotion to each other (Stanley Kramer made very effective use of such a shot for a similar purpose near the end of *On the Beach,* when he revolved his camera around the dancing, doomed protagonists portrayed by Gregory Peck and Ava Gardner)—but there are so many distracting camera movements of this sort in *The Untouchables* that after a while one wants to scream, "Enough already!" Similarly, the musical score (by Ennio Morricone) is often excessively dramatic, and several of the performances (notably De Niro's) are almost ludicrously overdrawn—all of which is, of course, in the classic De Palma tradition. Even Costner, in his magnificently minimalistic performance as Ness, comes dangerously close to excess—i.e., to overdoing his underplaying.

Nor has De Palma grown tired of perpetrating his famous *hommages* to great directors and films of the past. Given a choice between creating an original, realistic sequence and contriving a derivative one with an immediately recognizable filmic antecedent, he'll do the latter every time. For example, when Ness is waiting for a Capone bookkeeper to show up at Chicago's Union Station, and a woman and baby carriage appear at the foot of a nearby staircase, one knows immediately that De Palma is setting up an *hommage* to the famous pram sequence in *Potemkin*. Yet despite its derivativeness, this sequence is wonderfully effective—perhaps the best thing in the movie, in fact. The set-up—in typical De Palma fashion—is long and uneventful (remember Angie Dickinson's endless trek through the museum corridors in *Dressed to Kill?*), but once the action starts, so much happens in such a brief stretch of real time that De Palma shows it to us in slow motion so that we can take it all in. And, one might add, so that we can be impressed by the sequence's thrilling choreography. It's almost as if De Palma's playing teacher, offering us a sort of film-school anatomy lesson—a slow-motion dissection of a top-notch crime-film shoot-out. De Palma is in truth an academic sort of director, a man whose films, like the work of some academic poets, are extraordinarily contrived and extraordinarily conscious of their influences.

Needless to say, this tendency to devote more attention to coy allusions and camera tricks than to character development and dramatic structure has seriously weakened many of De Palma's films. But I was very pleasantly surprised by the degree to which *The Untouchables* held up in spite of this cinemacentric sensibility. For the truth is that, despite its superficiality and cynicism, this film is wonderfully entertaining. The story builds extremely well; there are viturally no dead spots; the editing and cinematography are impeccable; and the performances by Costner and Connery are truly impressive. Moreover, there are half a dozen action and suspense sequences each of which is so nearly perfect of its kind that, if it were transplanted into a typical contemporary crime picture, it would without question be the film's highlight. *The Untouchables* is, in short, a contrivance—but a decidedly first-rate one.

Like *The Untouchables, River's Edge* is based on a story of violence and retribution. But in tone and purpose the film—which was directed by Tim Hunter and written by Neal Jiminez—could hardly be more different from De Palma's glossy entertainment. *River's Edge* is based on a bizarre 1981 incident in a small northern California town: a high-school boy killed his girlfriend and showed several friends her dead body—which he'd left exposed on the banks of the local river—but none of them was as outraged or horrified as one might expect them to be; they continued to attend school, to hang out and party, and days passed before anyone reported the crime. The film focuses upon the murderer, a fat psychopath named Samson, a.k.a. John (Daniel

Roebuck), and upon his circle of friends, who are unable to recognize Samson's madness or to be deeply affected by his murder of their friend Jamie.

It's not that they're particularly scummy kids; indeed, most of them, though their lives revolve around dope and acid rock, would under ordinary circumstances probably pass as relatively decent. But something inside them is dead: they're unable to react to the murder with the grief and horror that normal civilized people would be expected to experience. To her credit, a girl named Clarissa is at least able to recognize her own inability to feel: she notes that she cried when "that guy in *Brian's Song*" died; why isn't she crying now? What is so remarkable about this film is that it makes these kids' anomie utterly believable. Even as one laughs—and, perversely, one cannot help laughing loud and long—at some of the extraordinarily insensitive remarks of some of the kids, one is profoundly disturbed. Indeed, I don't remember ever seeing a film that disturbed me the way this one did. *Blue Velvet* came closest, but one was able to remind onself, after experiencing its emotionally devastating (and, at the same time, weirdly funny) vision of the heart of small-town darkness, that it was a fiction; with *River's Edge* one has no such consolation.

What made these kids this way? The film places a good deal of the blame—and convincingly so—on the values and life-styles that became popular during, and continue to be associated with, the sixties. For the sixties mentality, in one way or another, seems to be responsible for the character of the adults who play the most significant roles in these kids' lives. Take the mother of Matt (Keanu Reeves)—a boy whose conflict of conscience becomes the film's primary focus, and who eventually turns Samson in. Matt's mom doesn't discipline her kids (even her twelve-year-old, Tim, is an earringed pothead); her house is a mess; her boyfriend lives with the family (Dad, apparently, walked out years ago). And she smokes dope: when Matt runs out of joints, he dips into her stash. Then there's the kids' history teacher. He's one of those ex-hippie teachers who try to "relate" to their students and preach "relevance" and "commitment," but who don't even try to instill in their students what the kids need most desperately—worthy ambitions, moral awareness, a respect for authority and for adulthood. Significantly, the adult whom the kids most look up to is the scummiest of them all: Fack (Dennis Hopper), a grotesque, one-legged hermit who killed *his* girlfriend twenty years ago and who regularly provides the local teenagers with free dope.

It's Fack to whom Samson describes the exhilaration he felt when he killed Jamie: "She was there dead in front of me and I felt so fucking *alive!*" To these kids, feeling alive is a rare experience; apparently the only thing they have to live for is the next high. ("Sometimes," Clarissa tells Matt at one point, "I think it would be a lot easier being dead." "No, that's bullshit!" Matt argues. "You couldn't get stoned any more.") What's more, like Fack, whose only friend is a plastic sex doll, none of them is really close to anybody. They think that they're one another's friends, but they don't even know the meaning of the word: Jamie, after all, was a "friend," and they can't even feel particularly bad about her death or get angry at her killer. Worst of all is Layne, a wiry, wild-eyed pill-popper who's almost as crazy as Samson, and who is rather pleased by the murder because it seems likely to bring them all even closer to each other—in defense of their friend Samson, of course. Ironically, when Tim says, "You're gonna pay for what you did," he doesn't say it to Samson but to Matt—whose act of squealing seems more of an obscenity, according to these kids' moral code, than the murder itself.

In general, the young actors are very good, though one spends a good deal of one's time worrying about Crispin Glover's performance as Layne. It's a broad, gutsy performance (sometimes uncomfortably reminiscent of Sean Penn's Jeff Spicoli character from *Fast Times at Ridgemont High*), and it may strike many viewers as *too* broad, more appropriate to a comedy than to a film like *River's Edge*. In Glover's defense, however, it must be said that there *are* young people who behave exactly like his Layne—who deliver lines with the same Valley-boy drawl, who indulge in the same broad gestures, who have the same dopey-eyed look.

River's Edge is the most frightening American film to come along in many a year—and it is frightening not because it makes us believe in an implausible tale of horror, but because it opens our eyes to a horror story that happened in our midst, and that—in a very real sense—is all around us still.

Yet another story of a real-life murder—and of its bizarre background—is told in the British film *Prick Up Your Ears*. The film, a biography of the irreverent sixties playwright Joe Orton, has been elegantly directed by Stephen Frears (*My Beautiful Laundrette*) from a literate script by Alan Bennett. Bennett's script is based upon the 1978 book of the same title by John Lahr. Like the book, the film is actually a dual biography, telling the story not only of Orton—a Leicester working-class boy who found the world of his parents bleak and unimaginative and fatuously conventional—but of Kenneth Halliwell, seven years his elder, whom he met at age eighteen when they were both acting students at the Royal Academy of Dramatic Art in London, and who became the most important person in his life.

"When Orton met Halliwell in 1951," Lahr writes, "he found a surrogate brother and formed the only family he would ever acknowledge." Orton also found in Halliwell the lover with whom he would spend the rest of his short life, and the mentor who would introduce him to the classics and to writing. For several years after they'd left RADA, the two of them, sharing a room in then-unfashionable Islington, collaborated on novels (which they couldn't get published) as well as on fake blurbs for the jackets of library books (a prank which landed them both in prison for several months); for years they were nothing more than misfits, weirdos, a couple of losers.

Then everything changed. In 1963 a play Orton had written, *Entertaining Mr. Sloane,* was produced in the West End and became a huge hit. Suddenly Orton was the toast of London. *Loot,* an even bigger hit, followed. Then, on August 9, 1967—soon after the thirty-four-year-old Orton had completed a play called *What the Butler Saw*—Halliwell took a hammer and smashed open Orton's skull, splattering his brain on the apartment's wall and ceiling. Halliwell then took twenty-two Nembutals with a grapefruit juice chaser.

Lahr's book opens with the murder-suicide; so does the movie. It's Orton's murder, after all, which makes Orton's life interesting—that, and the outrageous sexual escapades which he recorded carefully in his diaries. (*The Orton Diaries,* as I write this, is number one on the *Village Voice Literary Supplement* best-seller list—a reasonably good index of what's selling in literary bookstores in New York, where the film's been playing for several weeks; a reissue of *Prick Up Your Ears* stands at number six on the paperback list.) As for Orton's plays, which Lahr discusses at length (most of the second half of his book is devoted to plot summary and analysis), they are given relatively short shrift by Frears; a viewer who doesn't have much sense of what they are like will leave the theater with little more than a vague notion that Orton's work is as outrageous as he was.

And how outrageous was he? This the film shows us in spades. Leaving his mother's funeral, Orton (Gary Oldman) picks up a fat, unsavory workingman at the bus stop and loves him up in a nearby abandoned building. Later he takes his mother's false teeth and hands them to an actor in *Loot* to use as a stage prop. After accepting an award at a formal ceremony, Orton heads for a Holloway Road *pissoir* where he sets his statuette down on the floor and proceeds to have sex, in the dark, with half a dozen or so strangers. Rich and successful, he and Halliwell (Alfred Molina) fly to North Africa and surround themselves with scantily clad teenaged boys.

This is not, in short, *The Life of Emile Zola*. But it is unarguably a fascinating film. Despite all of the outrageous antics, though, what is most interesting to watch is the series of subtle transformations in the relationship between Orton and Halliwell. (Frears seems to specialize in the sociology of offbeat homosexual couples.) When they first meet, Halliwell is the sophisticated older man, Orton the cocky provincial boy whom he takes under his wing; but after *Entertaining Mr. Sloane,* Halliwell essentially takes on the role of Mrs. Orton—a cranky, prissy, neglected consort who cooks and answers the phone and identifies himself officially as the playwright's secretary. In the role of the cocky, narcissistic Orton (to whom he bears a remarkable resemblance), Oldman is splendid. As for the bald, bearlike Molina (whom fans of bad English cinema will remember as a Russian sailor in *Letter to Brezhnev*), he is certainly a compelling performer, but even when he is playing Halliwell as a young, relatively stable man at RADA he is already so scary and crazy-looking that one cannot for a moment understand Orton's attraction to him. (To judge by photographs, the real Halliwell was actually quite pleasant-looking—with, by the way, a much better-looking toupee than the one that Frears has slapped on Molina.)

Interpolated in the film are several sequences that take place years after Orton's death, and depict John Lahr's (Wallace Shawn) meetings with various survivors preparatory to the writing of his biography. Wallace Shawn—who is probably best known to audience from *My Dinner with Andre,* and as the "little homunculus" in *Manhattan*—is, I suppose, a good actor; but his peculiar appearance, voice, and mannerisms are highly disconcerting, and make if difficult to accept him as anybody other than Wallace Shawn. (Put it this way: If anybody hired him to play *me,* I'd sue.) The main link between these sequences and the body of the film is Peggy Ramsay (Vanessa Redgrave), Orton's agent, who provides Lahr with the playwright's diaries and shares her memories of Orton. Miss Redgrave handles this role quite professionally, but she is less a performer here than she is a lovely and stately presence: she seems to spend most of her screen time stepping elegantly out of cabs, applauding elegantly at awards dinners, and sitting elegantly at her desk. (I know the English are a lot classier than we are—but an *agent?*)

Why has Stephen Frears included these sequences? For one thing, he seems to be interested in pointing up the contrast between the low-key bourgeois life-style of John Lahr, Typical Writer, and the self-destructive, fast-lane life-style of Joe Orton, Literary Rebel (who, incidentally, started his life as John—he changed his first name, at Peggy Ramsay's suggestion, to avoid confusion with John Osborne). For another thing, Frears apparently wants to suggest a parallel between Lahr's wife—a devoted secretary-cook-typist whom Lahr takes for granted—and Halliwell. The sequences serve useful transitional purposes, too; and perhaps Frears also felt that these relatively low-intensity sequences would provide necessary breathers between high-intensity sequences about Orton. And perhaps he was right; but, though the Lahr segments are of interest, they don't strike me as having been worth the trouble, and certainly don't do much for the film's unity.

On the whole, however, *Prick Up Your Ears* is a very impressive film, a thought-provoking contemplation—like *My Beautiful Laundrette*—upon the themes of love, resentment, poverty, and violence. It provides further evidence—if any is needed—of the extraordinary inventiveness and sensitivity of Stephen Frears's directorial imagination. I look forward eagerly to his next project.

SUMMER FARE

The Squeeze
Spaceballs
Innerspace
Roxanne

The best one can hope for from most summer films is not that they will challenge one's intelligence, but that at any rate they will not insult it too brutally. Be warned that one of the more brutally insulting movies of this or any summer is *The Squeeze*. This tiresome comedy stars Michael Keaton as Harry Berg, a hapless schmo who lives on an abandoned Manhattan pier and spends his time (a) building giant sculptures out of working TV sets and (b) running away from people whom he's tried unsuccessfully to cheat at poker. Harry's a completely unbelievable, uninteresting character, but the hack writer (Daniel Taplitz) and director (Roger Young) who are responsible for this inert, murky mess doubtless think that he is kooky and lovable.

The film's witless excuse for a plot is as follows: Harry unwittingly stumbles upon a conspiracy to rig a $56 million "Lotto" drawing, gets chased by thugs through various discotheques and seedy motels, and along the way becomes romantically involved with a process server played by Rae Dawn Chong (have two less charismatic personalities ever shared a movie screen?). Yawn. It's one of those pictures in which the hero and heroine hate each other most of the way through—a sentiment which, in this case, is shared by the audience—and toss lines like "Oh yeah?" and "That's what you think" at each other in a tone that suggests these quips are brilliantly witty. The few truly funny lines in the picture, oddly enough, were plainly dubbed in after principal production was completed; apparently somebody decided that it might be a good idea to give the audience some clue that this was supposed to be a comedy.

In any event, the film doesn't develop so much as drag, and at the end—when Taplitz and Young, in a fatuously executed attempt to generate some climactic energy and drama, fill the deck of the aricraft carrier *Intrepid* with hundreds of screaming extras and a painfully unfunny John Davidson as the Lotto drawing's master of ceremonies—it falls completely apart. Nothing in this movie feels real: not the people, not the Lotto drawing (which strikes one as a moron's version of the end of *The Day of the Locust*), not even New York. To be sure, the creators of *The Squeeze* seem to think they've captured the megalopolitan atmosphere to a T (the ad shows a gigantic Keaton being squeezed between the World Trade Center's twin towers), but the fact is that I've never seen a film made in New York that so thoroughly succeeded in *not* capturing the feel of the city. Indeed, I kept forgetting that the film was shot in New York, and kept being surprised by the familiar landmarks that periodically turned up.

Mel Brooks's directorial career divides neatly into two phases. The early Brooks—of *The Producers, The Twelve Chairs, Blazing Saddles,* and *Young Frankenstein*—fussed over plot, lighting, and cinematography, stayed mostly behind the camera, and at times, for all the crudity of his humor, actually perpetrated sequences that were witty and sophisticated. The later Brooks—of *High Anxiety, Silent Movie, The History of the World Part One,* and *To Be or Not To Be*—became the star of his own pictures, which, compared to their predecessors, were less interesting visually, sloppier structurally, and even broader and more vulgar in their humor.

Though Brooks's new film, the egregiously titled *Spaceballs,* fits squarely into the later-Brooks mold, in many respects it is an outer-space variation on *Blazing Saddles.* In *Saddles* a passel of villains threatened to destroy the ridiculously idyllic frontier town of Rock Ridge; in the new film the evil planet Spaceballs (led by Mel Brooks himself as the sleazy, bumbling President Skroob, a retread of the Governor William J. Lepetomane role he played in *Saddles*) seeks to destroy the ridiculously idyllic planet Druidia (whose king is played by the worst actor in North America, Dick Van Patten). Many of Brooks's films have been parodies of various movie genres, and

Spaceballs is no exception: the film gags it up at the expense of the *Star Wars* series, and along the way also sends up *Alien,* the *Star Trek* movies, and even *Planet of the Apes.* (How long ago did Brooks, Thomas Meehan, and Ronny Graham write this script, anyway?) Though many of the parodic references are screamingly funny, too often they seem merely mechanical, as in the Hitchcock take-off, *High Anxiety,* whereing Brooks seemed determined to allude to as many Hitchcock films as possible.

In classic Mel Brooks fashion, the humor in *Spaceballs* consists mostly of sophomoric sexual and scatological jokes and outrageous Borscht-belt puns, often Jewish-related (the spoiled Princess Vespa of Druidia is a "Druish princess"; Brooks, in the role of the Yoda-like ancient sage Yogurt, says to Luke Skywalker-like hero, played by Bill Pullman, "May the Schwartz be with you"). Corny and lowbrow as it is, however, the movie is Brooks's most enjoyable in a long time. And its cleverest moments, interestingly, occur when the plot drops away and the characters start talking to the audience or discuss the fact that they're in a movie.

In one sequence, for instance, President Skroob and the evil but klutzy Darth Vader-like warrior Dark Helmet (Rick Moranis) fast-forward through a videotape of *Spaceballs* in order to find out where the princess (whom they want to kidnap) has gone. Then there's a funny bit in which Yogurt introduces the complete line of *Spaceballs* merchandise: lunchboxes, T-shirts, mugs, all emblazoned with the movie's title—and for the remainder of the movie, the set decoration includes official *Spaceballs* bedsheets, toilet paper, and so forth. There are, then, quite a few laughs here—although one does wish that Brooks would someday favor us with another production as brilliant as his classic *The Producers.*

Back in 1966 a director named Richard Fleischer made a movie called *Fantastic Voyage,* in which Raquel Welch and others were reduced to microscopic size and injected into the body of an Iron Curtain scientist for the purpose of removing a blood clot from his brain. In *Innerspace,* director Joe Dante and writers Jeffrey Boam and Chip Proser have taken this "concept" (as such things are called in Lotus-land) and explored its comic possibilities. This time, the fantastic voyager is a tough-talking test pilot named Tuck Pendleton (Dennis Quaid), who's in the employ of a Silicon Valley firm seeking to enter the hot new field of miniaturization; he and his inner-space capsule—which looks rather like a lunar module—are supposed to be injected into the body of a rabbit, but some high-tech thugs from a competing outfit (led by Kevin McCarthy) intervene and he ends up instead in the body of a nervous, hypochondriacal supermarket cashier named Jack Putter (Martin Short). Thanks to some useful devices in the capsule, Tuck is able to see through Jack's eyes, hear through his ears, and speak to him without anyone else hearing his voice. (The parallels to such recent films as *All of Me, The Man with Two Brains,* and *Oh Heavenly Dog* cause one to wonder whether the folks in Hollywood are having some sort of crisis of Self and Other.)

The plot is formulaic: in order to save Tuck (who's in danger of running out of air, just like the folks on Druidia), Jack has to swallow his timidity and take on the bad guys, who have stolen a component necessary to Tuck's deminiaturization; in doing this Jack learns to be as tough as Tuck, while Tuck, for his part, learns from Jack how to treat his extranged lady friend (Meg Ryan) with respect and consideration. Formulaic as it is, though, the plot is spun out with a charm and cleverness that at times recall *Tootsie.* And one relatively original touch is that the film takes an irreverent tone toward advanced technology—a refreshing departure at a time when American movies seem more fascinated by computers than by human beings.

Among the cleverest episodes in *Innerspace,* in fact, are those that parody the elaborate sequences, so common in recent films, in which impressive high-tech operations are shown or described in reverent detail; the film deliberately depicts the minaturization process as just plain silly, the scientists as absurdly solemn and self-important, the purpose of their experiment as ridiculously obscure. (Why do they want to shrink Tuck Pendleton and inject him into a rabbit? Mainly because they *can.*) Finally, the relationship between Tuck and Jack is funny and well developed and (for all its ridiculousness) even touching; both of the lead actors turn in strong performances, and Martin Short in particular does a virtuoso job in one of the more demanding comic roles in recent years.

Another virtuoso comic performance has been turned in this summer by Steve Martin. Martin has not, for the most part, been well served by the movies—or, to name names, by Carl Reiner, who has directed most of his vehicles. Reiner's got the same Borscht-belt sensibility as Mel Brooks, but lacks Brooks's comic genius; his strength lies in the realm of TV skits and sitcoms, and the bulk of his film work (the closest thing to an exception is *All of Me*) betrays a dismaying lack of visual imagination, as well as a prodigious indifference to such essentials as character, plot, and production values.

Fortunately, Martin's new film, *Roxanne,* has been directed by Fred Schepisi, and as a result it is, of all Martin's films, the least bumpy and murky, and the most pleasant to look at; not only the direction but the editing, cinematography, and production design are all considerably improved. The film's principal characters and plot are no small potatoes either—both having been borrowed, with a few major changes (e.g., a happy ending), from Edmund Rostand's classic play *Cyrano de Bergerac.* Martin himself wrote the surprisingly literate screenplay, which resurrects Cyrano as C.D. Bales, a small-town American fire chief with a nose the size of Wisconsin.

C.D.'s beloved, Roxanne (Daryl Hannah), is an astronomer who's in town for the summer, and Chris (Rick Rossovich), the handsome but none too bright young man whose love letters to Roxanne C.D. agrees to ghostwrite (in the original play this character was named Christian), is a young fireman who's also new in town. The film is more often amusing than it is hilarious, but it is consistently good-natured and charming; though Daryl Hannah brings less substance to the title role than one might hope (this is another example of a director trying to make an actress look intelligent by putting glasses on her), Steve Martin is wonderfully impressive in a role that requires him to be at once heroic and pathetic, romantic and ridiculous; he handles intimate dialogue, comic patter, and out-and-out slapstick with equal grace and self-possession. And in many ways his script is as impressive as his acting: it is especially entertaining to watch Martin come up with contemporary American equivalents for some of the situations and conflicts in Rostand's play (e.g., he has created a sequence in a bar in which C.D., like Cyrano before him, improvises twenty jokes about the size of his nose).

But what is most special about *Roxanne* is its respect for intelligence, sensitivity, and articulateness. In an era when American movie comedies tend to present us with heroes who are "common men" with a vengeance (i.e., inarticulate lunkheads) and with villains whose villainy is defined by their erudition and wit, it is very gratifying to see a movie in which the hero wins his beloved's heart because he can express himself intelligently. Perhaps there is hope yet for American film comedy—and (could it be?) even for summer movies.

KUBRICK GOES TO WAR

Full Metal Jacket

No main title, no establishing shot: at the beginning of *Full Metal Jacket* Stanley Kubrick takes us straight from a dark screen into the stunningly bright interior of a Marine Corps boot camp barracks on Parris Island, South Carolina, where a steely-eyed drill instructor—seen in frightening close-up—is busy delivering a blistering welcoming address to his newly arrived young charges. What Kubrick's doing to us here is essentially equivalent to what the D.I. is doing to his soldiers: he's attempting to shock us into paying attention to him, into heeding with awe and humility his view of the world. One's reaction to this opening sequence—which is succeeded by a number of episodes that further illustrate the D.I.'s tyranny over his men—embodies an interesting contradiction. On the one hand, the sequence has a very realistic feel; on the other, the only reason one knows immediately what's happening here is that one has seen other military movies, and the part where the cold-blooded, insulting boot-camp D.I. introduces himself to the new men is of course one of the all-time military-movie clichés.

This sort of thing happens throughout *Full Metal Jacket*. In sequence after sequence, Kubrick combines graphic realism—and a masterly sense of pacing (within the sequence, at any rate)—with motifs that were already old hat when Kubrick made *Paths of Glory* in 1958. For example, when a squad of Marines, picking its way through the ruins of a Vietnamese city, finds itself being shot at by a sniper, the viewer knows immediately that the sniper will turn out to be either a woman or child; similarly, when one of those Marines, in the course of inspecting a bombed-out building, happens upon a child's doll, one knows that he will touch the doll, and that it will explode.

The movie divides—somewhat before the halfway point—into two sections, each of which is structured in the manner of a short story and, accordingly, builds to its own climax. The first is set entirely on Parris Island; it is concerned with the effects of the D.I.'s rhetoric upon platoon number 3092, in particular upon a soldier named Lawrence, whom the D.I. singles out for special abuse. The second is set in Nam at the time of the Tet offensive. The two sections are bound together not by plot but, principally, by the fact that in both of them the point-of-view figure—who now and again provides bits of mostly gratuitous narration—is a soldier known as Private Joker (Matthew Modine). Though he is the central character in this film, we don't get to know Joker very well; all we know, really, is that he is a decent person, a writer, and a wise guy—a rather cocky sort who manifestly fancies himself an intellectual. In Nam—where he works as a reporter for *Stars and Stripes*—Joker habitually wears both a peace button and a helmet on which he has scrawled the slogan "BORN TO KILL." When an officer notices the contradiction and asks him to explain, Joker replies, "I think I was trying to suggest something about the duality of man—the Jungian thing, sir."

Joker is not the only person in the movie who is profoundly cognizant of the duality of man. On the contrary, if there is anything original about Kubrick's characterization of the D.I., it resides in the emphasis that he places upon the D.I.'s intuitive awareness of this duality, of man's innate capacity to make both love and war. For it seems to be the D.I.'s goal, during the eight weeks of training at Parris Island, to convert (as fully as possible) his charges' hunger for love into a thirst for blood. Hence he continually compares killing to sexual intercourse, and likens rifles to male members or to women. Holding up a rifle, the D.I. tells his men, "You're married to this piece—this weapon of iron and wood"; he teaches them to chant: "I don't want no teenage queen; I just want my M-14."

The D.I.'s speeches are obsessively sexual. He taunts his men by calling them women or implying that they are homosexuals or masturbators; the last thing he says to them at bedtime is "Good night, ladies," and the first thing he says in the morning is "Drop your cocks and grab your socks." (One is frequently reminded, by the way, of the D.I. portrayed by Louis Gossett in *An Officer and a Gentleman*—and indeed, one of Gossett's lines reappears in this film's opening sequence. When the D.I. asks a soldier where he's from, the answer is Texas, and the D.I. says, "Only queers and steers come from Texas.") He tries to tap not only his soldiers' sex drives, furthermore, but also their religious instincts, telling them that "God has a hard-on for Marines because we kill everything we see. . . . We keep Heaven packed with fresh souls." In short, the D.I. tries to turn the platoon into a collection of murderers. The Marine Corps, he informs them, "does not want robots—the Marine Corps wants killers." He declares that Lee Harvey Oswald and Charles Whitman (of the University of Texas massacre), who were both Marines, "showed what a motivated Marine and his rifle can do." He trains his men to answer the question "What do we do for a living, ladies?" with the words, "Kill kill kill, sir."

If the D.I. bears down particularly hard on Private Lawrence—a corpulent, simple-minded soldier whom he dubs "Gomer Pyle"—it is because Lawrence seems to be the member of the platoon least likely to turn into an effective killer. He's a wimp: he can't get through the obstacle courses, he hides doughnuts in his footlocker. Yet after he has been tormented enough by the D.I.—and by his fellow privates as well, who resent the punishments that the D.I. inflicts upon them on account of Lawrence's failings—the fat, pathetic isolato develops a pathological attachment to his rifle (which he talks to, and names Charlene), eventually becoming the best shot in the platoon. The D.I. congratulates Lawrence for his turnaround. But on the night before the platoon is to leave Parris Island, Lawrence—with a frightfully insane look in his eye—picks up Charlene, blasts a huge hole through the D.I.'s midriff, then shoves the gun's barrel in his own mouth and blows off the top of his head. So ends the first section of the film.

It is a breathtaking fade-out, but it is also decidedly melodramatic, and—in the final analysis—not only dramatically unnecessary but actually harmful to Kubrick's thematic intention, which apparently is, in part, to convince us that we live in "a world of shit." Kubrick plainly wants it to be assumed that the story he tells of these particular Marines is in some way representative of the military experience; for him to conclude the first section of the film the way he does, however, is to suggest that his film presents an exaggerated, even a romantic, view of its subject. How many Marines, after all, kill their drill instructors and then commit suicide?

The more one thinks about it, in fact, the less plausible the whole story of Lawrence and the D.I. begins to seem. For one thing, would a young man who was this fat, this slow-witted, and this psychologically disturbed be admitted into the Marines in the first place? Was any D.I., moreover, ever as thoroughly inhuman as this one? For Kubrick doesn't show us any side of the man other than his kill-kill-kill persona. Though he is one of the film's major characters, we don't know where he is from, how he became this way, what his personal life consists of (but then, this is more or less true of Joker as well); he comes across less as a human being than as a conception of evil in the shape of a man, a symbolically charged Kubrickian variation on a military-movie stereotype.

The second section of the film finds Joker in different surroundings and with a different supporting cast (the two main members of the previous supporting cast having been dispatched through the agency of Charlene). He and his photographer sidekick "Rafterman" are preparing to cover Ann-Margret's forthcoming visit to Nam when the Tet Offensive takes place. The results of the offensive are devastating. "It's a huge shit sandwich," Joker's editor tells a meeting of his staff, "and we're all gonna have to take a bite." (Joker's typically sardonic response: "Does this mean Ann-Margret's not coming?") Joker and Rafterman are sent to cover the fighting, and much of the rest of the movie consists of a sort of filmic equivalent of the article that one might imagine Joker writing. We are shown the bodies of a score of Vietnamese civilians murdered by North Vietnamese soldiers, shown a whore plying her wares among the American soldiery ("Sucky sucky?") and a thief snatching Rafterman's camera.

But mostly we're presented with vignettes of various types of American soldiers: the complacent, the thoughtful, the committed, the angry, the jaded. One soldier explains that "we are here to help the Vietnamese because inside every gook is an American trying to get out." Another says, "You think we waste gooks for freedom? If I'm gonna [kill] for a word, my word is poontang." And yet another complains, "We're supposed to be helping these people and they shit on us every chance they get." Every so often we come across a Xerox copy of Lawrence or the D.I. For instance, there's a soldier who brags about killing women and children, laughs crazily, and screams, "Ain't war hell?" all the while emptying his machine gun into a jungle from a speeding helicopter. And there's an officer who, after a skirmish with the VC, announces in a tone eerily reminiscent of the D.I. that "these people we wasted here today are the finest human beings in the world."

In order to provide a believable context for some of this speechifying, Kubrick shows a number of soldiers being interviewed by TV news reporters; it's a weak device, and Kubrick doesn't bring enough fresh insight to it to justify its employment here. He merely has the soldiers talk into the camera, each of them offering a different view of the war. ("I wanted to be the first kid on my block with a confirmed kill," says Joker, a smirk on his face.) Some of this material is effective, but much of it is familiar, and the fake-documentary style is unsatisfying.

Much of the latter section of the film, in fact, is unsatisfying. We're constantly waiting for a plot to develop, and waiting as well for some indication of how the second part of the movie is supposed to tie in with the first part. (We might as well be waiting for Godot.) We're constantly aware, too, of Kubrick sitting by the camera and pulling the strings. The ironies are invariably heavyhanded and unoriginal: for example, a soldier is killed while waiting for his discharge papers to come through. And Joker's somber narration (e.g., "The dead only know one thing: it is better to be alive") is often as facile and tired as his jokes. The last sequence in the film—in which a squad of soldiers, Joker among them, is attacked by a lone sniper—is perhaps the strongest; it is splendidly photographed and paced. But even this sequence—down to the last moments with the dying sniper ("What's she saying?" "She's praying")—is too familiar, too reminiscent of a hundred other war movies, and not especially good ones, either.

What is really missing from *Full Metal Jacket*—for all the grandeur of Kubrick's directorial style, in particular those blatantly symmetrical, eerily serene shots of barracks and corridors and such—is a strong shaping vision. There is, to be sure, something of a resolution at the end of the film; Joker is finally presented with a situation that he cannot bring himself to joke about, and is forced to become the killer that the facetiously inscribed slogan on his helmet proclaims him to be. But since one does not identify with this one-dimensional smart aleck anyway, the crisis that he undergoes—the "lesson," as it were, that he learns—has very little resonance. So uncertainly shaped is the film, in fact, that on the night I saw it, the audience began murmuring with surprise when the closing credits began rolling. "Is that it?" one voice cried out. In a way, I suppose it was a tribute to Kubrick's artistry that they waned *more;* the film had, after all, been visually striking, and at times quite gripping. But in the end it added up to little more than an assortment of memorable images and forgettable platitudes.

THRILLERS

The Big Easy
No Way Out

As the Cookin' Cajun on PBS would say, Jim McBride's new film *The Big Easy* is big on *at*-mose-phere. The picture opens with a series of helicopter's-eye views of the Mississippi delta and a generous helping of sultry, down-home Loo-siana style background music. The movie is grainy-looking, almost as if it were shot on 16mm stock, and it has an overcast look, for the most part, as if it were filmed on a couple of cloudy weekends in October. The idea here, apparently, is not to look *slick*—McBride wants a gritty, homey, y'all-take-ya-shoes-off tone. The film's setting, of course, is New Orleans, where Remy McSwain (Dennis Quaid) is the youngest man on the police force ever to be promoted to the rank of lieutenant. (Catch dat name, Remy? Dat's *at*-mose-phere.) Remy's from a police family: half the members of the force seem to be related to him. And they all have thick, syrupy Cajun accents.

Indeed, just about everybody in the film talks Cajun, with the major exception of Ann Osborne (Ellen Barkin), a Yankee-born-and-bred assistant district attorney who, Remy complains, "bust[s] cops for a living." This intelligent, strong-minded Yankee blonde is a strict believer in law and order who frowns on the easygoing way in which Remy and his Cajun-drawlin' colleagues enjoy their "perks." Remy tries to soften Ann up by taking her out for dinner, but when the meal turns out to be free—"his money's no good here," the restauranteur explains to Ann—she's incensed. How, she wants to know, is this any different from accepting a bribe? Remy tries to explain: "This is New Orleans. We have a certain way of doing things down here. Folks like to show their appreciation." He claims that there's a difference between taking advantage of "perks" and being a criminal—the real criminals are muggers, killers, burglars. "We're the good guys. We're all that stands between you and them, sugar." But she's implacable.

Remy doesn't give up, however. Ann turns him on, and before long it's clear that his cocky charm is getting to her, too, in spite of everything. For a while these two remind one, just a little bit, of Tracy and Hepburn—he the laidback, plain-talking man's man (who, we know, will prove capable of tenderness), she the high-strung, high-toned, no-nonsense career woman (who, we know, will prove capable of passion). Of the two Ann is the more interesting character, and when Remy finally does bed her down, she becomes even more interesting—an endearing combination of shyness, self-possession, and sensuality.

But *The Big Easy* ceases to be a latter-day Tracy-and-Hepburn film when Remy's arrested red-handed for taking graft from the owner of a topless bar. He goes to court (in what must be record time—less than a week after his arrest!) and Ann (who else?) is the prosecuting attorney. She's now full of contempt for him—and her contempt increases when his pals at the police department manage to get him off by destroying the evidence against him. "You're supposed to uphold the law," she snarls, "but instead you bend it and twist it and sell it. . . . You're not one of the good guys anymore." No *Adam's Rib,* this. It takes a series of local murders—which Remy at first attributes to a "drug war" among rival factions of the local mob, but which Ann suspects, correctly, to involve corrupt police officials—to make Remy forsake his family loyalty to the police department and its sleazy ways and to rejoin the "good guys."

The Big Easy is not a movie, then, that is calculated to warm the hearts of the Patrolmen's Benevolent Association. It appears to pride itself on its clear-eyed, unsentimental view of things. Rough as it is on cops, however, it's amazingly soft on assistant D.A.'s: Ann Osborne doesn't seem to have any political ambitions or, for that matter, any ulterior motives whatsoever; she believes purely in truth, justice, and the American way, and so apparently do her colleagues at the D.A.'s office. What a lovely fiction!

The movie appears to pride itself, too, on its realistic *at*-mosephere. But, though I've never been to New Orleans, it seemed to me that there were too many people in this film with Cajun accents; in New Orleans these days, the Cajuns are a small, colorful minority, aren't they? I'm informed by folks who know the city well that I'm right: the majority of its Caucasian residents are of Irish, Italian, or German heritage; the Cajuns are essentially a rural phenomenon.

This sort of thing would not be so disturbing except for the impression one gets, every so often, that McBride (who previously directed the Richard Gere epic *Breathless*) would like us to take this movie more seriously than it deserves. But the truth is that whereas *The Big Easy* is a genuinely entertaining romantic thriller—a glossy Hollywood picture with some of the gloss removed—it hardly provides a realistic view of New Orleans, of the judicial system, or (I suspect) of the real nature of institutional corruption. When Remy gies his heartfelt climactic speech about the way corruption, er, corrupts, it seems more forced than forceful; certainly it is nowhere near as dramatically powerful a moment as the makers of this film seem to think it is.

A couple of other quibbles: the sound is rather poor, the cinematography murky. But the film has energy and wit, and is blessed with a number of splendid performances. Ned Beatty is particularly good as a cop named Jack who's like a second father to Remy; and the late Charles Ludlam is weirdly amusing as a dandified defense lawyer right out of Tennessee Williams. Both the lead actors, moreover, are very appealing. Quaid had better be careful, though, or his prominent performances in this movie, as Gordon Cooper in *The Right Stuff,* and as the fantastic voyager in the recent *Innerspace* will stereotype him forever as the cocky-but-loveable type.

Roger Donaldson's *No Way Out* is yet another recent thriller in which a diverting plot has been yoked to an outsized moral about corruption within The System. Kevin Costner, who portrayed the terminally earnest Eliot Ness in this summer's *The Untouchables,* here plays yet another clean-cut, quietly forceful government man, Lieutenant Commander Tom Farrell. Like Remy McSwain, Farrell is a cocky fellow whose gifts have taken him very far for someone so young. A veteran of Naval Intelligence who is attached to the USS *Billings,* Farrell is brought back to Washington by his friend Scott

Pritchard (Will Patton), the right-hand man of Secretary of Defense David Brice (Gene Hackman). Brice wants to kill plans for an expensive sub called the Phantom, which he considers unnecessary but for which a Southern committee chairman named Duvall (Howard Duff)—with the support of CIA reports on Soviet naval buildup—has been lobbying hard; Farrell's assignment is to serve as liaison between the secretary and the intelligence community—especially the CIA, whose closely guarded raw data on Soviet sea power Brice wants him to obtain.

The film's extraordinarily convoluted plot revolves not around the Phantom sub controversy, however, but around a murder. Several months before going to work for Brice, Farrell meets a striking young lady named Susan Atwell (Sean Young) at an inaugural ball and—in what has become the film's most publicized sequence—makes love to her in the back seat of a limousine. A romance develops between them, although Farrell knows that Susan is the well-paid mistress of someone high up in government; Susan eventually confesses that the man in question is none other than Farrell's own boss, David Brice. Brice isn't aware of Susan's affair with Farrell, however; he doesn't realize she's been two-timing him until one night when he shows up at her house and sees Farrell—whom he doesn't recognize in the dark—leaving by the back way. Incensed, Brice slaps Susan around and inadvertently kills her. He goes straight to Pritchard, who comes up with a plan to save his skin: they'll declare that Susan was the mistress of, and was murdered by, a Soviet mole in the Defense Department named Yuri, whose existence has long been suspected by the CIA. This fiction will make it possible to keep the D.C. police out of the case, and to have a DOD hireling track down Susan's other boyfriend (the sole witness to Brice's appearance at her apartment on the night of the murder) and, on the pretense that he is Yuri, to have him killed. Naturally, the job of finding this "Yuri" is given to Brice's intelligence expert—Farrell.

Follow that? From there on it gets *really* convoluted, and, alas, sillier and sillier. There's the requisite chase scene, of course—in which Farrell hightails it through Rock Creek Park, a couple of Special Forces agents nipping at his heel—and another murder. But the whole film comes down in the end to a ridiculous race between two computers in the basement of the Pentagon. One of these computers, by means of a process the explanation of which didn't sound quite kosher to me, is gradually turning an all-black photographic negative found in Susan's house into an image of Farrell—and Farrell knows that the moment he's recognizable in the picture, Pritchard will have him killed. The other computer is printing out the Office of Protocol's gratuity gift list. Farrell hopes to find a reference on this list to a jewelry box which a Moroccan diplomat gave to Brice, and which was among the items found in Susan's house; to Farrell's mind, this is apparently the only way of establishing definitively that Brice himself was Susan's lover—and murderer. One wonders why Farrell doesn't simply ask the computer to search the file for mention of the jewelry box—a process that would take a few moments—instead of having it spend hours printing out the whole list; but this is the sort of movie in which the only real explanation is that, well, if he did *that,* there wouldn't be any movie.

The film has some things going for it: a few genuinely suspenseful moments, a couple of arresting reversals, a lively pace; for such a baroquely plotted picture, it moves along quite smoothly most of the way through. The acting is good, too: Costner brings to his role the same wonderful controlled intensity that made him so impressive in *The Untouchables;* Hackman offers a wise portrayal of a man who's not really malevolent, just cowardly; and Will Patton delivers a bravura performance as the psychopath who's determined to "save Brice no matter what it takes." But the most remarkable presence is that of Sean Young, whose vivacity, sensuality, and naturalness bring to mind the screen icons of generations ago. Every moment that she is on screen, the film has life, vigor, charm; she makes this silly thriller seem more distinctive than it is, makes these hokey proceedings seem *real.* The moment her character dies, the movie's dreary contrivance becomes manifest.

Like *The Big Easy,* this is a film that patently prides itself on its supposedly authentic *mise en scène,* its familiarity with the way things work in the corridors of power. But people I know in D.C. have been laughing it up over certain details in this film—for instance, over the anachronistic depiction of Duvall, the Senate committee chairman, as a bossy, drawling Southerner. What's more, though the film is competently shot and edited for the most part, there is one slip-up that particularly bothered me: when Brice and Pritchard are shown dining *al fresco* at the Hay-Adams Hotel, the film unit's big, white production vehicles are plainly visible in the background.

In the final analysis, *No Way Out* is yet another '80s romantic thriller, not much better or worse than—or, ultimately, different from—a score of others which have not only interchangeable titles (e.g., *Against All Odds*) but interchangeable pop-rock title songs of surpassing insipidity. (Like these other films, *No Way Out* forces you to listen to its theme song several times before the picture's through, the idea apparently being that if it irritates you enough you'll run right out and buy the record.) Aside from Miss Young's performance, in fact, the main thing that distinguishes this movie from other romantic thrillers of the day is its ending: I don't intend to give it away, but suffice it to say that the film's last moments contain a cheap dramatic twist that violates the most basic rules of dramaturgy and that sent this viewer, for one, out of the theater feeling cheated.

COLLEGE BOYS

Maurice

The reviews are exultant. Even a reader who ordinarily casts a jaundiced eye upon the critical encomia quoted in movie advertisements cannot help but be given pause by the quotations featured in the twenty-inch, four-column ads that the Merchant-Ivory people have been running in the *New York Times* and other papers: "A masterpiece. The greatest movie of the year" (Richard Freedman, Newhouse Newspapers). "A more remarkable achievement than *A Room with a View*" (Stephen Harvey, *Village Voice*). "The story is dramatic; the script is both literate and powerful; and the actors seem little short of perfection. One becomes involved, moved, shaken" (Mike McGrady, *Newsday*).

The film that these critics are writing about is *Maurice,* the latest offering from the distinguished producer and director team of Ismail Merchant and James Ivory. I'm afraid I can't join in their chorus of ecstatic praise. Let me say that after several months of viewing mindless comedies and romantic thrillers—many of which were fine enough, I suppose, but which were, after all, only *thrillers*—I very much looked forward to *Maurice.* I stood on line at the Paris Theater on 58th Street in Manhattan for an hour in the full expectation of being involved, moved, shaken—or, if not that, then at least bewitched by the grace, sensitivity, intelligence, and beauty of it all, as had been my reaction in 1986 when I saw Merchant and Ivory's *A Room with a View* (to my mind, the best film of that year).

From the reviews, *Maurice* (which, just in case you decide to drop the name of it at a cocktail party, should be pronounced in the British manner, to wit: *Morris*) sounded rather like a superior version of *Another Country,* a worthy pendant to the magnificent television miniseries of *Brideshead Revisited.* Based on the posthumously published novel by E. M. Forster (another of whose novels, of course, was the basis for *A Room with a View*), *Maurice* is the story of Maurice Hall (James Wilby), who in 1909, while a second-year student at King's College, Cambridge, befriends an extremely rich and strikingly handsome fellow student named Clive Durham (Hugh Grant). They become very close. Then, several months into their friendship, Clive makes a pass. Maurice is confused, not sure whether to return or to spurn Clive's embrace; later, when Clive takes him aside on the college quadrangle and announces "I love you," Maurice spits out his contempt—only to declare, soon afterwards, that he loves Clive as well. But Clive, embarrassed at what he has done, thinks Maurice is just trying to be gracious; not until Maurice climbs into his second-story bedroom window in the middle of the night, awakens him, plants a kiss on his mouth, and climbs back out the window does Clive believe that Maurice truly loves him.

They become lovers. And Maurice, who up to now has been a polite, quiet, and obedient young man, becomes unruly, skipping tutorials and chapel to spend time with his beloved, and behaving insolently toward profs and family alike. Shortly thereafter both young men leave Cambridge, Maurice for his mother's house in London and a bank job, Clive for his family's country estate, London town house, and a political career. They see each other frequently, often in the company of other young men and women, neither flaunting their sexuality nor hiding their closeness. Everything goes smoothly until the Viscount Risley (Mark Tandy), and old Cambridge friend (based on Lytton Strachey), is arrested, tried, and incarcerated for kissing a bellhop. Clive—who refuses Risley's request for help—is frightened by the courtroom spectacle, and, suddenly realizing that he is risking everything he has by romancing Maurice, tells him that henceforth they will be friends, nothing more. Presently he cements this resolution by getting married.

These developments throw Maurice into a tizzy. Desperate to rid himself of his homosexuality, he sees a hypnotherapist (Ben Kingsley) and pleads with the family doctor (Denholm Elliott) for an explanation, a "cure," for these longings that dare not speak their name. But nothing works. Resolution finally arrives, however, in the form of Alex Scudder (Rupert Graves), the earthy young gamekeeper on Clive's estate, who, during one of Maurice's frequent visits, climbs up to his second-story bedroom in the middle of the night and throws his arms around him. Once again Maurice finds himself being flabbergasted by a young man's embrace. He's thrown, too, by Alec's lower-class status and unashamed physicality. But after a period of guilt and mutual distrust, Maurice and Alec find love and happiness with one another.

Maurice is a beautifully and meticulously made movie—the direction intelligent, the photography and lighting exquisite, the set decoration sumptuous—and one certainly feels, once it is over, that one should be terribly moved by it all. But one isn't. The reasons begin with Maurice himself, and with the actor who portrays him. Wilby, as it happens, has no charisma and little charm, and he's not particularly handsome either—all of which make it hard to believe that not one but two very good-looking young men would fall for him *and* make the first move. Maurice is, furthermore, supposed to be a young man full of passionate longings; but in Wilby's hands he comes across as oafish, doltish, dull. There's no energy in him, no fire. He's supposed to be a chameleon of a character who turns speedily from a polite and apparently straight young man into a cocky homosexual comfortable with his sexuality; who then just as rapidly becomes distraught and confused about his sexuality; and who finally abandons his job and family, indeed his entire world, to live with a relative stranger. But Wilby is incapable of making the viewer buy a single one of these volatile changes or incarnations.

One doesn't feel, in fact, as if one knows Maurice very well at all. For that matter, one doesn't feel as if the filmmakers know him well either. Take his attitude toward the poor. When Clive dumps him, he starts giving boxing lessons to Cockney young men at a seedy local gymnasium (which is by itself a baffling enough turn of events: Maurice does not impress one as the sort of lad who could teach a Cockney anything about pugilism), and his pupils love him for his egalitarian ways. But later on in the film, just before his involvement with Alec, and apparently in order for his initial anguish over the gamekeeper's social inferiority and his subsequent distrust of the young man to make sense, the script puts in his mouth a few strongly condescending words about the lower orders. So which is it, anyway—snob or democrat?

Hugh Grant's performance is only marginally better. When he sneaks into the courtroom just in time to hear the verdict at Risley's trial, the worried look that comes over his face is of near-Kabuki broadness, and he skulks out of the courtroom like the villain in a nineteenth-century melodrama. Strangely, both Grant and Wilby come across as too old to be undergraduates and too young to be, respectively, a politician and an investment banker; one problem is that, though the film encompasses only five years in its characters' lives, taking them into their early twenties, Ivory seemingly wants to create the illusion that more time than that is passing. He puts a mustache on Maurice immediately after he leaves college, then takes it off after a couple of years (though partway through the mustache-wearing period, in a fleeting boxing scene that was obviously shot at the same time as a longer, and later, boxing sequence, Maurice is suddenly, briefly clean-shaven); after a while Ivory puts a mustache on Clive as well. In these post-Cambridge sequences, Ivory has both leading men look and act and carry themselves as if they're supposed to be in their forties rather than their early twenties—and it doesn't work; they come across like a couple of boys playing grown-up.

Nor does it help that there's virtually no chemistry between the two actors. Their affair is neither interesting nor convincing; imagine Tyrone Power romancing Martin Milner and you pretty much get the idea. One has no sense of what their affair is like—of the feel of it, the way it develops. Part of the reason for this is the rapid-fire presentation of the opening sequences; Ivory keeps making abrupt leaps of several months—one moment it's 1909, the next 1910—and too often, at the beginning of a sequence, he plunges straight into the action without a moment's foreplay. We watch Maurice and Clive meet; and then, before we can get to know either of them, it's suddenly months later, and they're best friends; and *then* a new sequence fades in, and Clive is in close-up, sitting at Maurice's feet, mumbling something (I think it was "Have you ever been in love?" but I'm not sure; much of the dialogue in this film is hard to make out) and reaching up to touch Maurice's face. It's the Big Moment and Ivory takes us right into it without any warning, without any preliminaries, without the slightest suggestion as to how it happened to come on this day, at this moment. We have no bead on these boys at this point—it's all happening too fast, in too much of a Monarch Notes manner; we feel as if we're seeing it all from outside.

If Maurice's affair with Alex is more compelling, it's because Graves is a very good actor. He has real urgency and passion; when he follows Maurice to London after their first night together, and offers declarations of affection in one breath and blackmail threats in the next, it all makes sense; one know exactly what he is going through. Whereas Maurice and Clive remain to the end something of a muddle and a mystery, Alex is utterly comprehensible, a far more sympathetic character—a more believable human being—than either of them.

To watch this movie is to be nagged at by a hundred little questions, doubts, irritations. We don't really learn till after the fact, for example, that Maurice and Clive's affair is platonic. And not until the Risley trial do we have a sense that they are playing a highly dangerous game which could destroy both of their careers. On the contrary, Clive is extremely reckless, cuddling with Maurice in front of the servants and laughing at his embrrassment. To both of them—and to the filmmakers—their romance often seems to be, more than anything else, a delicious little secret, an inside joke on the world around them. Especially on eligible young ladies: several scenes in the film exist for no other purpose, it would appear, than to bid us laugh at some poor girl who is obviously smitten with Clive and trying her best to win him, unaware that he's already taken by the man at his side. Ha ha. In any event, that it takes the Risley trial to make Clive realize what he's risking by being involved with Maurice—and that he so quickly undergoes a complete reversal of attitude in this regard—is thoroughly unbelievable.

Nor is it clear what his real feelings are toward the young lady that he marries. Does he love her? Is he really as capable of heterosexual as he is of homosexual passion, or is he just faking it? At the end of the film, having just learned that Maurice is in love with his gamekeeper, Clive stands pensively at his bedroom window, staring out into the dark, his sweet little wife resting her head lovingly, wonderingly, on his shoulder. We know he's thinking about Maurice, but this doesn't keep Ivory—whose touch is usually so certain—from unnecessarily splicing in a shot of Maurice back at Cambridge (looking, alas, very dopey and unappealing). Then Clive quietly closes the shutters—on his past, on Maurice, on the dark and uncertain and perilous night. Fade out; run credits. It should be a powerful ending. But Clive's feelings are such a question mark at this point that the closing of the shutters seems melodramatic, phony.

The more one thinks of it, in fact, the less one realizes one knows about the people in this film. How much are the boys' mothers aware of, for example (in contemporary jargon: what do they know and when did they know it?), and how do they feel about it? To be sure, many of the supporting characters in *Maurice* aren't there to think or feel anything at all, but simply to spout remarks which we are meant either to applaud or to jeer at. The hypnotherapist, for instance, who apparently makes his living trying to convert homosexuals into heterosexuals, nonetheless makes a crack at one point about the English intolerance for human nature—his implication being that homosexuality is a natural condition. When I saw the film, the audience erupted in laughter and applause at this line; nobody seemed to find it the slightest bit anachronistic or out of character. Then there's the minister who, thinking that Maurice's interest in Alec is merely charitable, delivers an improbably backward and fatuous speech to him about Alec's lamentable carnality, his commission of the dreadful "sin of sensuality." Patently, this minister exists for no other reason than to deliver remarks for us to scoff at. He's there to make us feel superior, virtuous, open-minded.

Preachy as he is, though, he's no more preachy than the filmmakers, who too often seem less interested in telling their story than in scoring easy points against the foolish prejudices of a society that no longer exists. In the Alec sequences, in particular, the contrast between Clive's wealth, life of artificial comforts, and sexual repression, on the one hand, and Alec's poverty, closeness to nature, and easy acceptance of sexuality, on the other, is much too simplemindedly conceived and heavyhandedly drawn—not to mention patronizing toward the lower orders. (It's the British equivalent of white Americans' romantic image of blacks as sensuous savages.) To be fair, insofar as this sort of thinking is concerned, the film is perfectly faithful to the sensibility of Forster, who, after making the discovery that the common folk had sexual organs too, got into the habit of writing about democracy as if he'd invented it himself. There's no egalitarian like an Oxbridge egalitarian.

Maurice, then, is positively riddled with flaws. Like the awesomely stupid *Another Country,* though, it's a movie I'd gladly see again just for the *mise en scène.* In any event, I do look forward to the next production by Ivory, Merchant, and (it is to be hoped) Ruth Prawer

Jhabvala, who usually writes these things but sat this one out in favor of Ivory and a young collaborator named Kit Hesketh-Harvey (a recent Cambridge graduate). In the meantime, let there be no misunderstanding: in a movie landscape populated by goonies and gremlins and robo-cops, even the failures of the Ivory-Merchant team are more deserving of respect, and of serious discussion, than most other filmmakers' successes. *Maurice* is a noble failure.

BACK TO THE NEWSROOM

Broadcast News

Our heroine is a cute, perky, sensitive, hard-working, highly principled, sexually square, auburn-haired television news producer. Her boss is a burly, balding, gruff-but-lovable fatherly type; her best buddy in the newsroom is a wisecracking, goodhearted, first-rate newswriter who's had a crush on her for years; her nemesis is a dumb-but-handsome anchorman.

"The Mary Tyler Moore Show"? No. The heroine I refer to is not Mary Richards but Jane Craig (Holly Hunter); the boss, not Lou Grant but Ernie Merriman (Robert Prosky); the buddy, not Murray Slaughter but Aaron Altman (Albert Brooks); and the nemesis—and love interest—not Ted Baxter but Tom Grunick (William Hurt). The movie is *Broadcast News*, which was written, directed, and produced by James L. Brooks, a co-creator and writer of "The Mary Tyler Moore Show."

Brooks struck sitcom gold with that series, and this time out he's very consciously working the same vein. Which, alas, is precisely what's wrong with *Broadcast News*: it falls uncomfortably in the no-man's-land between TV sitcom and movie comedy. What aggravates this problem is that it doesn't want to be just any movie comedy. No, it wants to be a *serious* comedy—a comedy about Human Relationships, a comedy with Something To Say, a comedy that simultaneously makes you think, makes you laugh till your sides split, and makes you feel warm all over. A comedy, that is, with aims much like those of Mr. Brooks's own *Terms of Endearment.*

Now, *Terms of Endearment*—which Brooks adapted very freely from Larry McMurtry's novel—was an odd movie. I didn't believe Shirley MacLaine for a moment as Debra Winger's possessive but emotionally inexpressive mama, but I bought it as a premise for the duration of the movie because so many funny situations were built upon it; nor, though his house was full of pictures of Saturn rockets and space capsules, did I believe that Jack Nicholson was an ex-astronaut; nor did I believe in Debra Winger's sudden fatal illness. Nicholson might just as believably have been a retired ballplayer, the ex-mayor of Chillicothe, Ohio, or the host of a syndicated teenage dance program; Winger, rather than dying of cancer, might just as convincingly have thrown herself under a train, gone into est, or taken up with a lesbian nun.

As in a sitcom, the dramatic complications and resolutions in *Terms* seemed not to have been coaxed delicately and sensitively out of the inner truth of the characters and the inner logic of the story, but to have been hammered out over bagels and cream cheese by half a dozen comedy writers. To be sure, Brooks pulled the strings well: I laughed my way through *Terms*, and when Winger died, my eyes teared up, but I left the theater thinking "How *phony*." If that doesn't happen with sitcoms, it's because their creators rarely stray beyond the genre's boundaries, never drag the phoniness out into the glare of sunlight. The lesson of *Terms* was that James L. Brooks doesn't know enough to stay out of the sun.

Broadcast News confirms that lesson. You may recall that *Terms* began with a prefatory childhood scene: MacLaine, the clinging mother, climbs into a crib in which her infant daughter is bawling her lungs out. It's cute, it's funny, it's a guaranteed laugh. It's also nothing more than a cheap visual gag—an unpromising way to begin a movie that wants not only to amuse but to be taken seriously. *Broadcast News* starts off in a similar fashion, with vignettes of the protagonists as children. Jane, age twelve or so, spends all her time writing; when her father calls her "obsessive," she dresses him down, in classic smart-TV-kid manner, for misusing a word whose precise clinical meaning by no means applies to her psychological state. Young Aaron, for his part, is an obnoxious high-school valedictorian who gets beat up by his classmates at graduation, then taunts them because they'll never make more than nineteen thousand dollars a year. And young Tom is a likable C-student who, as he explains to his dad, gets by on his great looks. (Though the actor who plays young Tom is only average-looking, we're apparently meant to take this self-description at face value.) At the end of each of these introductory vignettes, Brooks freezes the frame and superimposes a title (as at the close of *Animal House*) indicating how the kid will turn out; for instance, right after Young Tom's dad wonders aloud what the future might hold for a boy who's got nothing going for him but looks, we freeze on a close-up of the lad and Brooks superimposes the words "Future Network News Anchorman." That one gets a big laugh—mainly, of course, because of the cartoonish image of news anchormen that Brooks himself proffered on "The Mary Tyler Moore Show."

What's important about these prefatory vignettes is that none of them is dramatically necessary; they're the film's equivalent of the "teaser," that very brief scene which precedes the credits at the beginning of a sitcom, and which exists in TV-land only for practical purposes—namely, to make possible an extra commercial break. Good sitcom writers use the teaser to hook the audience in; Brooks does this at the beginning of *Broadcast News*, and simultaneously establishes that the film will be governed by a sitcom mentality. By the time the opening credits are rolling (as in *Terms*, they follow the teaser), we know that this is a film by a man who thinks of character as something that can be summed up in a single snappy exchange, a sharp one-liner.

From the credits we cut to Jane as a woman of thirty or so (i.e., Mary Richards's age when she got to Minneapolis). A segment producer for the news division of a Washington, D.C., network affiliate, Jane is introduced *in medias res* at a TV news convention, where she's delivering a heartfelt speech about the need for more substantial news programs. The audience finds her argument boring, and when she presents evidence of the superficiality of TV news—in the form of a network news-show videotape of a domino trick—her colleagues miss (or, actually, ignore) her point entirely and break into laughter and applause: they *enjoy* the dominoes. But Jane doesn't get any applause, and when the videotape is over the audience exits with unseemly haste. It's a funny sequence, yet it wants also to be taken seriously as stating a grim truth about the American media. And it simply doesn't do that. It's too glib, too exaggerated; no crowd of TV news people would find Jane's talk so dull, or those dominoes so fascinating.

But one person in Jane's audience stays to compliment her. Tom, a sometime sports reporter who's just been hired by her station as a newsman, is on his way up fast, but feels bad about it: "I'm no good at what I do," he confesses to Jane, whom he recognizes as having the intelligence, knowledge, and news sense that he lacks. Instead of respecting his honesty, however, Jane explodes in righteous anger: if he's incompetent, she tells him, he doesn't *belong* in this business, and should either educate himself fast or find some other line of work. Though they are drawn to each other, her explosion causes Tom to clear out pronto.

This opening sequence is a tidy job, I suppose: a few lines back and forth, and the film's main conflict is set up. Namely, Tom appeals to Jane but offends her most fervently held principles; as Aaron remarks later (as if we haven't already gotten the point!), "He personifies everything that you've been fighting against." Yet Jane's hostility to Tom doesn't make sense if you give it a moment's thought. The sequence at the news convention presumably means to suggest that TV news people are overwhelmingly amoral and unserious; Tom, who alone appreciates Jane's standards, would seem a relative paragon. Yet while Jane respects everyone else that she works with—is her news team different from all of those represented at the convention?—she has nothing but contempt for Tom. To be sure, over the course of the film she changes her attitude, and toward movie's end is ready to plight her troth; then it happens. Some time after Tom does an interview with a rape victim in which the camera cuts away to show him in tears, Aaron tells Jane that since Tom had only one camera crew, the cutaway must have been filmed afterwards and the tears faked. Horror of horrors! Jane is astonished and scandalized—a reaction which is downright ridiculous, since TV news cutaways are routinely faked. (This viewer, for one, assumed all along that Tom's cutaway was fake, and that it was understood to be so by all concerned; thus its magnification into the film's climactic issue lacked impact, to say the least.) Jane's forced to decide: love him or leave him?

So much for the plot, which at any rate does not develop so much as bounce from gag to gag; this film abounds with gimmicks that might be acceptable in a sitcom but must be counted here as structural flaws. Brooks drags Tom's father back into the story for no other reason than to set up a gag; Jane's romantic rival, a glamorous reporter named Jennifer Mack (Lois Chiles), is suddenly packed off in mid-movie to a long-term stint in Anchorage and is never heard from again. (Jane, by the way, is responsible for Jennifer's reassignment—an act which seems at least as morally objectionable as Tom's faked tears.) A major turning point comes when Aaron, having been given his big chance to anchor the weekend news, breaks out into a case of flop sweat so bad that within a couple of minutes his face is drenched and his shirt soaked through. It's a hilarious bit, but when it gives rise to a long sequence full of soul-searching and bitter accusation—all of which we are meant to take quite seriously—the picture seems like some bizarre collaboration between Mel Brooks and John Cassavetes. Another of the film's turning points, meanwhile, is overly evocative of the final episode of "The Mary Tyler Moore Show." Finally, several details in the film seem dubious: Would a local Washington reporter be sent to cover serial murders in Alaska? And what purpose does it serve to drag Jane and Aaron to Nicaragua for a brief, tonally incongruous sequence involving a contra-Sandinista battle?

At least Brooks gets good performances out of his stars. Holly Hunter is winning in a very Mary Tyler Mooreish way; Albert Brooks brings to the movie a wonderful zaniness which I'm sure is exactly what his namesake director wanted but which doesn't work at all when the film shifts into serious gear. As for William Hurt, he proves to be so frighteningly believable as a dimwit that one feels as if one should take another, more careful look at his previous work. Yet his is a problematic role. One wonders why Hurt took it on; it's a confusingly written part which requires him to be at once a self-seeking, know-nothing jerk—the embodiment of everything that's wrong with TV news—and a good guy, sweet and modest and well-intentioned. This combination is not easily imagined and, though Hurt does his best, the character never quite comes into focus. This is not the only unaddressed contradiction in his character: Tom's polished performance as anchor would seem to demonstrate, his (and the film's) claims to the contrary, that he is actually very good at what he does—that he is as skilled a talking head, in other words, as Aaron is a field reporter; but the film never reconciles this fact with its otherwise condescending view of him.

But then, the script of *Broadcast News* is a most rickety contraption indeed, and when in its final pages Jane must decide whether to love Tom or leave him, the whole fragile structure collapses. For neither choice is dramatically workable. If she chooses to go with Tom, she's opting for the predictable romantic-comedy ending, and making it obvious that her declared moral objections to him were just plot gimmickry, and the film's pretensions to seriousness precisely that—pretensions. If, on the other hand, she decides to reject his love because of that faked cutaway, such an inane attempt at a "serious" ending cannot but expose the real shallowness of the material—a shallowness that the audience has allowed itself to ignore most of the way through because the majority of the film's "serious" points have been made by way of rapid-fire jokes and sight gags.

How does the film end? I won't give that away; but I will say that once all this nonsense is supposedly wrapped up, we're given a "tag" (as they call it in sitcomland) in which we meet our three main characters "seven years later." (Since the movie proper appears to be set in the present, it must be assumed that the tag takes us into the mid-1990s.) Brooks patently thinks this denouement is the sort of epic touch that will send his audience out of the theater recognizing that *Broadcast News* is not a typical romantic comedy but a sensitive and respectable film—a *real* story about *real* people with *real* feelings. But its effect is quite the opposite: the sequence is so embarrassingly predictable and contrived, the sentiments so facile and phony, that one staggers out of the theater wondering at the ability of a genuine sitcom talent to make such a mess of things on the big screen. *Terms of Endearment* showed us, and *Broadcast News* reminds us, that James L. Brooks doesn't know the difference between persons and personifications, characters and caricatures, emotion and sentimentality. Nor—for all his carrying on about the topic—does his understanding of the moral dimension of journalism go any deeper than the pep talks on First Amendment rights and such that Lou Grant served up back at WJM. Brooks is a talented man who has stumbled pathetically into the wrong genre; one can only hope he finds his way back home.

SUNSTRUCK

Empire of the Sun
Hope and Glory
Moonstruck
Five Corners

The current films, *Empire of the Sun* and *Hope and Glory,* invite us to see World War II through the eyes of an English boy. Of the two, Steven Spielberg's *Empire,* which was written by Tom Stoppard and based on J. G. Ballard's autobiographical novel, is a major disappointment. The film tells the story of Jim Graham (Christian Bale), a bratty eleven-year-old who is separated from his parents during the Japanese invasion of Shanghai and spends the war in an alien internment camp. It should be a compelling story, but no such luck; Spielberg, who is more in tune with the fantasy life of the typical lighthearted American boy than any other director, proves himself incapable of understanding the effect war might have upon a boy's psyche. In Ballard's novel, the war manipulates Jim's mind in ways that are complex, curious, even (superficially) contradictory, but ultimately comprehensible: he idolizes his Japanese captors, cherishes violence, cheers an American air raid; he learns "that kindness, which his parents and teachers had always urged upon him, counted for nothing" and feels lightheaded "not because his parents had rejected him but because he expected them to do so, and no longer cared."

But Spielberg's benign *Weltanschauung* simply can't accommodate such unwholesome states of mind; nor does he seem comfortable with the idea of aliens (of the non-extraterrestrial variety) who are vicious rather than friendly. Accordingly he does his best to treat war as if it were one of his usual escapist themes. While the film puts Jim through essentially the same paces as the novel does, it skirts the darker places in the boy's soul—the only places where his behavior makes sense—and thus gives us an incoherent, unconvincing protagonist whose director simply doesn't recognize the degree to which he is *not* the same as the innocent California suburban kids in *E.T.* When the boy salutes a group of Japanese pilots about to take off on a bombing raid, for instance, there should be irony and pathos in the air, but instead there's just the usual Spielbergian joy and wonder; likewise, when Jim sneaks out of the camp to trap a pheasant, the tone is precisely the same as when Richard Dreyfuss sneaks onto the alien landing strip in *Close Encounters of the Third Kind.* We never feel as if we know this boy intimately; he moves through the film with an urgency that feels willed, and at various climactic points breaks into big phony eyepopping bursts of enthusiasm or sorrow—at which moments the music invariably swells up as if to tell us what to feel. Yet we *don't* feel.

A big part of the problem is the film's unsuitably lush visual style. With the help of his cinematographer (Allen Daviau), lighting director, and production designer (Norman Reynolds), Spielberg makes everything, from the war-torn streets of Shanghai to the hovels of the internment camp, look distractingly beautiful. Indeed, it hardly seems an exaggeration to say that the real subject of the film is its own cinematography. Spielberg appears to be more interested in lighting surfaces in pretty ways than in exploring the ugly depths of the material; to him, the way the light reflects off of the suitcase that Jim throws into the water in the film's last shot would seem to be more important than his reason for throwing it. Another shot—of Jim standing behind the barbed wire of the camp—looks just like a Ralph Lauren ad in GQ. To look at these images is to recognize that Spielberg has absolutely no comprehension of the life they are supposed to represent. And the music doesn't help at all: John Williams has contributed one of his patented sappy-and-jaunty adventure movie scores, which, while appropriate enough for a *Superman,* an *E.T.,* or an *Indiana Jones,* sounds particularly vacuous when coupled with images of a World War II internment camp.

Hope and Glory is another story entirely. Derived from writer-director John Boorman's own childhood, it depicts the Battle of

Britain as experienced by eight-year-old Billy Rohan (Sebastian Rice Edwards) and his lower-middle-class London suburban family (including Sarah Miles as Mum). Like *Empire of the Sun,* the film is episodic; but unlike Spielberg's movie, Boorman's is scaled to the perceptions of a child. It has an honesty, a modesty that *Empire* sorely lacks; Boorman doesn't strain after epic effects, doesn't engage in pointless displays of cinematographic brilliance. Most importantly, he coaxes from Edwards a performance of subtlety and coherence, with the result that we feel throughout the film as if we truly know and care about this boy. If the bombastic *Empire of the Sun* leaves one cold, one is surprised to find oneself being intensely moved by the simplest events and the smallest gestures in *Hope and Glory*.

In the author's note to his 1986 play *The Dreamer Examines His Pillow,* John Patrick Shanley muses as follows:

> Who am I? This is a courageous question. . . . I have, at one time or another, denied everything. Every fact of my specific self. My parents, my Bronx origin, my Americanness, my Irishness, my appetites, my mortality, my need for love and acceptance, my jealousy, my violence, my anger. . . .

But he's not denying those things anymore. No sir, these days young Mr. Shanley is embracing himself wholeheartedly and, alas, is charging us up to seven dollars a head to watch. Yet if Shanley's screenplays in two current films, *Moonstruck* and *Five Corners,* proves anything, it is that to accept one's background and to be capable of writing about it with intelligence, sensitivity, and perception are two drastically different things; to see these films is to be astonished at the crudeness and superficiality—the sheer *falsity*—with which both the principal characters and their lower-middle-class ethnic Outer Boroughs milieux are drawn.

By far the better of the two films is *Moonstruck,* directed by Norman Jewison and starring Cher, wherein Shanley substitutes Brooklyn for the Bronx and Italians for Irishmen. The film sets us down in present-day Brooklyn Heights, which in real life is Brooklyn's most expensive, highfalutin neighborhood, full of Wall Street yuppies and Benetton stores, but which has been cast here as a lower-middle-class Italian ghetto. The story could hardly be simpler. Cher plays a widow in her mid-thirties who has no sooner agreed to marry her unappealing, inarticulate boyfriend (Danny Aiello) than she falls in love with his equally unappealing, inarticulate estranged brother (Nicolas Cage). Everything about the film is pure Shanley. In place of characterization, he gives us goofy grotesquerie; in place of plot development, roller-coaster reversals. As ever, he confuses weirdness with wit: things are offbeat here for the sake of being offbeat. Cher's job? Office manager in a funeral parlor. The reason for the brothers' estrangement? A freak bakery accident, caused by Aiello, in which Cage lost some fingers, and which is described in such a way as to make the audience roar with laughter.

Everything in this film is played for laughs—and cheap ones at that. Yet every so often Shanley shifts abruptly from absurdist comedy into his own special brand of treacly sentiment: in one sequence, for instance, Cher, her mother, and her uncle all climb out of their beds in the middle of the night to stare at the moon and speak Great and Simple Truths to their respective bed-partners. Yawn. To enjoy the film on its own terms one must be willing to engage in Doublethink—to laugh, that is, at the cartoonlike qualities of Cher and Cage's romance, and yet to believe in (and to root for the triumph of) the romance; the soupy score—which draws on Puccini as well as the kitsch classic "That's Amore"—is there not only to amuse us with its schmaltzy excess but to touch our hearts. Aside from Cher's winning performance, though, what makes *Moonstruck* a palatable—and even, occasionally, a charming—entertainment is the fact that, for the most part, Shanley keeps it light.

Which is more than one can say for *Five Corners*. Directed by Tony Bill and set in a lower-middle-class Bronx neighborhood in 1964 (though it was actually shot in Queens), the movie covers two days in the lives of several local teenagers. Heinz (John Turturro) is a psychotic thug who's just returned home from prison; Linda (Jodie Foster) is the girl he tried to rape two years ago; James (Todd Graff) is her boyfriend; Harry (Tim Robbins) is the huge, tough Irish street kid who saved her from Heinz last time around, but who, in the wake of his dad's murder and thanks to the rhetoric of Dr. Martin Luther King, has become—presto!—a convert to nonviolence.

Or so Shanley wants us to believe. Or maybe he doesn't; it's hard to say. There is so much that is unbelievable in this movie—so many extremely unlikely coincidences, decisions, lines of dialogue, and changes of character—that one gets the feeling that Shanley doesn't *believe* in believability, that he feels if we see something happening on screen, we should accept it and keep still, and not bother him with questions of motivation. After all, the more goofily erratic a character's behavior, the more *interesting* he is. The main plot itself—Heinz abducts Linda, and James and Harry give chase—gets underway as the result of a thoroughly unbelievable decision on Linda's part: Heinz phones her and tells her to meet him at midnight in the park, and she complies. Why? Who knows? The fundamental rules of dramatic construction don't appear to be relevant in these parts; indeed, one of Shanley's remarks in the aforementioned author's note would seem to indicate that he has little use for those rules: "I see no difference between writing a play and living my life. . . . It is all the same thing." Somebody who thinks this way has no business passing a playwriting course, let alone writing a film script.

There are related problems with the film. Its dialogue is frequently padded and stilted (a flaw more common among bad plays than bad movies), and its exposition generally clumsy ("Harry got so serious after his father died"). There's also a ridiculous subplot involving the shenanigans of two vapid gum-chewing girls who, waking up one morning in a strange flat, engage in typically sparkling Shanley dialogue: "I ain't wearin' no clothes." "I ain't wearin' no clothes either." Like *Moonstruck,* too, the film seems at times to be little more than a catalogue of tacky, eccentric, and/or grotesque details: the white sequined dress on a middle-aged woman in a bar, the awful picture of Jesus on Harry's mother's living room wall, the plastic flowers in Heinz's mother's hair, the cop with one foot twice as large as the other, the high-school teacher killed by an arrow. (Some of these details are particularly reminiscent of *Moonstruck:* for instance, in that film the heroine's lover is missing fingers; in this one he has a limp.)

This is not the only violent episode in *Five Corners.* By the end of the film, several people will be killed—most of them, naturally, in zany ways. Indeed, what makes *Five Corners* so much more intolerable than *Moonstruck,* in the end, is that Shanley here takes *Moonstruck*'s already uncomfortable mixture of absurdist comedy and shameless sentiment and adds two further ingredients: violence and serious political theme-mongering. Now violence and absurdist comedy can be combined successfully: the Coen brothers did so in *Blood Simple.*

But to combine these elements with the sort of simpleminded sentimentality and genial screwiness in which Shanley specializes is to court incoherence; and when Shanley throws in platitudes about civil rights and nonviolence, the whole structure collapses under the weight of its own pretensions. The truth is that Shanley, for all the distinctiveness of his style, simply does not have a strong sense of tonal control. Yes, he may have stopped denying his Irish Catholic parents and the Bronx natives among whom he was raised. But he's not quite sure how he wants us to feel about such people—for he is still less than certain how *he* feels about them.

POLANSKI'S EMMANUELLE

Frantic

When I heard that *Frantic,* Roman Polanski's new thriller, was very much in the tradition of Alfred Hitchcock, I braced myself for a disappointment. Why, I wondered, had Polanski—the director of such wonderful films as *Rosemary's Baby, Chinatown,* and *Tess*—opted to straitjacket himself in such a fashion? All I could think was that *Frantic* would be another flatfooted, academic Hitchcock *hommage* like *Dressed to Kill,* Brian DePalma's pallid ripoff of *Psycho.* Hitchcock imitation, after all, is the *specialité de la maison* of the typical contemporary film-school graduate, the slick technician in search of a sensibility, the sort of person whose metaphysical cravings seem thoroughly satisfied by a diet of MGM B-movies, Republic two-reelers, and George Lucas space operas. To see Polanski—whose films always have the freshness of visions derived from life, not from other bits of celluloid—playing the *hommage* game with these second-raters was not, for me, a consummation devoutly to be wished. For heaven's sake, even the name of his film was unpromising: mentioning it in conversations, I kept confusing it with *Frenzy,* the title of one of Hitchcock's later, lamer efforts—an unpleasant echo which, it seemed to me, must almost certainly have been intentional.

Fortunately, however, my apprehensions proved to be remarkably unjustified. Engaging of style, compelling of tone, highly distinctive in its "look," *Frantic* is as fresh and original as any film that Polanski has ever made. And this in spite of the almost textbook-scale borrowing of motifs and images from Hitchcock—a borrowing that begins in the very first frames. (Of course, one man's obvious borrowing is another man's vague affinity; and certainly some of the instances of Hitchcock imitation, in this film, are a good deal more self-evident than others.)

Like many a Hitchcock film, *Frantic* opens with energetic, arresting music (by Ennio Morricone) and a riveting image that establishes the film's principal setting—in this instance, a point-of-view shot, from a moving taxicab, of the highway leading into Paris from Orly Airport. (The considerable length of this "take," by the way, is itself very Hitchcockian—remember *Rope*, which contains not a single visible cut?) From this we fade to a two-shot of the couple in the cab's back seat, Dr. Richard Walker (Harrison Ford) of San Francisco and his wife Sondra (Betty Buckley), who are arriving in town for a medical conference—a situation reminiscent of Hitchcock's 1956 version of *The Man Who Knew Too Much*, in which James Stewart plays an American doctor who is visiting North Africa with his wife and son after attending a Paris medical convention. (That film featured a similar opening two-shot of Stewart and Doris Day in front of a vehicle's back window: they were in the back seat of a bus, heading into Marrakesh.) Like Stewart's Ben McKenna, who "liberated Africa" during World War II, Walker has been to this part of the world before—he and Sondra came to Paris on their honeymoon—but doesn't know it well at all. "Do you know where you are?" Sondra asks him as the cab enters the city. His reply: "It's changed so much." When the taxi gets a flat tire it's a foreshadowing of the unexpected turn of events that will follow.

Yet everything about the hotel they check into later that morning is a model of order, serenity, familiarity: there are VISA and American Express plaques; the concierge speaks fluent English; even the predominant colors in the lobby and in their luxurious suite—a relaxing, complementary array of muted grays, blues, and off-whites—are in harmony with the colors of the Walkers' wardrobe. For the perfect touch of home, there is even a Pizza Hut adjacent to the lobby—an all-American eatery which, as the film heads further and further into darkness and entropy, will increasingly seem an ironic comment on the all-American niceness, naiveté, and normality that characterized the Walkers on arrival. With its disconcerting fire-engine red color, moreover, the Pizza Hut from the beginning screams out a warning that everything here is not as peaceful and orderly as it seems.

These opening sequences—in the cab and lobby, and especially in the suite—have a terrific naturalness; Polanski very swiftly makes us believe in these characters and in their easy, jokey, loving relationship. He also very swiftly makes us recognize—as they do not—how naked and vulnerable they are; when Walker, unable to open one of their suitcases, realizes that it is not theirs at all, and that Sondra must have picked it up by mistake at the airport, he sees it as nothing more than a frustrating inconvenience, while we panic—is there a bomb inside? Moments later, while he's in the shower (and in the foreground of the shot), Sondra (in the background) receives a phone call, slips into a dress (significantly, a *red dress*), tells him something (which he—and we—can't hear), and casually steps out of frame (thus do people disappear from each other's lives). From these simple, ordinary, everyday acts Polanski extracts an overwhelming sense of menace.

When Walker steps out of the shower—which is as important here, in its way, as a symbol of vulnerability as it is in *Psycho*—Sondra is gone. Nor does she show up for breakfast (Walker having placed a red rose on her pillow). Nobody in the lobby has seen her. The early-morning concierge, traced to a health club (its window frames and workout equipment all painted fire-engine red), informs Walker that Sondra left the hotel with a red-haired man. After a visit (inspired by similar scenes in *Topaz* and *Vertigo*?) to a flower shop across the street—whose proprietor tries to sell him a bouquet of red roses—Walker finds Sondra's bracelet in a nearby alley; a drunk claims to have seen her forced into a car by some men.

What we have here, then, is one of Hitchcock's favorite motifs, which he made use of in *The Lady Vanishes, Vertigo*, and a number of other films: the missing-person motif. Furthermore, since both the police and the American Embassy officers are reluctant to believe that Sondra has been kidnapped, Walker—like many a Hitchcock hero—begins the search for his missing person quite without assistance. Realizing that Sondra's disappearance might be related to the inadvertent suitcase switch, he jimmies open the mystery suitcase and finds, among other things, a matchbook (red-tipped matches) that leads him to a nightclub called the Blue Parrot (an *hommage*, to be sure, of a distinctly un-Hitchcockian sort—though the club's denizens are less reminiscent of the extras in *Casablanca* than of the circus freaks in Hitchcock's *Saboteur*), to the blood-spattered corpse of a lowlife named Dédé, and to an ally of sorts in the person of Michelle (Emmanuelle Seigner), a strikingly beautiful young punker and part-time transatlantic drug courier who worked for Dédé and belongs to the mystery suitcase. (Many of Hitchcock's heroines, incidentally, have names that begin with M: Madeleine in *Vertigo,* Marion in *Psycho,* Melanie in *The Birds,* Marnie in *Marnie.*) Walker learns that the men who kidnapped his wife are spies, that Dédé—and, in turn, Michelle—worked for them, and that a souvenir Statue of Liberty replica in Michelle's suitcase (an allusion to *Saboteur,* in which the title character falls to his death from Lady Liberty's torch) contains the top-secret "Kryton," a gizmo of American manufacture used for "triggering the detonation of nuclear devices."

Like several Hitchcock heroes, in short, Walker soon finds himself to be (a) deeply involved, thanks to an accidental turn of events, in international espionage intrigue, (b) turning for companionship and support to a comely stranger whom he cannot *completely* trust, (c) moving around a lot, meeting odd characters, getting the lay of the land, and (d) wrangling over a MacGuffin. No, not a McMuffin, a MacGuffin—a word Hitchcock used to refer to the contrivances, at once all-important and utterly insignificant, upon which many of his plots were built: the uranium hidden in the wine bottles in *Notorious,* the secret formula in *The Thirty-Nine Steps,* the clause of the peace treaty in *Foreign Correspondent.* The "Kryton" is a classic Hitchcock-style MacGuffin.

Walker also finds himself in circumstances of increasing disorder and slovenliness. The film begins at dawn, and ends at about the same time two days later; with each morning Walker looks more disheveled; every time he shows up at the hotel he looks a bit less respectable, and cares less about it. Though the plot unfolds in conventional fashion, Polanski infuses it with surprising wit and urgency; every scene brings yet another extremely provocative touch. For instance—as my references to the film's periodic bursts of red may have suggested—he manages to achieve a good deal of shock value, in this mostly muted-gray movie, by offering an occasional splash of bright color: a green garbage truck, Michelle's yellow Volkswagen (to which, peculiarly enough, she seems to have the keys, though a key ring in the suitcase containing her only apartment key also contained a VW key), a sexy red dress which Michelle wears in the last few sequences of the film (at last clearly spelling out her *Doppelgänger* relationship to Sondra, who might well have been this young and beautiful when she and Walker honeymooned in Paris twenty years ago).

Frantic is full of subtle motifs: animals (the dog in the replacement taxi, Dédês friendly cat, the drug-sniffing German shepherds at the airport, the pigeons engaging in intercourse outside Michelle's skylight), whose appearance often signals danger; telephones; money, which Michelle covets so eagerly and which Walker hands out with such abandon and in such abundance—to a bellhop, to the concierge (who refuses it), to Michelle (who finally gives it back), to several bartenders and waiters and cab drivers, to a coke dealer, to an airport parking-lot attendant—that the film represents, among many other things, a moral commentary on the whole business of getting and spending. There is also an abundance of keys—suitcase keys, hotel-room keys, the keys to Michelle's flat; there are even pairs of crossed keys on the lapels of the concierge's jacket—an image reminiscent of the crossed tennis rackets on Farley Granger's cigarette lighter in *Strangers on a Train.* Just as the crossed tennis rackets, in that film, symbolize the exchange of murders that Robert Walker proposes (might the name Richard Walker, in fact, be based on the name of that actor?), so the crossed keys on the concierge's jacket represent the mistakenly exchanged suitcases that set in motion the plot of *Frantic.*

Some of the Hitchcock echoes are amusingly familiar. For instance, like many of Hitchcock's movies—*Vertigo, North by Northwest, Saboteur,* and *Rear Window,* among others—*Frantic* contains a scene that plays with our fear of heights (the scene, in which Walker climbs over Michelle's slippery roof with her big, clumsy suitcase in hand, is particularly reminiscent of the clinging-to-a-rooftop climax of *To Catch a Thief*). Polanski makes witty, Hitchcockian use of music, too: to name just one example, when Walker phones the embassy toward the end of the film, he is put on hold and is forced to listen to a Muzak version of the theme from *Moulin Rouge,* a.k.a. "Where is Your Heart?" As our memory of his love for his wife grows dimmer (and as Michelle and her outfits grow sultrier), this is indeed one of the questions uppermost in our minds: where is Walker's heart? That he never explicitly betrays a weakness for Michelle's extraordinary feminine charms—the furthest he will go is to say "You look nice" when she puts on her red dress—doesn't keep us from positing a romantic interest; it only increases the ambiguity, hikes up the tension level. Finally, like *Vertigo* (which is set in the Walker's home town), *Frantic* ends on an embankment beneath a bridge—not at the Golden Gate, of course, but at the Seine, with all the landmarks of Paris in plain sight. This placement of chaos amid familiar symbols of civilization and order—the British Museum in *Blackmail*, Westminster Abbey in *Foreign Correspondent,* the Albert Hall in *The Man Who Knew Too Much,* the Statue of Liberty in *Saboteur,* the United Nations and Mount Rushmore in *North by Northwest*—is a vintage Hitchcock device, and Polanski makes very effective use of it.

What, for all these Hitchcockian borrowings, makes Polanski's vision distinct from Hitchcock's? Part of the answer is that there's a dark, genuinely disturbing quality here—a rather Conradian darkness (not so inappropriate, come to think of it, since Polanski, like Conrad, is a Pole-turned-Westerner) which is alien to Hitchcock; at movie's end Walker tussels with a man bearing a long knife, and all the Hitchcock allusions fly out the window, and the only thing we can remember is Jack Nicholson's nose getting sliced in *Chinatown.* What's more, several times in this movie one is made to recall the slaying of Polanski's wife Sharon Tate, and certainly one feels that at least something of Walker's reaction to Sondra's abduction must be derived from Polanski's memory of his own horror at Miss Tate's savage murder. (Significantly, the first names of the husband and wife in this film begin with the same letters—R. and S.—as do the first names of Polanski and Miss Tate.) This, at least, might help to explain why, for all its borrowings from the Hitchcock *oeuvre, Frantic* feels so real—so sincerely, strangely, and painfully felt—so much of the time. It seems, one might say, a *personal* film in a way that none of Hitchcock's films were; indeed, perhaps part of the reason for Polanski's elaborate use of borrowed Hitchcockian motifs and images was that, in making a movie that taps such profound wells of private grief, he felt an unusually strong need for an external principle of order. Whatever the case, *Frantic* is ultimately a doubly successful film—at once a dazzling entertainment and a disquieting work of art.

ZERO FOR FOUR

Bright Lights, Big City
The Milagro Beanfield War
Masquerade
Biloxi Blues

Much as I admired Jay McInerney's clever novel *Bright Lights, Big City,* I fully expected the movie to be awful. Yes, the book has a zippy pace, a clean storyline—our unnamed young hero, supposedly anguished over his wife's recent desertion and over his inability to get a writing career underway, drinks too much vodka and snorts too much coke and consequently screws up royally on a fact-checking assignment at the *New Yorker*-type magazine that he works for, thereby losing his job—but otherwise it's far from promising feature-film material. For one thing, it's largely about writing and editing, and though fiction that contemplates such things can be quite compelling, it is exceedingly difficult to make them anything but deadly dull on screen. Who, after all, wants to see a Major Motion Picture about fact-checking? Equally problematic is that the book's most distinctive feature is its second-person narration: the hero is referred to throughout as "you." This device gives the book a very special feel—and how to translate *that* to film?

Given these formidable impediments to cinematic adaptation, the movie that McInerney and director James Bridges have fashioned proves to be rather a pleasant surprise. It is remarkably faithful to the novel, both in structure and spirit; I was impressed by how well the filmmakers have managed, sequence by sequence, to capture the tone of the original, and amazed by the degree to which some of the scenes looked the way I had imagined them when I read the book.

To be sure, the film doesn't really work as a whole in the way that the novel does. Toward the end one realizes that there is simply no way that Bridges and McInerney—who are clearly about to follow the novel faithfully to its conclusion, wherein we learn what's *really* tormenting our hero—will save this picture from falling apart. For one perceives that the eleventh-hour revelation—namely, that our hero's mother died exactly a year ago of cancer—won't wash on film. If McInerney got away with it in the novel, it's because the novel's whole chic, nightclubby environment utterly ignores the existence of such things as mothers and families, and the ending exposes the phoniness of this environment in a quietly effective manner that is perfectly in key with the contemplative state of mind of an individual reading a novel—a state of mind to which the protagonist's kinetic *Lebensart* is bound to feel alien, wrongheaded. In the highly charged social setting that is a movie theater, however, the ending of *Bright Lights* feels like a cop-out. Having presumably sensed that this ending would seem less justified on film, McInerney drops a few hints along the way, mostly in the form of brief memory flashes of our hero's bedridden mother writhing in pain; far from solving anything, however, these addenda come off as feeble attempts to disguise a structural flaw.

Yet if the film ultimately collapses, it offers many pleasures along the way. Aside from the fine direction and superb cinematography (by Gordon Willis), it's rich in memorable characterizations: Swoosie Kurtz's sympathetic co-worker, Frances Sternhagen's spinsterish supervisor, Jason Robards's has-been writer. (Alas, John Houseman's imposing editor-in-chief is the usual Professor Kingsfield retread.) Most striking of all is Dianne Wiest, seen in flashback as the mother; despite the brevity of her on-camera time, her performance is rich and strong and acutely moving. And there are funny moments—notably a sequence involving a ferret and a goofy line delivered in a perfect deadpan by a blond transvestite.

Even Michael J. Fox, an actor of narrow range, is often surprisingly effective as the leading character (who's been dubbed Jamie Conway). But Fox's modest size and boyish appearance create problems. When he stares bleakly at his dissipated self in a bathroom mirror, he looks less like a drug-ravaged wreck than like a Cub Scout who's had one too many malteds; likewise, when he drags himself out of his disheveled bed, wearing only underwear, after a day-long post-party snooze, he looks as if he's all of eleven years old. Once or twice (e.g., when Swoosie spurns a sexual come-on and mothers him instead), this childlike appearance seems a plus; but more often it works against the filmmakers' intentions. At times, moreover (e.g., when he opens Swoosie's medicine cabinet and exclaims, "Valium—all *right*"), Fox falls back noticeably upon the limited repertoire of gesture, expression, and inflection that is Alex Keaton, the character he plays on the TV series "Family Ties." Even more miscast is Phoebe Cates as his fashion-model wife Amanda; though attractive, she is hardly the "gorgeous, gorgeous creature" that everyone in the film considers her to be. She certainly doesn't look much like a fashion model; indeed, she's hardly taller than Fox.

About fifteen minutes into *The Milagro Beanfield War,* the friend I'd brought with me leaned over and whispered: "I'm so glad this movie isn't taking sides!" He was being sarcastic. Boy, was he being sarcastic. This picture—the first to be directed by Robert Redford since his Oscar-winning directorial debut in *Ordinary People*—is so crudely tendentious that it brought back memories of some of the more shrill and phony populist movies of the 1930s. The good guys here are the dirt-poor, predominantly Hispanic, salt-of-the-earth residents of tiny Milagro, New Mexico (*milagro* is Spanish for "miracle"); the bad guys are the Anglo developer Ladd Devine (Richard Bradford) and his political cronies (among them the governor, played by M. Emmett Walsh) who are planning to surround the town with the Mircale Valley Recreation Area, "the largest leisure-time development" in the state's history. And believe me, such evil-looking fat cats haven't been seen on film since the days of Edward Arnold.

The "war" of the title—actually more of a skirmish—begins when Joe Mondragón (Chick Vennera) defies the Anglos' plans by irrigating (with public water) and then seeding his beanfield, which, we learn, is "in the middle of what's going to be the thirteenth fairway" of the Miracle Valley golf course. Milagro activist Ruby Archuleta (Sonia Braga), the local auto mechanic, is heartened by Joe's action; watching the stolen water pour onto his land, she declaims (to no one except us, and in a voice reminiscent of La Pasionaria at her most *apasionada*): "I knew José Mondragón couldn't go through his whole life without attempting at least one great thing."

What flatness, what preachiness, what solemnity! (*Ordinary People,* you'll recall, was likewise something of a stiff sermon masquerading as poignant human drama.) Vennera walks through the whole picture with a single expression of fatuous, bemused defiance; Braga, for her part, plays Ruby as one of those awful liberated women who seem to have exchanged all their warmth and gentleness for a sexless, steely determination—and of course we're supposed to admire the hell out of her for it. But it's impossible to admire any of the too-numerous characters in this film, because it's impossible to feel anything for them; they're not human beings, they're one-dimensional icons of noble poverty, courtesy of the cliché-infested, liberal-guilt-ridden imagination of a rich white movie star.

Like others of his breed, Redford patronizes Hispanics without even realizing it: arguably, the film's real hero is not a Latino but an Anglo, Charlie Bloom (John Heard), a Milagro newspaperman and "progressive lawyer" who says things like, "These are not the sixties . . . nobody gives a shit anymore." Since Heard looks quite a bit like Redford, and delivers a performance chock-full of Redfordisms, it is hard not to identify him with Redford—especially when the feisty-but-unlovable Ruby, stung by his initial reluctance to join her revolution (well, there has to be *some* drama), spits out an accusation: "You're a tourist. . . . When things get rough you run away to somewhere comfortable." This is, most assuredly, a tourist's film; watching it, you picture Redford sitting in his Fifth Avenue apartment, sipping cappuccino and trying out script ideas on his valet: "How does this sound, Pablo?"

What a bad movie! In one scene the peasants actually sing "Cielito Lindo." Among the unsatisfactory supporting players is Christopher Walken, whose performance as a slimy lawman named Kyril Montana is not only wooden but inchoate (why does he suddenly seem to turn friendly at the end?). Though Robbie Greenberg's cinematography, moreover, is (inappropriately) gorgeous, the dubbing and continuity are often surprisingly sloppy (Joe's bean plants, for instance, inexplicably shrink from one scene to the next). And though Redford aims essentially for a *Grapes of Wrath*-style poetic naturalism, he also features a disconcerting touch of south-of-the-border "magic realism" in the form of a Shakespeare-quoting angel (Roberto Carricart) who is invisible to everyone except Milagro's oldest resident, the devout Amarante Córdova—played by Carlos Riquelme, who gives the second most endearing performance in the film (the most endearing is that of his pet pig).

What's more, there are several utterly gratuitous characters, notably Herbie Platt (played by the irritating, overexposed Daniel Stern), an NYU grad student in sociology who has (quite unbelievably) come to Milagro for six months to write his thesis, and who—although Redford doesn't seem to realize it—comes off as impossibly stupid, even for an NYU grad student in sociology. (His first question to old Amarante: "What does Milagro mean?" He hasn't even bothered to learn Spanish!) Based on the novel by John Nichols and filmed from a script by Nichols and David (*The Sting*) Ward, this is a film that only Phil Donahue could love.

For an equally silly look at the other end of the economic scale, there's *Masquerade,* which is set in the Hamptons and is positively awash in mansions, yachts, dinner jackets, dinner parties, and stately WASP surnames. It's an entertainingly dopey thriller—with an increasingly byzantine (and increasingly improbable) plot—of the marry-her-and-murder-her type; as in all these films (*Dial M for Murder, Suspicion*), the big question is whether the sweet young heiress's penniless-but-dashing young consort will actually knock her off. Meg Tilly, in the role of Olivia Lawrence ("the richest nice kid on the East Coast"), is probably the best performer here, but she has little to do except to look innocent and credulous and to gaze adoringly into the utterly vacant baby blues of Rob Lowe, whom director Bob Swaim and writer Dick Wolf expect us to buy as a yacht captain ("the youngest guy on the Southern ocean racing circuit"). The nicest thing one can say about Lowe is that, for once, he's not the movie's major deficiency; indeed, not only is *Masquerade* very poorly directed and written (a commonplace enough phenomenon in expensive Hollywood pictures), but its lighting, sound, and cinematography are of low-budget-horror-movie quality; the editing is so incompetent that I sometimes thought I was viewing a rough cut. To an astonishing degree, *Masquerade* is itself a masquerade—an amateurish production being marketed as the work of pros.

In *Biloxi Blues,* on the contrary, we see an astonishing example of professionalism gone awry. What writer, after all, has won more renown than Neil Simon—who adapted the screenplay from his hit Broadway show—for his sheer *craft,* his gift for slick contrivance? Yet *Biloxi Blues,* which follows Brooklyn boy Eugene Morris Jerome (Matthew Broderick), the hero of last year's *Brighton Beach Memoirs,* to boot camp in 1945, suffers from Simon's congenital weaknesses—formulaic characters, plots, and situations; cheap sentiment; predictable jokes about the heat and the food—without partaking of any of his usual strengths: shape, focus, and a generous proportion of big laugh lines. The supposed reason for the lack of structure and for the relatively paltry number of good jokes is that the story is autobiographical: according to Eugene's wrap-around voice-over (which we are plainly being begged to accept as the voice of Simon), everything in the picture really happened to the writer when he was young. But if this is the case, then why are the characters here even more plastic than is usual in his work? Besides, shouldn't consummate pro "Doc" Simon know better than most of us that being true doesn't make a story worth telling?

For there simply isn't much worth telling here: Eugene isn't that interesting, the other guys in his platoon aren't that interesting, and very little that happens to them is that interesting. Granted, it's funny when Eugene loses his virginity to a prostitute—but it's funny more because of the boy's clumsiness, as enacted by Broderick and directed by Mike Nichols, than because of any lines in Simon's script. The rest of the movie consists mostly of disconnected episodes with no dramatic point and little or no comedic payoff: Eugene meets and romances a girl named Daisy (who, to all intents and purposes, remains nothing more than a name); his intellectual platoonmate Epstein (who at times comes off as a Woody Allen parody) challenges the disciplinary methods of creepy, laconic Sergeant Toomey (Christopher Walken again—one is tempted to say naturally); his platoonmate Hennessey is caught *in flagrante* with a fellow soldier and carted off to prison. And so forth. Result: a good chuckle here, a sober moment there, a few touches of sentimentality. But nothing more. Every now and then Simon seems to be taking fitful stabs at some large and serious theme or other, some statement about memory and youth, or love and war, or differences and prejudice. The images never cohere into a vision, though, and in the end the film seems little more than a harmless assortment of nostalgic clichés.

COMMUNISTS AND KITSCH

The Unbearable Lightness of Being
The Manchurian Candidate

If I've taken this long to get around to seeing *The Unbearable Lightness of Being,* which came out last winter and has been playing two blocks from my home for weeks, it's because every time I passed the theater the notion of sitting through a 172-minute movie based on a European novel of ideas filled me with despair. Nor did it seem promising that the novel, written by the distinguished Czech émigré author Milan Kundera and published in 1984, was born of a philosophy that implies, among other things, a contempt for movies. For above all, Kundera despises kitsch, a term which (in his recent collection of essays, *The Art of the Novel*) he defines broadly: "Kitsch is the translation of received ideas into the language of beauty and feeling. It moves us to tears of compassion for ourselves, for the banality of what we think and feel." In Kundera's lexicon, kitsch embraces all social and cultural phenomena—sentimental pop songs, clichéd TV news reports, and, yes, Hollywood movies—which are designed to please the crowd. The concept of kitsch figures crucially in the novel *The Unbearable Lightness of Being*.

Indeed, though the ordinary reader might consider Kundera's novels to be powerful indictments of Communism, to Kundera this sort of interpretation is itself only a sign of the ubiquity of the kitsch mentality. He plainly identifies with his character Sabina when she cries, "My enemy is kitsch, not Communism!" Kundera interprets the entire global situation in terms of kitsch. "The model of Communist kitsch is the ceremony called May Day," he writes, describing the gulag as "a septic tank used by totalitarian kitsch to dispose of its refuse." Then there's "American kitsch," a sensibility which Kundera sees reflected in catch phrases like "powerful indictment of Communism"; in his eyes, even to speak of the evils of Communism—to which his work testifies powerfully—is to indulge in American kitsch. Although Kundera (who has lived in Paris since 1975) clearly appreciates the value of living in the Free World, he seems compelled, for some reason, to play affirmative-action games when making moral comparisons between West and East, to find something—even if it's only the tackiness of New York buildings, the banality of the American media, or the schlockiness of Hollywood films—to stack up alongside Communism's legacy of crimes against humanity. (Pardon my American kitsch.)

To make an American movie out of *The Unbearable Lightness of Being,* then, seems a paradoxical proposition. Not to mention a difficult one. How, after all, can a film adaptation effectively convey ideas which in the original book are communciated largely by way of leisurely discursive passages? (Though the novel's story is meant to make a statement about kitsch, without Kundera's intercalated glosses the typical reader could hardly be counted on to understand it.) What, moreover, can a filmmaker do with a text whose chief structural principle is not plot but argumentation, and whose characters are less flesh-and-blood humans than emblematic ciphers?

What the director Philip Kaufman (*The Right Stuff*) and his coscenarist, Jean-Claude Carrière (*Belle du Jour, The Discreet Charm of the Bourgeoisie*), have done is to isolate the narrative segments of Kundera's novel, to put them in chronological order (with a couple of significant exceptions), and to throw in an occasional line or two of dialogue that makes an awkwardly obtrusive reference to one or another of Kundera's central themes. The result is an unconventional but medium-voltage story about a randy young Prague brain surgeon named Tomas (Daniel Day-Lewis) and a sweet and charming country girl named Tereza (Juliette Binoche) who, against all odds, makes him her husband. The story's principal complications include (a) the aforementioned Sabina (Lena Olin), a sexy avant-garde artist who is Tomas's frequent bedmate and who, we are told, understands him best; and (b) the 1968 Soviet invasion, in the wake of which Tomas and Tereza move to Geneva (where they live very well), then back to

Prague (where he must work as a window washer, she as a barmaid), and finally to a collective farm (where they find bucolic bliss).

The film is temperate, steadily paced, strikingly photographed (by Sven Nykvist), moderately disjunctive, and (in spite of the inevitable T. & A.) surprisingly tame. But what, for a viewer who hasn't read the book, does it all add up to? My guess is that, while such a viewer will probably recognize the filmmakers' intention to convey a host of complex and recondite ideas, and might well find this intention vaguely impressive and even intellectually challenging, he would not, in the end, quite be able to make out what those ideas are. Indeed, even a reader of the novel has the feeling, while viewing the movie, that the significance of one story development after another is constantly hovering just beyond his grasp.

Take Tomas and Tereza's departure from Switzerland. Why, a viewer innocent of Kundera may wonder, do they abandon the comforts of Geneva for certain misery back home in Prague? All one has to go on is Tereza's enigmatic remark to the effect that life in Switzerland is too "light," and that she pines for the "heaviness" of life in Soviet-occupied Czechoslovakia. In the novel one understands this peculiar motivation, more or less, for Kundera helpfully expatiates upon the concepts of "heaviness" and "lightness," which along with kitsch, form the book's thematic foundation. But in the film, the return to Czechoslovakia seems quite incomprehensible. Similarly, such matters as Sabina's hat fetish and Tereza's attraction to photography, which in the novel are pregnant with meaning, seem arbitrary details when they occur in the film, divorced from Kundera's thorough explanations. Then there's our supposed hero, Tomas. "You are the complete opposite of kitsch," Sabina tells him in bed, and presumably we're meant to see that he deserves this compliment in some way, that he embodies some fundamental Kunderesque ideal. But mostly, alas, the Tomas of the film comes off as a jerk; only toward the end, when he becomes a devoted husband, does he begin to earn one's sympathy.

Interestingly, the film's most successful sequences are frankly sentimental, and would almost certainly be classified by Kundera as kitsch. I'm speaking of sequences which show Tomas and Tereza content together at last in the countryside; which show them suffering over their dying dog, Karenin; and which feature a good-natured elderly villager and the beloved pet pig who accompanies him everywhere. (If nothing else, this has been a good year for endearing performances by pigs—see my review last month of *The Milagro Beanfield War*). Though Kundera mentions the old man and his pig, and dwells at some length upon Tomas and Tereza's rural life and upon their love for Karenin, the film's treatment of these matters is considerably more expansive than the novel's. What's more, the film's very effective ending doesn't come from Kundera's book at all, and the point which that ending makes, wonderfully touching and appropriate though it is, doesn't have much of anything to do with the themes that animate the novel.

If, in spite of all this, the film is highly engaging, one major reason is its wealth of strong performances. Juliette Binoche is perfect as the sweet Tereza, and Lena Olin manages to capture both the vivacity and the vulnerability necessary for the role of Sabina. The astonishingly versatile Daniel Day-Lewis, who played a Cockney street tough in *My Beautiful Laundrette* and an effete Edwardian snob in *A Room with a View,* proves equally convincing here as the libidinous young Czech doctor; *The Unbearable Lightness of Being* is worth seeing if only to watch this splendid actor at work.

Also worth seeing is *The Manchurian Candidate,* the 1962 John Frankenheimer political thriller which is currently in re-release. Adapted by George Axelrod from the novel by Richard Condon, this weirdly forceful film introduces us to Staff Sergeant Raymond Shaw (Laurence Harvey), who wins the Medal of Honor in the Korean War for taking out a company of enemy infantry; to his rich, domineering mother (Angela Lansbury) and his despised stepfather, Senator John Iselin (James Gregory)—a Joe McCarthy-type demagogue—who are eager to make political hay out of his success; and to Captain Ben Marco (Frank Sinatra), who, believing himself to have witnessed Shaw's heroic action during a four-day period when they and their Army patrol were incommunicado in the Korean countryside, recommended him for the medal.

Once everyone's back in the States, however, Marco begins to have nightmares which present a shockingly different version of that four-day period. He comes to realize that the encounter with the enemy company is a fiction, and that during those four days he, Shaw, and their entire patrol were abducted, flown to Manchuria, and brainwashed by a team of Soviet scientists, who erased the memory of their abduction and imprinted on their minds a "memory" of Shaw's imaginary heroic action. But to what evil purpose? Gradually we—and Marco—discover that the Soviets have rendered Shaw vulnerable to post-hypnotic suggestion, and that they seek, through him, to gain control of the biggest prize of all: the Presidency of the United States.

It's a bizarre, audacious story, which at times seems to be making fun of Americans who attribute too great a capacity for elaborate and evil ingenuity to the Communists and at other times seems to share their fears, and Frankenheimer's characteristic tone and style—dark and intense, hard-edged and high-contrast—suits the material perfectly. At various points one recalls such other Frankenheimer films as *Seven Days in May* and *The Train* (which, like *The Manchurian Candidate,* is a story of totalitarianism and large-scale deception—the only difference being that in *The Train* the good guys are the ones doing the deceiving).

But one is reminded especially of his 1966 film *Seconds,* in which a frustrated middle-aged businessman contracts with a secret medical conglomerate that fakes his death and transforms him surgically into a handsome, virile, and young-looking Rock Hudson; yet the conglomerate has more surgery planned—shall we say?—than the man bargained for. Like *Seconds, The Manchurian Candidate* offers a stark, black-and-white, tilted-camera's-eye vision of a Kafkaesque world in which things are not as they seem. Both films present an agreeable illusion—in *Seconds,* an illusion of the possibility of starting a new life, and in *Candidate,* an illusion of wartime heroics—beneath which lies a horrific reality; in both films the horror consists in the use of ultra-sophisticated (indeed, well-nigh fantastic) scientific processes in the service of a clandestine, subversive, and profoundly evil power.

To be sure, *The Manchurian Candidate* is not quite the classic that some reviewers have claimed it to be. It seemed to this viewer, for one thing, that there would be much easier ways for the Soviets to get someone to do their bidding than to devise such an elaborate and improbable scheme. But the film is nonetheless very gripping, more compelling by far than most thrillers of the present day. Perhaps the best thing about its re-release is that it draws deserved attention to a director, John Frankenheimer, who is responsible for some of the most striking films of his time.

SUMMER FLICKS

Funny Farm
Big Business
Big

When it comes to your typical summer movie, the question is not whether the filmmakers have come up with a new idea, but whether they've managed to do anything interesting with an old one. And there's no question but that *Funny Farm* makes use of one of the most ancient and wheezy of story ideas: an urban couple, eager to escape the rat race and get acquainted with nature, move to the countryside, only to discover that (in the words of the current movie's ad copy) life in the country isn't all it's cracked up to be. Now, if you've seen a few episodes of the Eddie Albert-Eva Gabor sitcom "Green Acres" (or the old movie *The Egg and I*), you know that this story idea comes equipped with a less-than-infinite number of comic complications, to wit: the charming house that our couple move into proves to be in astonishingly primitive condition; their simple, goodhearted country neighbors are revealed to be morons, hucksters, and screwballs; the natural world that appeared so beautiful shows itself to be dangerous and uncomfortable.

Though our heroes, this time around, are played by the ever-genial Chevy Chase and by an oddly lackluster actress named Madolyn Smith, *Funny Farm* is pretty much a "Green Acres" retread. If Manhattan-lawyer-turned-gentleman-farmer Eddie Albert had to climb up a telephone pole every time he wanted to place a call from his Hooterville hovel, so Chevy Chase—in the role of Andy Farmer, a sometime Upper West Side sportswriter who has retired to the countryside with his wife, Elizabeth, to write his first novel—must get used to feeding quarters into the public phone which has inexplicably been installed in his kitchen.

Jeffrey Boam's screenplay, then, is exceedingly derivative. What's more, it's very episodic, moving from gag to gag with all the shamelessness of a Henny Youngman. Plot doesn't count for much here, nor does character: Boam takes the Farmers and their feelings no more seriously than the writer of a Road Runner cartoon takes a fall from a cliff by Wile E. Coyote; it doesn't seem to occur to him not to have Andy or Elizabeth do something funny (e.g., hit a dog over the head with a frying pan) simply because it would be out of character. If the center of the story keeps shifting, moreover, it's apparently for no other reason than that Boam, at various junctures, happened to come up with boffo plot twists that had little or nothing to do with the direction the story happened to be taking theretofore. Even the broadest of movie farces generally operates by stricter rules than this.

If *Funny Farm* nonetheless has its moments—inspired, original, wonderfully loony moments—the main reason may be stated in three words: George Roy Hill. In fact, this film is something of a textbook lesson in the difference that a top-notch director can make to a basically feeble screenplay. Throughout the movie, you can feel the wit of the director working its magic upon the witless material. To be fair, some of Boam's inventions (e.g., a scene involving an order of lamb fries) would likely be amusing even in the hands of a Carl Reiner; but the majority of them (e.g., the world's one-millionth Dutch-door gag) are funny and memorable primarily because of the way Hill visualizes and times them. Of course, the director of *The World According to Garp* shouldn't be wasting his time on such mediocre fare in the first place—but that's another story.

Like *Funny Farm, Big Business* tries to find humor in the contrast between city and country. Try to follow this: forty-odd years ago, in Jupiter Hollow, West Virginia, a dirt-poor local woman name Ratliff and a rich Manhattanite named Shelton are both delivered of twin daughters named Rose and Sadie; a befuddled nurse switches two of the infants, so that each mother unwittingly goes home with one baby that's hers and one that isn't. Cut to the present: in Manhattan,

Sadie Shelton (Bette Midler) is the brassy, obnoxious chief executive officer of her family's huge conglomerate, the Moramax Corporation; her meek, friendly "sister" Rose (Lily Tomlin), who's never felt quite at home in New York or in the corporate world, is more interested in collecting stray dogs than in her role as the firm's v.p. Things are the other way around down in Jupiter Hollow: there Rose Ratliff (Lily Tomlin) is a take-charge type, at harmony with her surroundings, while her "sister" Sadie Ratliff (Bette Midler) feels out of place and aches to see the big city. Sadie's opportunity comes when her urban namesake decides to sell off one of Moramax's smaller holdings, the Hollowmade Furniture Company in Jupiter Hollow. Since Hollowmade is the burg's chief industry, Rose Ratliff is deeply concerned about Moramax's plans; with Sadie in tow, she travels to New York on the eve of Moramax's big stockholders' meeting to seek assurances that Hollowmade will not be closed down following the sale.

If the opening sequences sound cumbersomely expository, they are. The purpose of these sequences, needless to say, is as simple as the sequences themselves are complicated: to place twin Lilys and twin Bettes in adjoining hotel suites, unaware of each other's existence, and set them loose on an increasingly confused supporting cast. In order to get the fun under way, however, the film must first ask us to swallow a rather dubious complication: namely, that even though Moramax's corporate headquarters are in New York, the stockholders' meeting is held at the Plaza Hotel, and the Sheltons (who live in Manhattan) spend the night before the meeting in a Plaza suite.

Neither the complexity of the set-up nor the unbelievability of the complications would matter much, of course, if the ensuing sequences were brilliant. But *Big Business* is never as amusing or clever as one would like it to be. In order to be maximally effective, a mistaken-identity comedy must build steadily, sharply, and smoothly; but from the beginning this film is creaky and clumsy, which appears to be rather less the fault of the uneven script by Dori Pierson and Marc Rubel than of Jim Abraham's consistently uninspired, and sometimes even inept, direction. There are laughs, to be sure, but they're scattered, and most of them are occasioned not by terrific mistaken-identity situations but by the two lead actresses' talent for making a great deal out of very little. (Simply by spitting out a single word—"Eurotrash!"—Bette Midler can make one laugh uproariously.) The climactic recognition scene, moreover, is utterly disappointing; and the humor of the final sequence depends altogether too much on the fact that Sadie Ratliff watches "Dynasty"—and it seems ill-advised for a film as thin and cartoonish as this one to refer to (and incorporate a snippet or two from) a TV series which, compared to the film itself, looks realistic and profound.

The two-pairs-of-identical-twins gimmick has an honorable lineage, of course, leading back to Shakespeare's *Comedy of Errors* (and back beyond that to Plautus). But there are several practical problems with it here. To begin with, Lily Tomlin is celebrated for her ability to transform herself into very different characters; but she can't do that here, because her two Roses must be similar enough to be mistaken for each other. As for Bette Midler, she's best at playing herself—or, more specifically, at playing loud, vulgar, wisecracking, swaggering, street-smart Mae West-type know-it-alls—which works perfectly for Sadie Shelton; but Midler must also play the naive, wide-eyed country girl Sadie Ratliff, a character that doesn't really come off at all. Aside from Sadie Shelton, indeed, none of the film's protagonists seems perfectly in focus; one can't *believe* in all four of these women. And this makes it difficult to apportion one's sympathy in the way the filmmakers would like. (It's impossible, by the way, to isolate one of these four as the film's heroine.)

To be sure, apportionment of sympathy is always a problem when you have an actor playing multiple roles. The late actor Ronald Colman knew this; that's why he insisted that the producer David Selznick not give him both the Charles Darnay and the Sydney Carton roles in *A Tale of Two Cities,* even though the two characters were supposed to resemble one another. As Selznick later said, "I'm glad now that he held out for that, because I think a great deal of the illusion of the picture might have been lost had Colman rescued Colman and had Colman gone to the guillotine so that Colman could go away with Lucy." (If Colman played two roles in *The Prisoner of Zenda,* it was only because there was no conceivable alternative.) *Big Business* has precisely this problem: simply stated, it's hard to feel too emotionally involved when one Sadie knocks the other Sadie down and locks her in a closet.

Another problem here is that at times the film seems to be endorsing certain unpleasant stereotypes. For a while, one suspects that the story will conclude with the revelation that, appearances to the contrary, the two Sadies are—surprise—the real Ratliffs, and the two Roses are the real Sheltons. But no way; it's clear in retrospect that we're supposed to have recognized all along that the two Sadies are born "New Yorkers," in the middle-American "code" sense of the term (meaning, of course, that whenever some middle Americans want to say unpleasant things about Jews without being explicitly anti-Semitic, they speak not about "Jews" but about "New Yorkers").

One thing must be said: it's good to see a movie starring two funny women. Midler and Tomlin are a considerably more promising pair than Midler and Shelley Long (in last year's *Outrageous Fortune*), and one would very much like to see them together again. Yet they would have been well advised, this time around, to have junked the far too elaborate premise of *Big Business*—salvaging, perhaps, the delicious character of Sadie Shelton—and found some other script more worthy of their gifts.

A year ago or so, I remarked in this space upon the profusion of recent comedy-fantasies—such as *All of Me* and *Oh Heavenly Dog*—in which characters found themselves inhabiting bodies other than their own. Since then the trend has escalated. We've had films in which fathers and sons exchange bodies (*Vice Versa, Like Father, Like Son*), and even one (*18 Again*) in which a grandfather and grandson change places. And now there's *Big,* in which thirteen-year-old Josh Baskin (David Moscow) wakes up one morning to discover that he's been transformed into a twenty-years-older version of himself (Tom Hanks).

Given the extreme familarity of its concept—and the fact that it was co-written by Steven Spielberg's sister Anne (with Gary Ross), produced by the insipid James Brooks (of TV comedy and *Broadcast News* fame), and directed by Penny ("Laverne and Shirley") Marshall (most of the members of whose family know more about churning out vapid sitcoms than about making films)—one could be forgiven for not expecting much from *Big*. Surprisingly, however, the film proves to be one of the most delightful comedies in recent memory. And among the most gently moving, too. Superficially it may resemble *Vice Versa* and the like, but it has a deeper affinity to such strange and affecting fairy tales as *Charly* and *Being There*. Both the script and the direction are first-rate, and Tom Hanks, whose talents have rarely seemed more than modest, does an absolutely extraordinary job of convincing one that he is a boy in a man's body. His performance is at once tender and hilarious, full of perfect small touches (e.g., the tentative way he peeks into his underpants after looking in the bathroom mirror and seeing a grown-up); at every turn, the awkwardness, exuberance, and innocence of this boy-man feel exactly on target, never overdone or sentimentalized. Like *Big Business,* to be sure, this is one-joke film; the difference here is that the joke keeps building, that it builds with wit and perception and sensitivity, and that (for all its ridiculousness) it is on some level taken perfectly seriously: Marshall and company make us believe in, and care about, this character precisely because *they* believe in and care about him.

They also make us care about Susan (Elizabeth Perkins), a jaded young businesswoman who, during the course of a most peculiar affair with Josh, gradually learns to be vulnerable, to trust, and to love. Perkins is smart, funny, and often astonishingly touching in this role; an actress of rare expressiveness, she lets us see Susan open up, step by subtle step, like a mimosa leaf, lets us watch her various reactions to Josh—curiosity, perplexity, wariness, amusement, ardor, wonderment—playing across her face, vying for control. It is reported that Perkins was James Brooks's original choice for the Holly Hunter role in *Broadcast News,* and that when he took that part away from her he gave her *Big* as a consolation prize. This revelation only reinforces one's already low opinion of Brooks's taste: Hunter is an arresting if narrow performer, a grating sitcom type; Perkins is incomparably finer, an actress of subtler effects, wider range, lovelier presence. But then Perkins should probably be grateful for Brooks's decision, because *Big* is unquestionably superior to *Broadcast News.*

RABBIT, RUN

Who Framed Roger Rabbit

You've probably already seen *Who Framed Roger Rabbit*, but if you haven't, whip off those reading glasses and hop like a bunny over to your nearest theater. This film—which does a breathtaking, state-of-the-art job of combining live action with animation—is, quite simply, the closest thing I've ever seen to a perfect piece of film entertainment. Not only is it wonderful, it reminds you what the word *wonderful* really means: it excites wonder, astonishes you, causes you to marvel. And don't wait for it to show up on cable either, or on broadcast TV: this is the kind of movie you have to see at a movie theater.

It is, in short, an exhilarating, magical experience. At this writing, I've seen *Roger* four times (in two weeks), and as far as I'm concerned, you have to see it at *least* three times: the first time to gasp in amazement at the technical achievement and, after fifteen minutes or so, to forget the technical achievement entirely and fall into a glorious, childlike belief in the whole magnificent illusion (and laugh at the jokes); the second time to follow the Byzantine suspense plot more carefully, to note that virtually everything in the second half of the film is foreshadowed in the first half, and to recognize how wonderfully organized and tightly plotted it is (and laugh at the jokes); the third time to look closely at all that technical stuff and drive yourself crazy trying to figure out how the hell they did it (and laugh at the jokes). With each visit, you notice delightful, funny little details that you hadn't noticed before; you grow increasingly respectful of the actors—especially Bob Hoskins and Joanna Cassidy—for their ability to make you believe that they actually are interacting with Roger and Jessica Rabbit; and you get more and more tickled with Roger himself (splendidly dubbed by Charles Fleischer), a cartoon character as memorable, lovable, and hilarious as any you can name. After watching this movie, you think endlessly about how many things could have gone wrong—a single part miscast, a single scene in which the illusion just didn't come off—and how disastrous it would have been if just one of them had, and how incredible it is that none of them did. You think about what a mess the typical movie is (and after seeing *Roger*, how easy a typical movie seems to make!), and what a flawless piece of work this most technically challenging and directorially problematic one has turned out to be.

Among other things, *Who Framed Roger Rabbit* is a tribute to the golden age of the American cartoon, an age which peaked around 1947, the year in which the film is set. Most of the major cartoon characters of that era—Disney's Donald Duck and Mickey Mouse, for instance, and Warner Brothers' Bugs Bunny, Tweety, Yosemite Sam, and Daffy Duck—are featured in cameos (with, as always, the versatile Mel Blanc doing many of the Warners voices). The film is, in fact, a co-production of Steven Spielberg's Amblin Entertainment and Touchstone Films, a division of Disney; the Disney Studios, and Walt himself, are both name-dropped in the script. But the film's look and feel and *Weltanschauung* are pure Warner Brothers—and thank goodness. For, Disney's grand *Fantasia* notwithstanding, those zippy, sophisticated Warners cartoons of the early postwar years—the "Looney Tunes" and "Merrie Melodies"—represent the zenith of American cartoon-making: they had a sensibility, a species of humor, and a wacky but thoroughly consistent set of physical laws all their own. If a Warners character found himself in midair, for instance, he didn't fall until he looked down and *noticed* he was in midair. What's more, the Warners cartoon characters were unkillable: Wile E. Coyote routinely got blasted to bits in one scene and was perfectly fine again in the next. (This was not at all the rule in Disney cartoons: remember Bambi's mother?) These same physical laws apply for the cartoon characters in *Roger*. Likewise, the Warners cartoons had a colorful vocabulary that was all their own. Words like *simoleon* and *zillion* proliferated; if an American city was mentioned, it was likely to be some place with a funny name like Walla Walla, Cucamonga, or

Kokomo; if a commercial product appeared onscreen, its brand name was invariably "Acme." These details, too, are remembered in *Roger*.

What makes *Roger* different from the golden-age cartoons is that, in the world imagined by this film, the cartoon characters live in the same dimension as the rest of us. They're not mere drawings but actual beings known as "toons" who live in a Los Angeles community called Toontown, and earn a living by acting in cartoons that have been written, directed, and produced by humans. It doesn't seem possible to sustain such a conceit for nearly two hours, but director Robert Zemeckis, writers Jeffrey Price and Peter Seamon (whose script is adapted from Gary K. Wolf's novel, *Who Censored Roger Rabbit?*), and an army of animators (*Roger*'s credits seem to last almost as long as the picture itself) succeed in integrating the human and toon physical laws, as well as the distinct human and toon ways of viewing the world, with remarkable wit, coherence, and imagination. (They also manage to work in a multitude of funny allusions to famous detective movies, among them *The Maltese Falcon* and *Chinatown*.) Only a moment passes before you buy the gimmick completely, and at no point in the film—not even when the hero, human private-eye Eddie Valiant (Hoskins), pays a visit to Toontown (a sequence that might easily have gone a bit too far and destroyed the illusion completely)—does your belief in it all falter.

Roger, to say the least, whets your appetite for animation. But to look at Saturday morning TV after seeing this film is to be reminded just how witless and inelegant most children's cartoons are nowadays, and how rare an exception *Roger* really is. Some critics have been saying (it's the closest thing most of them have to a major complaint about the film) that *Roger*, splendid though it may be, is for adults more than it is for children. To borrow a phrase from the Warners lexicon, that's a load of succotash. Once upon a time it was understood—by cartoon makers and critics alike—that wit and sophistication were not for adults only. I know that my own favorite cartoons, in my childhood, were those in which an occasional joke routinely went over my head. Though I didn't fully grasp them, I was entertained by these cartoons; I recognized and appreciated their cleverness; they created a world that was, to a small child, rich, baroque, and mysterious—indeed, well-nigh symbolistic. Those cartoons succeeded for the same reason that *Roger* does: their creators didn't condescend to the audience; they wrote and drew things that made *them* laugh, simple as that. Since those days, cartoons have suffered a fate similar to that of elementary-school textbooks: they've been watered down, dumbed-down, vetted by humorless educators and child psychologists for social responsibility and political correctness; they've had all the magic and the joy committee-meetinged out of them. As if that weren't bad enough, the high price of animation has, in addition, drastically reduced the technical quality of most cartoons; thus watching Saturday morning network fare nowadays is, in more than one way, a grim experience. If the achievement and reception of *Who Framed Roger Rabbit* don't do something, at least, to reverse this trend, nothing will.

Film notes: Some thoughts on colorization and the law. On June 30, a *New York Times* story by Andrew L. Yarrow reported that the House of Representatives had voted to establish something called the National Film Preservation Advisory Board, which would be empowered to "select up to 25 films a year that represent 'an enduring part of our nation's historical and cultural heritage.' " Those films selected "would be included in a National Film Registry and given a commission seal that could be used for promotion. If altered versions of these films were distributed or exhibited, they would have to be labeled as 'materially altered' or 'colorized,' with a disclaimer that 'certain creative contributors did not participate.' " The thirteen-member board would include among its members the presidents of the American Film Institute, the Directors Guild, and the University Film and Video Association, as well as the chairmen of the film departments at UCLA and NYU. Ye gods.

Now, I deplore the coloring—or "colorization," as the process has come to be known—of films without the consent of the producer or director. If you've ever seen Claudette Colbert flashing bluish-green teeth in *Boom Town* you know what I mean. Perhaps something *should* be done to prevent it. But an advisory board most certainly isn't the answer. It's simply not the government's business to decide which American films—or books or musical compositions, for that matter—are classics. If the creators of one film have the right to be accorded disclaimers in cases of colorization, then the creators of all films have that right.

One can imagine supporters of this measure comparing it to the practice of giving certain buildings landmark status for the purpose of protecting them from drastic alterations or the wrecker's ball. But this analogy doesn't work. Buildings play a civic role that films and novels don't, and landmarking is simply one of many ways—along with zoning laws, building codes, and safety regulations—in which government exercises its regulatory rights over them. Besides, classic films exist in multiple copies; buildings don't. The production of colorized prints of, say, *It's a Wonderful Life* doesn't entail the destruction of the extant black-and-white copies of the film.

Nor can this proposed board be compared to one of the national endowments, such as the NEA or the NEH. Though I'd hardly jump at the opportunity to defend those endowments (whose work often amounts to little more than government-subsidized literary or academic log-rolling), it can at least be said that they don't presume to accord preferential legal status to certain artists and art works; they just hand out money.

The other day, while I was perusing two adjacent newspaper advertisements—one for *Coming to America*, in which Eddie Murphy towers over the New York skyline, and the other for *Crocodile Dundee II*, in which Paul Hogan and a curvaceous friend likewise tower over the same skyline—it occurred to me that someday our descendants will watch a few representative American movies of the eighties and will conclude that there weren't any cities in America besides New York. How many more times are we going to have to watch an awestruck out-of-town protagonist (whether Hogan in *Crocodile Dundee* or Bette Midler in *Big Business*) gaze at everything from the skyscrapers along Sixth Avenue to the lowlifes in Times Square? When are scriptwriters going to grow tired of setting scenes in Rockefeller Center, cinematographers cease dwelling upon the reflection of the Manhattan skyline in the East River, directors stop aiming their cameras down Park Avenue toward the Pan Am Building? In a world as big as this one, I found it ridiculous that both *Big* and *Big Business*—to speak only of recent films—contain major sequences set in the famous Fifth Avenue toy store F. A. O. Schwarz. Among other reasons, I go to the movies to see places I've never been; most of the location shots in *Big Business* took place within three blocks of the theater I saw the movie in.

Woody Allen? An exception. He has something to say about New York; it's the part of the world he knows and understands best. In the movies I'm talking about, by contrast, New York's not even a setting, really—it's just a backdrop.

THE STATELY HOMES OF ENGLAND—AND AMERICA

A Handful of Dust
Mr. North

Want a foolproof recipe for a critically successful late-eighties English film? Here, copy this down: first, get somebody to write a screenplay that is based very faithfully upon a novel by Evelyn Waugh—the miniseries version of whose *Brideshead Revisited,* you'll remember, was largely responsible for the current spate of films about prewar gentlefolk and their grand houses. Next, fill the lead roles with James Wilby and Rupert Graves, the stars of *Maurice,* the most recent production by the acknowledged masters of the grand-houses genre, James Ivory and Ismail Merchant. Then, arrange for beautiful photography, sumptuous production design, exquisite period costuming. Finally, offer a relatively small but colorful role to Sir Alec Guinness, whose very presence in a film is universally recognized as a guarantee of its wit, elegance, and all-around class. *Voilà:* a stately, sophisticated, lovely-to-look-at film, guaranteed to please any audience of hoity-toity Brits, stateside *New Yorker* subscribers, or Anglophile voting members of the Academy of Motion Picture Arts and Sciences (who, after all, gave the Best Picture nod a few years back to the tedious but raffiné *Chariots of Fire*).

This, at least, would seem to be the sort of sharp thinking responsible for the existence of *A Handful of Dust,* the execrable new British picture that has been adapted from Evelyn Waugh's wonderful 1934 novel. To watch this film—which was directed by Charles Sturridge (who also directed *Brideshead*) from a script by himself, Tim Sullivan, and Derek Granger—is to have the feeling that while everyone involved in the project may have read the book, not one of them managed to understand it.

The novel, in case you've forgotten, tells the story of a disastrous love triangle. Tony Last is a callow, rather absurdly solemn young husband and father with a fanatical attachment to Hetton, his ugly neo-Gothic country house (each of whose rooms is named for a character in the *Morte Arthur*), and to the English traditions that it symbolizes. His fellow clubman John Beaver is a thoroughly superficial young bachelor-about-London with no job, no prospects, and (aside from his indulgent mother) no visible means of support. And Lady Brenda Last is Tony's lively, charming wife, who detests Hetton and is beginning to grow tired of her dull, trusting husband; so it is that when Beaver pays a weekend visit, it is less sexual attraction than sheer boredom and whim that draw Brenda into an affair with the unsavory young man. The ensuing events are grim: the death of the Lasts' little boy is followed hard upon by a heartless divorce suit. And the conclusion is perfectly bizarre: a disillusioned Tony journeys to a remote corner of South America, where he finds himself trapped in the jungle, condemned to live out his days reading Dickens to a courtly tyrant named Mr. Todd. Meanwhile, back in England, Tony is presumed dead, his beloved mansion inherited by cousins; and a penniless Brenda—thrown over by Beaver—marries Tony's best friend.

Bizarre though it is, however, Waugh's ending works, because it makes perfect sense within the context of his comprehensively ironic vision of the way of all flesh. Throughout the novel, it should be emphasized, Waugh's tone is darkly but assuredly comic: this is a book, after all, that contains people named Lady Cockpurse and Colonel Inch, Souki de Foucault-Esterhazy and Mr. Graceful, Lady Anchorage and Princess Abdul Akbar; Tony's best friend, moreover, is an MP whose method of researching a speech on farm policy is to ask friends over cocktails whether they know anything about pigs. Unquestionably, *A Handful of Dust* is one of the funniest novels of the century. Yet it is, at the same time, a deeply serious novel which borrows its title from *The Waste Land* ("I will show you fear in a handful of dust") and which, like Eliot's poem, communicates a profound anguish concerning the moral and spiritual poverty of modern man. Waugh, like Eliot, reveres God and tradition; and he finds both comedy and tragedy in the utter failure of his characters to do the same. His vision encompasses sympathy as well as bitter scorn for Tony, Brenda, and Beaver alike. (For the hapless, obtuse Tony—though some of his instincts, at least are correct—is hardly Waugh's idea of a perfect modern Englishman.) The novel's signal achievement is that its combination of serious purpose and comic method works splendidly; to read it is to have the rare feeling that this is a writer who thoroughly understands the people he has created.

To view the film adaptation of this novel, by contrast, is to have the feeling that its director doesn't understand the book at all. Though exceedingly faithful in the specifics of its plot—and even in details of setting and dialogue—Sturridge's film fails utterly to capture the spirit of Waugh's novel; it is as sumptuous and glittery as Waugh's novel is spare and stiletto-sharp. Indeed, Sturridge directs the film as if it took place in the same graceful, soft-focus, gently lit demesne as *Brideshead Revisited* or *Maurice* or *A Room with a View,* and not in the distinctive, sardonically imagined world of Waugh's thirties novel. This difference is a crucial one, and among its consequences is that, in Sturridge's film, the South American sequences simply don't work: the very un-Waughian tone that Sturridge has established in the earlier part of the film simply doesn't allow for such an outré conclusion to Tony's story; the transition feels abrupt, and the entire episode with Mr. Todd—which is so wackily on target in the novel—comes across like a misplaced reel from another movie.

Sturridge's casting likewise does damage to Waugh's material. The film's Beaver (Rupert Graves) and Brenda (Kristin Scott Thomas) are so attractive, and its Tony (James Wilby) so hollow a vessel (why does this vapid and incompetent actor keep getting cast in lead roles?), that, in the earlier sequences at any rate, Brenda's infidelity seems perfectly understandable, and for a good portion of the film one actually finds oneself applauding Brenda and Beaver's romance—a response utterly at odds with Waugh's intentions. That this romance is meant to symbolize the amorality and irresponsibility into which men and women descend when they lose their respect for faith and tradition is thoroughly obscured. Though it is engaging, then, and though it contains at least two strikingly good performances—namely, those by Alec Guinness in the role of Mr. Todd, and by Anjelica Huston as a rich American woman named Mrs. Rattery—this adaptation of *A Handful of Dust* is lamentably off the mark.

A Handful of Dust is a young man's novel; *Theophilus North,* published in 1973 by Thornton Wilder (who was born in 1897, six years before Waugh), is a work of old age. If anything, Wilder's setting is even more upper-crust than Waugh's: while *A Handful of Dust* takes place in a number of highfalutin English residences during the early part of the Depression, *Theophilus North* is set in the mansions of Newport, Rhode Island, during the summer of 1926. Despite the similarity of their milieux, however, there are striking differences betwen the two novels. Whereas the grimly humorous young Waugh intends, in *A Handful of Dust,* to express his high regard for the stately homes of England and all they represent, as well as his contempt for the social and political forces that have conspired to destroy the symbolically named Tony Last, the elderly (and considerably sunnier) Wilder, in *Theophilus North,* seeks to celebrate the irreverence of youth amidst the stuffiness and mendacity of some of America's own stateliest homes; if *A Handful of Dust* concerns itself with tragic endings, *Theophilus North* is a novel of happing beginnings. Wilder's treatment of the Eternal Things is different too: whereas most of Waugh's characters are notable for their extreme detachment from God, the very name of Wilder's protagonist suggests that he enjoys the special affection of the deity.

Theophilus North—which is, as it happens, heavily autobiographical—takes the form of an elderly man's memoir of long ago. In the first couple of chapters we meet the eponymous hero, a 1920 graduate (like Wilder) of Yale who, having taught for several years at a boy's prep school in New Jersey, heads for Newport, takes a room at the YMCA, and begins working as a tutor and reader to the wealthy and their children. Theophilus explains that at various times in his youth he'd had various ambitions—to be a saint, an anthropologist, a lover, an actor, a magician—but notes that what united all of these ambitions was the desire to be "a free man."

"Notice all the projects I did not entertain: I did not want to be a banker, a merchant, a lawyer, nor to join any of those life-careers that are closely bound up with directorates and boards of governors—politicians, publishers, world reformers, I wanted no boss over me, or only the lightest of supervisions. All these aims, moreover, had to do with people—but with people as individuals." And, in fact, each of the remaining chapters of *Theophilus North* recounts our hero's introduction to one or more very distinctive individuals: an extraordinary pair of rich children named Charles and Eloise Fenwick, a poor but literary young Italian named Mino, and so forth.

The film that has been based upon this novel—which Danny Huston has directed from a script by Janet Roach, John Huston (the director's late father), and James Costigan—is called *Mr. North* and is based primarily on two of these chapters, both of which are named for the estates at which they take place. " 'Nine Gables' " is the story of Theophilus's encounters with James McHenry Bosworth (played in the film by Robert Mitchum), an elderly millionaire; with Bosworth's avaricious daughter Sarah (Tammy Grimes), who has convinced the old man that he is ill and non-ambulatory; and with his granddaughter Persis (Anjelica Huston). In " 'The Deer Park' " Theophilus's use of his "electric hands" on an ailing seventeen-year-old (he has "a certain gift for soothing, for something approaching mesmerism") lands him in a degree of trouble. These stories are altered considerably in the movie: the filmmakers, for example, turn Persis into Theophilus's love interest, and make her at once more mysterious and (by casting the director's gifted but mannish sister in the role) less beautiful than she is in the novel; and they complicate the "electric hands" incident with a resentful Scots doctor (played by David Warner) who—in the film's weakest sequence—drags Theophilus into court for practicing medicine without a license. The film's happy ending, furthermore, bears no resemblance to anything in the novel.

In terms of story and character, then, *Mr. North* is nowhere near as true to its original as is *A Handful of Dust.* Yet Huston's film is by far the better adaptation. I say this as someone who went to *Mr. North* with fond, if considerably faded, memories of the book from which it is derived. Wilder's novel is a strange and delightful work, suffused with a gentle, romantic nostalgia for the energy, ideals, and ambitions of youth. I was fortunate enough to read it during my nineteenth summer; and though, years later, I could not recall many of its details, I retained an extremely vivid image of the character of Theophilus and of Newport in the summer, and a strong overall impression of light and air and charm. The film that Danny Huston has made is surprisingly congruous with these lingering images and impressions. Indeed, though *A Handful of Dust* is, in most of the ways that can be quantified, more consistent than *Mr. North* with its source material, the latter film is more faithful in the way that really counts: its feel, its sensibility, are wonderfully close to those of the novel; Huston *fils* makes it possible for a person who has experienced a strong affection for Wilder's novel to leave the theater with the feeling that his affection has been shared, comprehended, and reanimated.

There are, to be sure, problems with the film, and they begin with Anthony Edwards, the young actor who plays the title role. Physically, Edwards is right for the part, but there are times when the dialogue—which is deliberately somewhat formal, even unnatural, in its diction and syntax—sounds a little *too* unnatural coming from his lips. Some of Mitchum's line readings, too, old pro though he is, have the same stilted quality—the reason doubtless being that, Mitchum's impressive range (for a Hollywood movie star of his generation) notwithstanding, a courtly late Victorian plutocrat with a consuming passion for the writings of Bishop Berkeley may be a bit of a stretch for him. Nor does Mitchum seem even slightly helpless and sickly; it is difficult to imagine this bear of a man being bullied by a Tammy Grimes into staying indoors for several years. Yet these are minor cavils. All of the major roles are, for the most part, engagingly acted, and the film is full of strong, interesting supporting performances—notably by Lauran Bacall (as a stylish landlady) and Harry Dean Stanton (as a *faux*-English gentleman's gentleman). Indeed, *Mr. North* is on the whole a most appealing film—a first-rate adaptation that might have pleased Thornton Wilder himself, and made Evelyn Waugh more than a mite envious.

SUPERSTAR

The Last Temptation of Christ

Given all the furor, it seemed a sure bet that *The Last Temptation of Christ* would at least be interesting to watch. Wrong. It's sheer torture—one of those deadly boring films, like Barbra Streisand's *A Star is Born,* that drag along so numbingly that you get the feeling they *want* you to walk out. And believe me, I would've cleared out of *The Last Temptation* after twenty minutes or so if I hadn't already decided to write about it.

Fundamentalists who are lucky enough not to have seen this picture decry it as a willful, indeed cynical, act of sacrilege, a crass exploitation of Christianity. Not at all. Sacrilegious this film may be, but not intentionally so: on the contrary, it's the work of people who plainly thought they were doing something devout. After all, when competent movie people set out to make a few bucks off of Christianity, they don't turn out a picture like *The Last Temptation;* they give us crowd-pleasers like *The Robe, Quo Vadis, Ben Hur*—glossy platitudinous spectacles marked by stilted dialogue, excellent posture, syrupy musical scores, and a thoroughgoing (if thoroughly fake) reverence toward Holy Writ (or, more accurately, toward the crudest popular twentieth-century American conceptions thereof).

No, *The Last Temptation* seeks not to exploit Jesus but to know him, to understand him; if those old Hollywood Biblical movies held Christ at arm's length, this film—based on the novel by Nikos

Kazantzakis, and directed by Martin Scorsese from a script by Paul Schrader (his collaborator on *Taxi Driver* and *Raging Bull*)—tries to climb into Christ's skin, to get inside his head. This is a noble motive, perhaps; but it's also an exceedingly dangerous one, for to break down the barriers that those vulgar old Hollywood epics tacitly observed is to risk a degree of vulgarity—and, yes, a degree of profanity—that even Cecil B. DeMille never approached. So it is that *The Last Temptation,* whose advertising would lead us to believe that it manifests a dignity, intelligence, and even godliness unprecedented in Jesus movies, in fact takes the genre to new depths of bad taste, fatuity, and moral offensiveness.

Willem Dafoe, who will be remembered for his portrayal of the Christ figure Sergeant Elias in *Platoon,* plays the Nazarene as a high-strung hippie—an oversensitive Haight-Ashbury type who spends most of his time whining to his apostles about his inner conflicts, confusions, doubts, and longings, and having impromptu rap sessions with them about such things as the relative importance of the soul and the body. (You keep expecting the boys to pass around a joint.) He's Jesus as seen through the filter of *Godspell* and *Jesus Christ Superstar,* of est and Transcendental Meditation, of Jim Morrison and John Lennon. When he's not whining he alternates between crying jags and shrill pronouncements about sin and death and the hereafter—none of which is the least inspiring, for the script deliberately robs the Gospel of its poetry. When some men attempt to stone an adulteress to death, Christ doesn't say, "He that is without sin among you, let him first cast a stone at her"; no, he picks up a stone and says: "Who has never sinned? Who? Whoever that is, come here, and throw these." In the Sermon on the Mount, he doesn't say, "Blessed are the meek; for they shall inherit the earth. Blessed are they which do hunger and thrist after righteousness: for they shall be filled." No, he says, "The meek will be blessed. And the righteous will be blessed too." With an act like this, the real Jesus would never have made it to the big time. (This Jesus doesn't even know his grammar: he says "if I was" instead of "if I were," uses *like* for *as*, and announces that "it's me the prophets preached about.")

The idea here is clearly to remove Christ from the pages of Scripture, to make him more human. (The film shows him, for example, dancing at a wedding: Jesus as regular guy.) But what results is one of the most inarticulate protagonists ever to fill a movie screen. Lack of eloquence, you see, equals sincerity. This is a Lite Jesus—a timid, sniveling, banal, seedy-looking, not particularly bright Saviour who's utterly without majesty or depth or what junior high school teachers used to call "leadership qualities." There's no sense of profound love or goodness here, no sense of a huge soul in torment. There's not even any *warmth.* We're supposed to see him struggling with temptation, struggling against the necessity of his final sacrifice ("Do I really have to die?" he whimpers. "Is there any other way?"); yet he's not only tempted but weak, surly, vacillating, and impotent: a hollow vessel who occasionally has delusions, hears "voices," and acts like a guy on acid at the Port Authority in New York. Speaking in public, he usually doesn't even know what he's saying: "When those soldiers were torturing Magdalene I wanted to kill them and then I open my mouth and out comes the word love. . . . I don't understand." When he's with Mary Magdalene (who is played by the lovely and gifted, but ever-spacey, Barbara Hershey), the two of them look and behave like one of those aging flower-child couples who live in Topanga Canyon, drive around in pick-up trucks, and analyze each other in pop-psych fashion ("You were hanging onto your mother," Mary Magdalene tells Christ, "then you were hanging onto me, now you're hanging onto God").

You get the feeling that Dafoe and Hershey's way of getting into the characters was to decide that Christ and Mary Magdalene must have been pretty much like George Harrison and Mia Farrow after a visit to their Indian guru. Lennon-style homilies abound: preaching his New Order, Jesus says, "All I'm saying is the change will happen with love, not with killing." And sex figures importantly; to Scorsese and company, the interesting thing about Jesus is that he was *human,* and to be human, in their view, is to be preoccupied with sex and self-gratification. Thus, in the course of his fantasy marriage to Mary, sister of Lazarus, Jesus tells her: "Don't ever leave me. I'm happy." And having reached (in that fantasy) a ripe old age, he tells a cantakerous St. Paul: "I enjoy my life—for the first time I'm enjoying it." (Jesus as "Tonight Show" guest!)

The Last Temptation is overacted throughout; Dafoe and Hershey in particular seem incapable of saying hello without putting on an intense Actors Studio expression. The portrayal of Christ's followers is strictly revisionistic: where the old Biblical movies presented them as gentle and soft-spoken, possessed of an inner peace, all the adherents of Christ in this film—John the Baptist, the disciples, St. Paul—are loud and pushy and obnoxious, selling salvation as if it were a cheap suit.

The film is freighted with obtrusive dissolves, excessive atmosphere (camels, turbans, sand), and a musical score that relies too heavily on ditsy recorder music and a hard-rock African drumbeat; it contains too much talk and too little narrative drive; and, like all of Scorsese's movies, it offers violence and gore aplenty, an abundance of yukky things that force you to look away from the screen.

But the most troubling thing about the film is that its theology is a mess. Yes, Christ was both human and divine; but a Christ horny for Mary Magdalene and tempted by the dream of a wife and some cute kids is simply not consistent with Biblical teachings. Nor is a St. Paul who, when Jesus (in his fantasy) identifies himself and demands that he stop preaching, declares, "I don't care whether you're Jesus or not. . . . If I have to crucify you to save the world, I'll do it." To ascribe such a pragmatic view of Christ to St. Paul is indefensible. But then there isn't much intellectual rigor here to speak of—or, for that matter, any real sense of engagement with the idea of God. When Jesus abandons his fantasy of a married life and accepts his fate on the Cross, you get the impression that he's doing so because it's a good career move.

Silly and offensive though this film is, to be sure, the filmmakers' intentions were patently not frivolous, nor their motives basely pecuniary. Martin Scorsese is a serious artist; he has done extraordinary work (*After Hours* remains one of my favorite films of the eighties); he is a master when it comes to making movies about whacked-out-all-American anti-heroes. His mistake in *The Last Temptation of Christ* was to have taken on a subject extremely ill-suited to his grim, grubby, visceral, violence-obsessed, and utterly contemporary intellect. He has robbed Jesus of historicality, of divinity, of all but the most superficial sort of humanity, and—yes—of a heroic dimension. And what remains, I'm afraid, is not very much at all.

STREETS OF NEW YORK

Punchline
Crossing Delancey

One of the more dire recent developments in American pop culture has been the glorification of the stand-up comedian. Comedy clubs and "Comedy Relief"-type benefits have proliferated; films of comedy routines by Bill Cosby and Eddie Murphy have been released theatrically and reviewed as if they were actual movies; yesterday's stand-up comics become today's movie stars. In the eighties, stand-up comics put on airs: the *Playbill* for comedienne Sandra Bernhardt's recent one-woman show in New York referred to her as a "rock-and-roll performance artist." Wasn't it Thucydides who observed that a society enters upon an inexorable process of decline once it begins to take stand-up comedy seriously?

All this is by way of getting around to *Punchline*, which was written and directed by David Seltzer, and which is just as awful as it looks in the ads. Tom Hanks plays Steve Gold, an aspiring stand-up comic who works regularly at an obscure New York club called the Gas Station. Steve is also a med student, but not for long; in the opening sequence, he's kicked out for failing a junior-high-school-level oral exam in anatomy. But hey, he wasn't made to be a doctor, like his dad and brother—he was made to be *funny*. Instead of identifying parts of the large intestine, he entertains his examiners with "poop-chute" jokes. Hilarious.

Also appearing regularly at the Gas Station is a New Jersey housewife named Lila Krytsick (Sally Field). Lila's not as good as Steve—or so, at least, we're supposed to understand. His comedy, you see, comes from his *guts*: hers comes from a list of gags. Indeed, she gets in hot water with her hubby (John Goodman) by spending the family vacation money on Polish jokes. Hubby doesn't understand why she's wasting her evenings at this seedy comedy club for $15 a night. She tries to explain: "I love being a mom. I love being a wife. And I love being able to make people laugh." Her tone is solemn, subdued: Mozart was never this serious about his art.

And seriousness is very much the point here. "Is everything a joke to you?" Steve's prof demands. Later, Lila asks the same thing. Steve's reply: "Lady, nothing's a joke to me. That's why I do stand-up comedy—and *that's why you don't.*" (This is Seltzer's idea of a profound line; it's supposed to Make Us Think.) Seared by this insight, Lila begs Steve for pointers; he complies. For he believes she's naturally funny—and while he'll lie to a woman about a lot of things, he wouldn't lie about that sacred subject: "I don't mess around with *funny*." All Lila needs, he insists, are "the right gags." He instructs her to draw upon her own life: "All our lives are funny. We're God's animated cartoons." Apparently, we're supposed to look upon this as brilliant advice; certainly Lila seems never to have heard it before.

So Lila starts telling jokes about her family and becomes a socko comedienne—easy as that. (Except that she doesn't *really* tell jokes about her family: the supposedly good and original material she does at the end of the movie is in fact as bad and contrived as the stuff she does at the beginning.) Meanwhile, Steve's hitting the skids: the same emotional distress that makes him a great stand-up comic threatens to destroy him, *verstehen*? When a TV talent scout expresses interest, Steve says, "If you're sending someone down you'd better send him fast, because funny Steve is goin' down." When a second round of scouts appears, Steve cracks up on stage, collapsing in tears after choking out a gloppy psychiatrist's-couch monologue about his med-school failure, his macho dad's love of deer hunting, and his own fear of the sight of blood. It's a very weird scene, pathetic and overplayed and unconvincingly motivated; instead of feeling sympathy for Steve, we feel embarrassed for the scriptwriter.

Predictably, the film winds up with Lila and Steve facing off in a comedy contest. The audience (at the Gas Station, not in the movie theater) laughs itself crazy; their fellow comics tell Lila and Steve that they're "brilliant." We're plainly supposed to think so, too. But the comedy routines are as lame as the plot. It's amazing that somebody could make a big-budget film about stand-up comedy and not manage to get any fresh, funny material. Throughout the movie, the jokes are standard eighties stand-up fare: formula gags about genitals and breasts and vibrators, pointless references to baby-boomer pop-culture icons (e.g., "Gilligan's Island"), faux-confessional stuff about the comic's sexless marriage or crummy dates or screwy folks. Even Hanks's best lines, in his climactic routine, sound familiar; and his every gesture and inflection is a stand-up cliché. Like the worst sort of comedian, director Seltzer seems to think that anything will get a laugh if you give it a glib, snappy delivery. Seltzer's own script and direction, to be sure, are anything but snappy; the film is half an hour longer than it should be, and is full of slack, dramatically unfocused sequences.

What's most irritating of all about *Punchline*, however, is its governing pretense—or delusion—that the slick recitation of a set of canned jokes constitutes a serious form of self-expression, if not art. We're supposed to buy the idea that Lila "finds herself" through *schtick*, that Steve is a tormented genius—Nijinsky as stand-up comic. We're supposed to identify with the feelings of the talent scout when she watches Steve's act with a reverential awe, as if he's Joan Sutherland or Caruso. What could be more grotesque? Watching this film, it's hard to believe that once upon a time Hollywood movies customarily made heroes of people like Zola, Chopin, and Michelangelo; most of the films themselves were far from art, but at least they honored art and recognized it as a moral force, as something in which truth and beauty inhered, as a separate and serious entity. The only thing that a characteristic eighties writer-director like David Seltzer seems to take seriously, by contrast, is showbiz itself.

Back in 1974, the director Joan Micklin Silver gave us a movie called *Hester Street*, in which a young Jewish immigrant woman—played by Carol Kane—made a life for herself on the Lower East Side of early twentieth-century Manhattan. Now Silver has moved ahead a few generations and up a few blocks, has found herself another small, delicately pretty actress with frizzy hair, and has come up with *Crossing Delancey*, an extremely charming contemporary romantic drama starring Amy Irving.

Written by Susan Sandler (who based the script on her play of the same title), the film is about Isabelle Grossman, a single young Jewish woman who lives on the West Side of Manhattan and works in "New York's last real bookstore," New Day Books. Isabelle loves her job, loves the readings and book parties and literary soirées that go with it, loves meeting the famous writers who show up in the store from time to time. She has a particular fondness for Anton Maes (Jeroen Krabbe), a celebrated Dutch novelist who lives in the neighborhood and whose latest novel she has kept in the window of the bookstore for several weeks. ("What I like most about your writing," she tells the suave, hunky Anton, "is its deceptive accessibility.") She is, in short, the very model of a sophisticated and modern young urbanite, a cosmopolitan girl for whose life-style Helen Gurley Brown herself would be proud to take the credit.

But her old Jewish grandmother—her "Bubby," to use the movie's Yiddishism—isn't having any of it. Bubby (Reizl Bozyk), who lives in a gloomy Lower East Side high-rise, feels that Isabelle's life is empty and meaningless without a husband: "No matter how much money you got, if you're alone, you're sick." Consequently she engages the services of Hannah (wittily played by Sylvia Miles), a loud, vulgar old matchmaker right out of *Fiddler on the Roof.* In Bubby's kitchen, Hannah introduces Isabelle to Sam Posner (Peter Riegert), an unprepossessing young man who lives in the old neighborhood, goes to *shul* every day, and runs a pickle stand on Delancey Street. Isabelle finds the matchmaking process embarrassing and prehistoric, and finds the pickle merchant himself totally unsuitable. "I live uptown," she tells him patronizingly. "A million miles from here." She's in love with a famous Dutch novelist, for heaven's sake.

But the stolid, no-nonsense pickle man doesn't disappear from her life. He's attracted to her, and she gradually finds herself being attracted to him. It's the oldest story in the world, of course—the young woman coming to recognize the superior worth of the less glamorous but more truly substantial of two men. Audrey Hepburn went the same route in *Sabrina*, Katharine Hepburn in *The Philadelphia Story*, Jean Simmons in *Desiree*, and so forth. With this sort of movie, one invariably has the conclusion figured out pretty early on; the pleasure comes from watching the heroine reverse herself. And in *Crossing Delancey*, I'm happy to say, Isabelle's reversal is managed with remarkable finesse and charm. It is the ultimate measure of the success of this film, in fact, that the match with Sam seems, in the early scenes, like the height of absurdity, and by the end seems wonderfully right. You start out thinking, *God no, they're not going to try to convince us that this vibrant, happy, literate girl should marry this fellow?*—and by the end, to your considerable surprise, you *are* convinced.

There are, as it happens, a lot of wonderfully right things about this movie. To begin with, Amy Irving's performance is luminous and endearing. She captures Isabelle's confusion—her sense of being caught between two worlds—with marvelous naturalness; for all her little lies and self-deceptions, one never feels less than utter sympathy for her. Also notable are the modest but deeply poignant images of the loneliness of a single woman's life in New York: grabbing dinner with girlfriends at a corner hot dog stand, jawing over coffee in a diner, haunting the take-out salad bar at the Korean delicatessen after work. I've complained previously about how few films manage to capture the feel of life in Manhattan; this ones does so, with astonishing sensitivity and without making a fuss about it. Likewise, while American films tend to be notoriously bad at capturing the way literary people look and talk and behave, this one does a pretty good job of it.

To be sure, not everything about *Crossing Delancey* is perfect. In seeking to create a decidedly traditional young Jewish man, Sandler has imagined someone who, if his kind actually existed, would have to be the least successful Jewish guy in New York. (An intelligent, articulate young Jewish CUNY graduate selling pickles out of barrels on Delancey Street? Tell me another.) Peter Riegert's Sam, moreover, is so down-to-earth and secure about his identity that he sometimes comes across as downright smug and self-satisfied. And Sandler gives him at least one line of dialogue—"What's wrong with my world? You think it's so small? You think it defines me?"—that should have gone unspoken; it makes Sam sound less like a Lower East Side pickle merchant than, well, a Dutch novelist.

As for the Dutch novelist, one gets the feeling that Sandler made him Dutch because the Netherlands is right next to Germany and because "Dutch" sounds like "Deutsch" and because when we see Isabelle mooning over this big, strapping fellow we're supposed to feel, deep down: What's this nice Jewish girl doing falling for this *Nazi*? Finally, while the musical score is mostly quite serviceable, there are times when the fast, loud, and aggressively rhythmic numbers supplied by the Roches (a group of girl singers) seem just a bit too distracting. On the whole, however, *Crossing Delancey* is a delightful film—fresh and affecting and lovely.

WOMEN AND MORE WOMEN

The Accused
The Good Mother

Based loosely on a real event, *The Accused* tells the story of a young waitress named Sarah Tobias (Jodie Foster), who one night walks into The Mill, a white-trash bar in Washington state, and finds herself being raped by three strange men on a pinball machine. Sarah's not the most respectable type—she lives in a trailer with a dope dealer, talks tough, dresses provocatively, and was drinking and smoking pot at the time of the rape—and so the prosecuting attorney, deputy D.A. Katheryn Murphy (Kelly McGillis), decides that rape convictions will be hard to secure and makes an out-of-court settlement at a reduced charge. Sarah—who wanted the crime officially recognized as rape, and herself certified as a victim—is furious, and feels betrayed by Katheryn. So frustrated is she that when she is taunted in a shopping-mall parking lot by one of the bar patrons who witnessed her shame and who urged the rapists on, she rams his pickup with her car, sending both of them to the hospital. Katheryn feels that this development is her fault, and consequently puts her career in jeopardy by bringing a precedent-setting suit: she takes three of the rape witnesses to court on a charge of egging the rapists on. Finally, Sarah gets a chance to tell her story and to be recognized as a victim.

In many ways this is a very conventional movie. The formula could hardly be more familiar: we open with a crime and end with a trial, and in between we watch the victim and prosecutor work their way through mutual suspicion and learn gradually to trust and understand one another. There is little doubt as to what the final verdict will be. If the film nonetheless feels vivid and original, and even quite powerful at some points, it is because Tom Topor has written a solid script, Jonathan Kaplan has directed it expertly, and the cast—especially Miss Foster—has enacted it with wit and sensitivity. Sarah's story feels *real.*

This naturalism is even more of a triumph because the film, though it doesn't come across as a shrill tract in sexual politics, has a strong polemical bent. When you think about it afterward you're surprised to realize how effectively you've been manipulated. Indeed, it may not be till you try to describe *The Accused* to a friend, and realize that it is next to impossible to do so without dipping into feminist rhetoric ("victimization," "sisterhood," "solidarity," "consciousness raising," etc.), that you'll see how subtly the filmmakers have faked you into buying a nightmarish view of the relations between men and women—relations which, though the director and writer are both men, are observed entirely from the women's perspective. Men are regarded here less as opponents in some frothy Tracy-and-Hepburn-style battle of the sexes than as threatening figures who, whether friends or lovers or strangers, could at any moment turn into attackers. Every man, in short, is a potential rapist. Even Katheryn's fellow lawyers at the D.A.'s office talk about Sarah's case in a manner that is subtly but chillingly reminiscent of the ignorant, aggressive creeps at The Mill. The film seeks to show, in incidental ways, how men's images of women are fed by everything around them: at The Mill, in the distant background, we see a close-up of a sexy pair of lips on a TV commercial; the pinball machine itself is called SLAM DUNK and is illustrated by a picture of a curvaceous blonde stuffed into a basketball hoop. And the director slips in images of violent sports (Katheryn and her fellow lawyers discuss legal strategy at a hockey game, where the men explode with excitement when something savage happens on the ice; the TV at The Mill broadcasts a boxing match), as if to imply a connection between men's enjoyment of these sports and the inclination to commit an act of rape.

The idea here is that it's women against men, and Katheryn's big achievement is her recognition, finally, that her principal bond is not to her fellow lawyers (all male) at the D.A.'s office but to her fellow woman, Sarah. When at the beginning of the film she is assailed for her insensitivity by Sarah's rape counselor, Katheryn barks: "I'm not a rape counselor. I'm a prosecutor and I have to make a rape case."

By the end of the film she's realized that, hey, it's part of *every* woman's obligation to be a kind of rape counselor. *The Accused* offers women the opportunity to say to themselves, "Men! They're horrible!", and it offers men who have never committed, contemplated, or encouraged rape the opportunity to enjoy their moral superiority to the vermin who attack Sarah. The film's offense is that, in the course of indicting men who regard women as mere hunks of flesh, it ends up suggesting that most men are themselves sexist beasts.

(P.S. to Mr. Kaplan: Next time you direct a film in Canada that's supposed to be set in the U.S., don't show a sign in the background which reads *Media Centre.*)

"Can a court tell us how we should raise our children?" The trailer for Diane Keaton's new film, *The Good Mother,* based on the 1986 novel by Sue Miller, implies that this question—read in voice-over by a deep, solemn male voice—has something to do with the content of the film. But the question that this movie actually addresses is: "Should a man who couldn't give his ex-wife an orgasm be allowed to have custody of their six-year-old daughter?"

Let me explain. The daughter in question is Molly (Asia Vieira), your typical cute, bright movie kid. Her mother is Anna Dunlop (Miss Keaton), a piano teacher and lab assistant who lives with Molly on the second floor of a small, shabby house in Cambridge, Massachusetts. Her father is Brian Dunlop (James Naughton), a sober, affluent businessman who lives in D.C. and of whom we get the briefest of glimpses—just enough to support Anna's contention that he's a prude. Anna herself, mind you, was once like Brian—she was, she tells us in voice-over while we watch scenes of her own childhood, a "shy" girl, a "conformist." But the influence of her cigarette-smoking, boy-chasing Aunt Babe—a teenager who dismissed Anna's conventional parents and grandparents as "assholes"—was critical. "In her presence," Anna tells us, "it just seemed as if everything was possible. . . . I wanted to be like her, wanted to take risks and be passionate." And yet, presumably in thrall to her own conventional impulses, she married Brian, and stayed married for seven years. "Sex between us was nothing," Anna says. What's worse, Brian—the wimp!—didn't *realize* it was nothing. They divorced, and Anna built her life around Molly, whom she adores.

So the situation stands until Anna meets Leo Cutter (Liam Neeson), a passionate, earthy Irish sculptor whose apartment is full of pieces with names like "Celtic Twilight" and "Drunken Boat." (Remember Alan Bates in *An Unmarried Woman?* Same idea.) Their first time in bed, Anna confesses, "I don't think I'm very good at it." "We can fix that," Leo says generously, and proceeds to give Anna her first orgasm. They fall in love, and he becomes a fixture around Anna's house and a friend to Molly. But this happy ménage self-destructs when Brian refuses to return Molly (the child having been shipped off to D.C. to visit him and his new wife) and sues for custody on the grounds that Leo—in accordance with Anna's "relaxed and natural" household rules about nudity and such—has permitted Molly to touch his genitals.

Yes, another movie that ends up in court. "I tried to raise Molly freely," Anna tells her lawyer, Mr. Muth (Jason Robards). "I didn't want her to be ashamed of her body and think of it as something to hide. . . . We had been naked around her, it's true, but it was all part of this world Leo had opened up to me where I was beautiful and he was beautiful and Molly was part of our life and our love." Anna emphasizes to Mr. Muth that she was frigid with Brian but not with Leo, and that this revolutionary sexual breakthrough "was good for Molly."

This last comment is typical of Anna. The truth is that while Anna thinks she's interested in what's good for her little girl—and while the director (Leonard Nimoy, of all people) and screenwriter (Michael Bortman) seem to think so too—the girl's well-being consistently takes second place to Anna's karma. When Molly's taken away, Anna's upset not for Molly's sake but for her own; the child is an integral part of the life she's made for herself, the identity she's forged. Molly, as she's told Leo, is her "commitment"—the point being not that she feels an innate, ineradicable sense of obligation to the child, but rather that Molly has come in handy as an organizing principle in her life, and that she has accordingly made a conscious decision to make Molly's needs a priority. But after the court decision goes against her, and Molly seems miserable living with her father, Anna rejects her lawyer's advice to use this misery as the basis for an appeal: "I didn't want to use her misery, I wanted to end it." The logic here is striking; Anna seems to be admitting that she's been "using" Molly all along, that her legal attempt to recover custody did not represent an attempt to end Molly's misery but to preserve her own happy little world of orgasms and purposeful motherhood.

In any case, by the end of the film it is extremely clear that Molly is not the point—if in fact she ever really was. Shorn of both daughter and lover, Anna tells her grandmother, "I'm starting all over again." Molly might just as well be a piece of community property whose loss she has to accept in order to (in the popular phrase) get on with her life. What preoccupies her, at the end, is not whether Molly has the best of all possible family lives but whether she herself is a "good mother." As I wrote in a review of Sue Miller's novel a couple of years ago, "Anna seems less concerned about what happened to Molly while in her care, and about how it may have affected the child emotionally, than with the question of how the whole sordid incident reflects on *her*. (Thus the book's title.)"

Yet the movie is considerably easier to take than the novel. Anna's grandmother (beautifully played by the radiant Teresa Wright) is more congenial here, Leo is less slimy and obnoxious (in the book he collects pornographic pictures and is "fascinated with the inability of painting, print, to convey a sense of the pornographic in the way photography did"), and Anna herself (mainly because she's played by our Diane) is more sympathetic. In the novel, Anna was pretty humorless; Keaton has eliminated that problem, though she doesn't do much to convince us that Anna is an especially loving mother. In the scenes between her and Molly, which are meant to establish the closeness of their bond, the child might just as well be a favorite niece, for all the intimacy that the scenes communicate. It should destroy us when Molly is taken from Anna; it doesn't. In fact, there's very little warmth in *The Good Mother;* only Elmer Bernstein (*To Kill a Mockingbird, The Great Santini*), who wrote the musical score, seems to have understood completely what this story required of him.

THE SCREENPLAY'S THE THING

Perhaps the most difficult part of reviewing movies for any monthly publication above the level of *Teen Beat* is deciding which one to write about. What makes this task difficult, however, is not that there are so many movies to choose from, but that there are so few. Omit the foreign releases, and the limited-distribution films that 95 percent of your readers will never get a chance to see anyway, and what remains? In the average month, very little. Among those currently on tap: something called *Mystic Pizza* that proudly advertises itself as "this year's *Dirty Dancing!*"; the latest specimens of post-*E.T.* space garbage, namely *Cocoon: The Return* and *My Stepmother Is an Alien* (these days, the unusual twist would be a stepmother who *isn't* an alien); and an obviously-not-destined-to-be-a-classic one-joke "comedy" in which Danny DeVito and Arnold Schwarzenegger play twins. (Get it? One of them is very short and plump and the other is tall and muscular! This is "high-concept" moviemaking at its lowest.) Leafing through the movie advertisements in your daily newspaper, you feel as if you've seen all these films before, every last one of them—and not months or years ago but the day before yesterday.

To be sure, every year miraculously brings a handful of fine and memorable American movies. But the overwhelming majority of new commercial films are as mindlessly conceived, constructed, and composed as they are competently produced. Indeed, many an intelligent moviegoer in the late eighties may well conclude that movies are technically as impressive as ever (and in some ways more impressive), but that the scripts are just plain awful. Well, for what it's worth, I agree, and so does Stanley Kauffmann, the longtime film critic of the *New Republic.* In a recent issue of that journal, Kauffmann unburdened himself of some interesting observations about contemporary American screenwriting. "Screenwriting," he remarked, "lags behind every other aspect of filmmaking. . . . Week after week in this column and in the box on this page [i.e., of "Films Worth Seeing"], I note films in which all the elements except the scripts are commendable." Why is this the case? Largely, he argued, because arty, quirky, personal, and/or message-bearing films like *The Hired Hand, Pocket Money,* and *Go Tell the Spartans* (ugh!), which proliferated in the seventies, are no longer being made in great numbers. And why aren't they? Largely, Kauffmann argued further, because filmmaking expenses have gone through the roof and producers, eager to reach the widest possible audience and thereby recoup their investments, have quashed "the spirit of adventure" that flourished in the seventies. "Most American screenwriting," Kauffmann wrote, "now seems a bid at a roulette table, neither slick engineering for a reliable audience [as in the old Hollywood] nor personal conviction [as in the seventies]."

Kauffmann is, of course, absolutely correct about the awfulness of most contemporary screenplays. The average American film script today is more artificial and more cynically contrived than ever, and is aimed at a far more puerile mentality than mainstream Hollywood pictures ever have been. This being the case, however, I don't understand how Kauffmann can suggest that current movies don't represent "slick engineering" geared to a specific audience. On the contrary, American movies—on the whole—are slicker than at any time in history. They're aimed at teens and pre-teens. And what's most woefully missing from them is not the "spirit of adventure" of the seventies but the relative sophistication and dramatic craftsmanship that routinely characterized the better American movies of two or three generations ago.

No doubt, one would be hard put to defend most of the products of Hollywood's so-called Golden Era as art. But to watch even some run-of-the-mill Hollywood movies of the thirties and forties is to marvel, time and again, at the intricacy and tautness of their dramatic structure, and at the economy and wit of their characterization. (Relative, that is, to contemporary commercial films.) The most recent innovation of the Ted Turner empire is a network called TNT (for "Turner Network Television"), which devotes most of its airtime to half-century-old B-movies that Turner picked up a while back in a package deal with MGM; the remarkable thing about these films—the majority of which are so obscure (Ina Claire in *Rebound?* Dick Powell in *The Singing Marine?*) that they are new to even the most fanatical of contemporary cineastes—is how watchable they are, how well they hold up. They'll never be mistaken for masterpieces, God knows, but they "work," because they're put together properly; they have focus, shape, conflict, tension.

The principal weakness of today's films, by contrast, is that most of them are written by people who don't know anything about dramatic structure or character development, who have seen every movie in the last ten years but have never read a word of Aristotle or Aeschylus or, for that matter, Noël Coward. Does this tell us anything profound about the *gestalt* or the *Weltanschauung* or whatever of the contemporary American screenwriter? No, it doesn't (Kauffmann's fancy analysis to that effect notwithstanding). Rather, it reflects an extremely simple—but thoroughly devastating—failing on the part of the producers and studio chiefs who select and approve and initiate projects. For the plain fact is that—as anyone in certain sections of Los Angeles, anyway, is well aware—a considerable proportion of the population of Southern California is writing screenplays nowadays. People who have never read a book are writing them; people who wouldn't write a short story because they can't manufacture a coherent grammatical sentence are writing them. And there would be nothing harmful in this state of affairs—let them scribble away, if it makes them happy!—except that the film business today is largely dominated by people who don't know anything about drama, either, and who have no respect for writing or writers.

Now, the old studio bosses and producers were hardly connoisseurs of art. They didn't read literature, didn't care about books like *The Great Gatsby* or *The Sound and the Fury*. But they knew enough to recognize the importance of good writing to a movie, and when a writer like Fitzgerald or Faulkner made a name for himself as a literary figure, the studio bosses, who had knowledgeable subordinates around to inform them about such occurrences, were quick to respond with job offers. Yes, they sometimes treated their contract writers abominably—switched them without explanation from one script to another, had their work rewritten and rewritten again by other contract writers, and suchlike. But their goal was always the same: the best-written script possible. And many of the scripts that became films, under their auspices, were wonderful ones. Can one even imagine a script like *The Women,* for instance—in which Anita Loos and Jane Murfin actually improved on the play by Clare Boothe—being produced nowadays? Or, for that matter, *Mr. Skeffington* or *Ninotchka* or *Pride and Prejudice* or *Spellbound* or *The Story of Louis Pasteur?*

It seems impossible. Not because the scriptwriting talent isn't there, but because the people selecting scripts typically don't know a bad one from a good one. Indeed, many of them don't even think of a film in terms of its script—they think of it as a "project," a "concept." To them, the script is almost a peripheral consideration, a set of pages no more or less important to the production than the daily call sheet. That writing is a special talent, that different people have it in different degrees, that there is such a thing as dramatic structure, that any of this might have more than a casual connection with the ultimate quality of a film: of all this and more the average studio executive of today is astonishingly innocent. To such an individual, what's important is (a) that a film have a hot star in the lead, (b) that it tell a story which can be related in one sentence, and which is similar to the story of at least one recently successful movie, and (c) that it not be above the heads of *anybody*. Not above the heads of the youngest children, or the most brain-dead and rock-obsessed teenagers, or the slowest of the slow. In such a marketplace, obviously, the screenwriter with an original idea and a talent for literate dialogue is actually at a disadvantage, and the unlettered amateur with a thoroughly derivative story idea and the mentality, vocabulary, and emotional maturity of a 12-year-old has pretty much everything he needs in order to achieve fame and fortune.

Not that he will necessarily be successful, of course. There are so many bad scripts circulating out there that whether *your* bad script will be optioned and produced is something of a crapshoot. Stanley Kauffmann is right, then, when he suggests that most screenwriting in this country is like "a bid at a roulette table." But the bidding takes place not at the writing stage, as he seems to think, but at the submission stage. Writing scripts, nowadays, is very much like buying a lottery ticket.

And, Kauffmann to the contrary, these circumstances do not represent a dramatic departure from those under which people like

Robert Altman and Peter Fonda operated when they made "personal" and statement-oriented movies like *California Split* and *Easy Rider* two decades or so ago. As a matter of fact, it was precisely such films that helped to give professionalism in scriptwriting a bad name, and to make the idea of "good writing" passé in Lotusland. Certainly the decline of the old Hollywood was in many ways a good thing; there are remarkable pictures of various kinds made in America these days (one thinks of *After Hours, The World According to Garp,* and *Blue Velvet,* among others) which would have been unimaginable in the days of Louis B. Mayer and Jack Warner. But it can't be denied that the present pathetic state of the typical American screenplay is very much a consequence of the rise of the Altmans and Fondas. As Kauffmann observes, those filmmakers thought of themselves as speaking to the hip teenagers and twentysomethings of the Vietnam Era, members of what Kauffmann calls "the Film Generation"—a generation identifiable not only by their tendency to make film their art of choice but by their elevation of it above all the other arts (about which they, in many instances, knew little or nothing). It was in an attempt to reach this audience (which was much more comfortable with moving images than with words) that Altman, Fonda, and company effectively brought the level of discourse in mainstream American movies down a notch. The creators of the pre-teen fare that constitutes most of America's movie product in the late eighties have simply followed their lead, lowering the level another notch or two.

Kauffmann speaks admiringly of the "verity" of dialogue in contemporary American film, as compared to the dialogue in Hollywood pictures of two or three generations ago. Yes, the characters in most movies nowadays do talk like real people. Real dumb people. They all, in fact, sound the same. Forget all the special effects; the best way to astonish a middle-American movie audience these days would be to have a character say something witty or clever. If Woody Allen's movies seem brilliant to so many people, in fact, it's mainly because he doesn't conform to the unwritten rules that govern these matters. His characters don't deliver many profound lines; they just talk like educated people, which makes them the rarest of rarities in movieland today.

THE WINTER OF OUR DISCONTENT

The Accidental Tourist
Dirty Rotten Scoundrels
Talk Radio

Winter has brought with it a blizzard of widely heralded new films, the most lauded of which is probably *The Accidental Tourist*, directed by Lawrence Kasdan from a script by Kasdan and Frank Galati. Based on a novel by Anne Tyler, this movie—which reunited William Hurt and Kathleen Turner, the stars of *Body Heat*—has been called "perfect," "a triumph," and "one of the best movies in many years," and was cited as Best Picture of the Year by the New York Film Critics' Circle. The night I went to see it, New York had been hit by a snowstorm and traffic was almost at a standstill; nonetheless, the two large adjoining Upper East Side theaters in which *The Accidental Tourist* was playing had both sold out an hour and a half early, and though it was only nine o'clock I had to buy a ticket for the 11:45 showing. Now, when you get crowds like that on a snowy night in Manhattan for a non-Woody Allen movie, you know you're in the presence of something special—namely, The Prestige Film of the Year, the latest answer to *Amadeus*, *On Golden Pond*, and *Gandhi*, the movie-to-beat at the Academy Awards.

Of course, Prestige Film doesn't necessarily mean Bad Film, and there was no reason not to expect that at least some of the critical encomia were justified. Yet *The Accidental Tourist* proved to be a first-rate disappointment—an incredibly lifeless and programmatic concoction, the most solemnly dull award-winner since *Chariots of Fire*. What pretension! Hurt plays a middle-aged Baltimorean named Macon Leary, author of a series of travel guides for on-the-go businessmen who want to visit "the most exotic places in the world without feeling they'd left home." Want to know which hotel in London has the best plumbing? where to find a Burger King in Paris? Leary's books have the answers. Always take a book with you on an airplane flight, he advises, so as to avoid being bothered by your seatmate. His guidebooks speak to the most banal, unadventurous side of the business traveler, and we are meant to understand this as a metaphor for his approach to life in general. For he moves through life like an accidental tourist, doing his best to avoid contact with other lives, to evade new experiences, to cushion his somber and solitary progress through the world.

In part, this *Lebensart* is a family trait. Macon's aging, unmarried sisters and brothers—who live together in the family manse—are all anal retentives who spend their time alphabetizing groceries and road maps, and who get lost if they wander so much as a block off their usual neighborhood routes. Unlike his siblings, Macon *is* married, but since the sudden, shocking, recent death of his 12-year-old son, he has reverted to type: his wife, Sarah (Kathleen Turner), has left him, and he's moved back in with his pathetic, eccentric clan.

In other hands, this material might have been truly affecting. But there isn't much to get attached to in Hurt's Macon. He plods across the screen like Frankenstein's monster, his face pale and eyes dead, and delivers every line in the same robotic monotone. "There's something so muffled about the way you experience things," Sarah complains. Alas, in seeking to convey this quality, Hurt has muffled his very expressivity. Watching him, one has increased respect for the late Peter Sellers, who in *Being There* took an equally numb, shambling, and matter-of-fact character and made him truly affecting. Hurt's Macon, by contrast, is uncompelling, a cipher.

And all the people around him—excepting the ever-natural Sarah—are utterly bizarre. The grotesques in Flannery O'Connor and Carson McCullers have nothing on this bunch. Seated in the family parlor, the Learys look as if they're awaiting an appointment with Diane Arbus. The jobs here are invariably goofy: Macon's brother Charles makes bottlecaps for a living. ("It's not half as exciting as it sounds," he tells Macon's publisher.) Weirdest of all is Muriel Pritchett (Geena Davis), a young obedience trainer for dogs, who is inexplicably attracted to Macon. The film's attitude toward these folks is schizophrenic: it feigns compassion even as it ridicules them, making (for example) a cruel running joke out of the numerous and exotic allergies of Muriel's small son, Alexander.

It would be an exaggeration to describe this film as having a plot. The development seems random, pointless: first Macon ignores Muriel's attentions; then she manipulates him into a relationship; then Sarah talks him into a reconciliation. In the end, he picks one woman over the other, because "she's given me another chance to decide who I am—to step out of the Leary groove and stay out." Why does Macon suddenly achieve this sense of resolution? No apparent reason. Why does he feel that this woman more than the other would help him to escape his rut? Beats me. "It's a mistake," he declares, "to plan everything as if it were a business trip"—and this feeble insight is actually meant to constitute an epiphany, a profound moment of truth. It's almost embarrassing to sit in the theater and realize that one has been taken on so long a journey for so little. Macon is like nobody one has ever known, and the "lesson" he ultimately learns is one at which the filmmakers have been tiresomely hammering away since the opening frames.

Synthetic as it is, though, this movie *looks* profound. A composition in brown and gray, it's lugubriously paced and equipped with a solemn, self-important John Williams score; the actors have the serious air of TV stars doing an Arthur Miller play on PBS. All this may well be more than enough to convince the Academy voters, come spring, that *The Accidental Tourist* is a worthy successor to *Terms of Endearment*.

Speaking of which, they've been comparing Bette Midler's new picture, *Beaches*, to *Terms of Endearment*. Up to a point, it's a valid comparison: like *Terms*, *Beaches* follows a relationship through its ups and downs, from childhood to an early death, and was directed by a man (Garry Marshall, in this case) who is famous for his TV sitcoms. But Midler's movie feels realer, truer than Shirley MacLaine's. And whereas *Terms* gave us a mother and daughter, *Beaches* presents us with two women, Ceecee Bloom (Midler) and Hillary Whitney (Barbara Hershey), who meet on the beach in Atlantic City as 11-year-old children and remain best friends for thirty years. They're as different as can be: Hillary, a proper little rich girl from a San Francisco suburb, ends up attending Stanford and becoming a high-profile lawyer; Ceecee, a brash kid from the Bronx with dreams of showbiz success, goes on to spend years singing in shabby nightclubs and acting in off-off-Broadway plays before finally becoming a star. But they're united by their fascination with each other: Ceecee is awed by Hillary's preppie-ish way of life; Hillary envies Ceecee her talent and determination. At various points over the years, the two women room together, fall for the same man, become estranged; both of them lose direction (and husbands), and each helps the other get back on track.

It could be argued that the film (written by Mary Agnes Donoghue) contains too many episodes, and that they are too loosely strung together. But the two women's performances are wonderful, their chemistry is perfect, and the way their lives develop and intersect has a naturalness about it that is very engaging and, in the end, astonishingly tender. Hershey is lovelier and more *simpática* than ever, and Midler is superlative at every turn—funny, touching, and in great voice. Yes, the film has major weaknesses, among them a maddening series of false endings, and a loud, idiotic rock song that almost ruins the film's moving climax. For all this, however, it's extremely gratifying to see a contemporary film that's set over a long period of time, and that regards friendship and its attendant responsibilities with sympathy and respect.

Like *Beaches, Dirty Rotten Scoundrels* makes use of an "odd-couple" pairing. But that's where the similarity ends. *Scoundrels* is a farce of prelapsarian wit and elegance. Michael Caine plays an adroit, sophisticated English con man named Laurence Jamieson, who routinely takes wealthy ladies for millions in a Riviera resort town; Steve Martin plays a slovenly American named Freddy Benson, a small-time operator who tries to crowd his turf but who, finding himself outclassed, blackmails Jamieson into teaching him (as Robert Redford does Paul Newman in *The Sting*) how to pull off The Big Con. When school's over, though, Benson refuses to leave town. So they make a wager: whoever can bed the pretty young heiress Janet Colgate (Glenne Headly) can stay; the other must go. You can see the dénouement coming all the way down the Riviera, but the fun is in watching it work itself out. The screenwriters (Dale Launer, Stanley Shapiro, and Paul Henning) keep things moving deftly from reversal to reversal; Caine and Martin never stray from character, and Frank Oz's direction (though it could be tauter) never loses its light, charming touch. It's a top-notch contrivance.

In *Talk Radio*, Eric Bogosian brings new meaning to the word obnoxious. Bogosian—a New York "performance artist" who, with director Oliver Stone, adapted the film from his off-Broadway play—stars as Barry Champlain, the host of "Night Talk," an infamous radio phone-in show in Dallas, Texas. Champlain is an opinionated loudmouth. "This country," he declaims, "is in deep trouble, people!" And the only hope for a solution would seem to lie in his show. "It's the last neighborhood in town!" he insists. "People just don't talk to each other anymore!" He's at once paranoid, messianic, apocalyptic. "This show is about saying what's got to be said!" he screams into his mike, and mostly the movie consists of his doing just that: arguing with bigots, talking down would-be suicides, ranting about everything from drugs to the Holocaust.

Bogosian's character has been compared to so-called shock-jock Howard Stern (whose morning radio show is heard in New York, Philadelphia, and Washington), but though Bogosian seems to have copped a few of Stern's trademark gags, there's no real similarity. Stern's a comic who puts down his own program and the pretensions of radio people; Champlain takes himself more seriously than Jerry Falwell. Stern is a pro with a natural-sounding delivery; Champlain (as we learn from a clumsy flashback) is a former suit salesman who got into showbiz because a radio deejay walked into his store one day and said, "You've got quite a voice. You ever do radio?" Quite a voice, indeed! It's one of those slick, phony-from-the-word-go radio voices, and it makes everything Champlain says sound utterly insincere (an effect that would seem to be unintentional, since this is how Bogosian really talks).

Needless to say, the salesman-to-superstar flashback is hard to buy. So is a scene at a basketball game (one of the few episodes set outside the radio studio), where Champlain—supposedly a ratings king—is booed by the entire audience. (What's even more unconvincing is that he seems astonished by the reception: Doesn't he know how the city feels about him?) So is the way the KGAB management treats Champlain—not telling him about a syndication deal, for instance, until three days before it takes effect. (Who's his agent?) So is the fact that practically every other caller is a rabid anti-Semite. And so, finally, is the film's gruesome conclusion—which cynically rips off the sensational demise of real-life Denver deejay Alan Berg, for no better reason than that this feebly plotted, dreadfully stagey talkfest has to wind up *somehow*.

Talk Radio is desperate to make a point. But what is it? Champlain talks endlessly about America—yet his message amounts to little more than a garbled replay of Peter Finch's "I'm mad as hell and I'm not going to take it anymore!" spiel in *Network*. Forget about America, though—Stone and Bogosian don't even have a half-way intelligent take on their central character. "The most important thing," Champlain's ex-wife tells him, "is you've got to start loving yourself!" That's about as deep as this movie goes. Only KGAB's station manager appears to have the picture in focus. "All you are," he tells Champlain, "is a f-----g suit salesman with a big mouth." Amen.

FAIRLY FUNNY

Working Girl
Who's Harry Crumb?

Working Girl is the archetypal eighties comedy. It's cast entirely with bankable names (Melanie Griffith, Harrison Ford, Sigourney Weaver); it's so glossily produced that you sometimes feel as if it would be much, much funnier if only it didn't look so *expensive*; it has a distracting Top-40-type score (by Carly Simon) that doesn't really suit the picture at all; it has a glamorous setting, and a get-to-the-top-of-the-heap plot, and a love interest, and a gratuitous sex scene or two; it's funny enough, and even sort of touching at times, though there's not a thing about it that you haven't seen a hundred times before. And while you'll probably leave the theater feeling entertained, you'll know that there's not much about the picture that will stick in your mind a week later.

Here's the story: Griffith plays Tess McGill, a tacky-dressing, gum-chewing, English-language-fracturing 30-year-old white-trash secretary who resides in working-class Staten Island and works at a brokerage firm on Wall Street. Like all the other white-trash secretaries who ride the ferry to work every morning, she lives in a dumpy apartment and has a going-nowhere, good-for-nothing, macho-dumbbell boyfriend (Alec Baldwin). But there's one thing that separates her from the other white-trash secretaries: she's brainy. Over the past few years, she's earned her MBA in night school, and she's determined to move up in the firm. Things look hopeless, however.

She's up against a host of Ivy Leaguers—most of them men—who speak correctly, dress properly, and have the Right Look. To them, Tess is nothing more than a sex object. It doesn't help that she's utterly without tact; when one of her superiors does her wrong, she abuses him—before the entire company—on the electronic tickertape. We're supposed to like her for this: she's not stuffy like these other Wall Street types, she's *spunky!*

Not surprisingly, her spunkiness gets her fired. At her new job she finds herself with, thank heaven, a woman boss—the beautiful and sophisticated Katharine (Sigourney Weaver), who proves to be a year younger than she is. And who proves also to be a great deal less of a blessing than Tess had thought, because when Tess comes up with an investment idea for a client, Katharine doesn't hesitate to rip it off. It's when Katharine fractures her leg on the slopes, and is hospitalized in ski country for a week or so, that Tess does something—well, spunky: she covertly steals her investment idea back and, pretending to be something more than a secretary, joins forces with Jack Trainer (Harrison Ford), a first-class, fast-lane deal-maker at another brokerage firm. In partnership with him, she proceeds, within a matter of days, to negotiate a multimillion-dollar acquisitions deal for a major corporation. Needless to say, in true-to-formula fashion, Tess and this hunky wheeler-dealer fall quickly in love—for he's not like all the other big-time Wall Street operators, you see: he *hates* networking, hates talking about money, hates the whole downtown crowd. (Sure—and Sammy Davis, Jr. hates show business.)

At any rate, in order to pull off this breathtaking coup behind Katharine's back, Tess must effect a major transformation in herself—and who else to use as a model but Katharine herself? It's weird: this young lady whose lower-middle-class look and voice and carriage have kept her from joining the ranks of the Masters of the Universe manages somehow to turn herself overnight into a replica of the cool, elegant Katharine. What gives? Why is this transformation suddenly so easy for her to carry off, and why in heaven's name hasn't it occurred to her—or hasn't she been able—to do it before? And while we're busy asking questions, what species of morality is operating here? We're expected to feel that Tess justified in her subterfuge because Katharine has betrayed her. But Tess isn't simply getting back at Katharine—she's putting at risk the reputation of the company that employs her, not to mention the entire career of her unwitting and innocent partner in the deal, with whom she is supposedly smitten.

What's more, the film's class values seem rather confused, to say the least. Consider this: in the tried-and-true tradition of Hollywood moviemaking, Tess and her lower-middle-class girlfriends are (without apparent exception) good and decent folks; the upper-middle-class types in the executive suites are almost entirely rotten. The only problem with Tess's life (aside from the fact that her boyfriend is a creep) is that her home, wardrobe, and neighborhood are pretty tacky—but that's not even a problem, really, because she doesn't *know* they're tacky. By her own standards, then, Tess's life doesn't seem to be missing anything important. Yet she wants nothing more than to escape from the world she knows and to move up into the world of these Ivy League snobs whom she despises—and we're supposed to cheer for her. Why?

These logical inconsistencies aside, *Working Girl*—written by Kevin Wade and directed by Mike Nichols—is admittedly a very slick contrivance, in the best and worst senses of the phrase, its plot as neatly worked out as it is improbable. As is usual in a film of this sort, the fat cats are rather too broadly played, but Nichols does capture nicely the atmosphere of those gray, Pennsylvania-steel-town-like working-class communities that line the northern tier of Staten Island. And he captures the residents of these communities too: one of the film's most memorable images is the sight of Joan Cusack—in the role of Tess's best friend—wearing matching orange-and-blue earrings and eyeshadow. But the question remains: Are we supposed to laugh condescendingly at these people or identify with them? Nichols and Wade apparently want to have it both ways.

The leading cast is a mixed bag. Griffith possesses the sort of annoying, monotonous voice that a couple of generations ago would have kept an actress from becoming a movie star (and with good reason). Nonetheless she is appropriately endearing, for the most part (although she fails to make Tess's penchant for the occasional vulgar insult seem anything but ugly), and carries out with aplomb her character's metamorphosis into a graceful swan. Ford, meanwhile, in the role of the driven-yet-decent mover-and-shaker who is also Tess's love interest (and who, incidentally, embodies a contradiction or two of his own), exudes the requisite middle-aged-boyish charm and energy. Yet it is Weaver who lingers longest in the mind. Her character, Katharine, may be a devil, but she's got a lot more style and poise than most heroines in American movies nowadays, and Weaver plays her with great verve. This is a role that the young Katharine Hepburn would've sunk her teeth into, and Weaver does it proud.

Who's Harry Crumb? Long answer: he's a bumbling oaf of a private investigator, "the last in a long line of great detectives," who has been exiled by the successful, upscale family agency, Crumb and Crumb, to an extremely seedy branch office in Tulsa, Oklahoma. At the beginning of the movie, Harry gets the call that he's obviously been awaiting for years, summoning him to the agency's L.A. headquarters to investigate a crime—a kidnapping, to be specific. And investigate he does, with remarkable fatuity and incompetence.

Short answer: Harry is Inspector Clouseau, of the Pink Panther films, without a script, a director, or an accent. Or, of course, without the late Peter Sellers to give him that certain *je ne sais quoi*—although it must be said that John Candy, the heavyweight star of this featherweight comedy, has his own special something. That something, unfortunately, does not include a talent for choosing scripts. Not that there's anything wrong, necessarily, with a film that sets out to amuse 12-year-olds; but when you get the feeling that the script was *written* by a couple of 12-year-olds, you've got trouble.

Granted, there's a lot of funny stuff in this picture, virtually all of it slapstick. For instance: Candy, at the wheel of a speeding car whose brakes have been cut, pulls out a book entitled *Emergency Driving Made Easy*. Candy, to dramatize a point, slams his hands palms downward on a desk, thereby impaling himself on a dozen or so fishhooks. Candy, at the racetrack in a jockey outfit, gets stuck in a tiny phone booth labled "Jockeys Only." Candy, spying on a kidnapping suspect from inside an apartment building ventilating system, ends up being propelled through the labyrinthine ducts at breakneck speed when the suspect sets the air-conditioning on exhaust. It's not the most sophisticated kind of humor, but it does make you laugh.

Through all these episodes, Candy mugs it up more than adequately, and for those in search of an utterly uncerebral entertainment, the half-dozen or so sequences of this sort are probably worth the price of admission (as prices of admission go these days). Other viewers, however, may well leave the theater feeling undernourished. For even in Candy's funniest moments, the wit of Blake Edwards's Pink Panther movies is sorely lacking. This patron, for one, left *Harry Crumb* with a newfound appreciation of Edwards's ability to build a sight gag, his sense of timing, and his avoidance of overkill. Neither *Harry Crumb*'s director, Paul Flaherty, nor its screenwriters, Robert Conte and Peter Martin Wortmann, seem to know when enough is enough.

Nor do they have a very clear bead on their principal character. They apparently think it is sufficient, for their comedic purposes, to have Harry say and do one blatantly stupid thing after another. But even within the framework of sheer farce there are rules about credibility and consistency of character. The makers of the Pink Panther films recognized this; the makers of *Harry Crumb* don't. Part of what's funny about Clouseau is that even in his most ridiculous moments he doesn't know he's ridiculous. He has a self-possession, a sense of dignity, that makes his bumbling all the more hilarious. Sometimes Candy and company appear to be going for this quality with *Harry Crumb*, and sometimes they don't. The film's uncertainty of tone is disastrous: indeed, a couple of scenes involving a listless, cross-eyed, heavy-lidded butler are so unfunny, and feel so out-of-place, that they have a positively surreal effect. (But then, the whole supporting cast gives the impression that it's killing time waiting for a better movie to come along.) Finally, the screenwriters' gift for amusing dialogue is virtually nil: this is, alas, yet another of those eighties comedies in which the typical snappy comeback is "Says you." If *Harry Crumb* nonetheless provides quite a few laughs, it is thanks mostly to Candy's native drollery, winsomeness, and vivacity.

TALES FROM THE CITY

New York Stories
Dangerous Liaisons

New York Stories sounded like a good idea. Imagine—a trilogy of short films directed by Martin Scorsese, Francis Coppola, and Woody Allen, set in a city which all three directors have captured memorably on celluloid but which scores of their inferiors have, in recent years, reduced to a collection of visual clichés and caricatures. What a wonderful opportunity, one thought, to rescue this subject matter from the Hollywood hacks and to offer three striking visions of *real* metropolitan life. And what richer trove of material could there be? As they used to say on "Naked City," there are eight million stories here, and a considerable percentage are downright fascinating.

Why, then, is *New York Stories* so bad? Mainly because its directors have chosen not to look beyond the aforementioned clichés. In "Life Lessons," Scorsese—whose taut, ironic *After Hours* represented for many of us the last word on SoHo and its art scene—goes over to the enemy, as it were, with a flaccid, flabbergastingly earnest rendering of the ultimate SoHo cliché. Written by the ever-vulgar Richard Price, "Life Lessons" depicts the frantic attempts of Lionel Dobie (Nick Nolte), a successful middle-aged abstract expressionist, to keep his beloved young protégée, Jean Paulette (Rosanna Arquette), from returning to her white-bread family somewhere beyond the Hudson. There's not a fresh touch in either character: Dobie is your standard possessive, misogynistic, tempestuous, egocentric painter-in-a-movie, and Jean Paulette is a one-dimensional version of, say, Zelda Fitzgerald or *Reds'* Louise Bryant, the jealous, neurotic female appendage who takes her lack of artistic talent out on the gifted man who loves her.

Jean Paulette's character is completely summed up in such lines as "Just tell me if you think I have any talent or if you think I'm just wasting my time!" And: "Am I good? Will I ever be good?" It's hard to say which is more annoying: Arquette's endless nagging to this effect (she really doesn't have anything else to say or do in the film) or Nolte's interminable slopping of paint onto a wall-sized canvas while his boom-box blares out hyperloud, and *very* abrasive, rock music. It must be said, though, that while Arquette—a whiny, irritating actress of extremely limited range—does absolutely nothing for the picture (no, Rosanna, you never *will* be any good), Nolte at least invests Dobie with a degree of energy, humor, and pathos. As for Scorsese, Congress should pass a law making it a federal crime for him ever again to take a movie camera into a loft.

From Scorsese's SoHo, we move to Coppola's Upper East Side—though his segment, "Life Without Zoe," might just as easily be set in Rome or Paris or Mexico. It is an indication of his lack of seriousness about this assignment that Mr. C wrote the script with his teenaged daughter Sofia. It's loosely based on *Eloise* (and loose it most assuredly is), the main difference being that the twelve-ish, poor-little-rich-girl heroine of his piece (Heather McComb) lives not at the Plaza Hotel but at the Sherry-Netherland across the street. The daughter of a famous flautist (Giancarlo Giannini) and a celebrated photographer (Talia Shire), both of whom are usually out of town, Zoe is your typical precocious movie kid, whose daily digestion of *Women's Wear Daily* and inability to catch the school bus on time (she always ends up taking a cab) we're supposed to find charming.

Needless to say, we don't. This segment is worse than Scorsese's—not only thin but drastically uneven, clumsily told, and overflowing with a thoroughly fake cuteness. It requires a special kind of talent to make a satisfactory movie of this sort—a talent for taking your story and characters seriously while maintaining a light touch. (George Roy Hill, for one, carried it off nicely in *The World of Henry Orient.*) The man who directed *The Godfather, The Conversation,* and *Apocalypse Now,* however, has yet to demonstrate that he knows the meaning of the phrase "light touch"; he plainly looked upon this project not as a challenge to expand his directorial range but as a chance to "have fun," to be glib and self-indulgent, while varying little from his usual heavy style (and, one might add, allowing cameraman Vittorio Storaro to employ a rich, golden-yellow palette more appropriate to a film version of Puccini). In this age of synthetic New York films, "Life Without Zoe" is as phony as they come.

After these two strikeouts, Woody Allen's bunt single looks almost like a home run. "Oedipus Wrecks"—the director's first comedy in years—is a genuinely funny *jeu d'esprit* about Sheldon Mills (Woody Allen), a partner in a big midtown law firm whose tiny, tirelessly kvetching Jewish mother (Mae Questel) is the bane of his existence. Rather than give away the plot, I'll simply say that Allen's is the only one of the film's three segments that veers into out-and-out fantasy—and yet, at the same time, it's the only one that's in touch with the rhythms of real New York life, the only one that reflects a sincere affection for the city, the only one whose protagonist we can believe in and sympathize with. To be sure, Allen, like his collaborators, has made use of a New York cliché—in this case, the overly possessive Jewish mamma—but unlike them he recognizes it as a cliché and makes fun of it.

Of Allen's previous films, "Oedipus Wrecks" most resembles *Zelig* and *A Midsummer Night's Sex Comedy*—though in fact it's tidier, less unbridled than the typical Allen comedy. (Actually, its strongest affinity is with a couple of hilarious post-Kafka short stories which appear in his books *Without Feathers* and *Side Effects*.) Compared with the busy, self-conscious camera movements of the previous segments—Scorsese's nervous and jerky, Coppola's fluid and operatic—Allen's static camera communicates a satisfying sense of confidence in his story and characters, a heartening reluctance to rely too much on cinematographic athletics to captivate his audience. This is not to suggest that the director of *Annie Hall* and *Hannah and Her Sisters* is in top form here; "Oedipus Wrecks" is minor Allen (though it represents a definite recovery from his recent failures *September* and *Another Woman*). If his segment of *New York Stories* prove anything, indeed, it's that even his less ambitious, more offhand work can be quite entertaining—which is, alas, more than one can say for Scorsese or Coppola.

Les Liaisons Dangereuses, the 1782 novel by the French writer Choderos de Laclos, tells the story of a pair of corrupt sophisticates, the Marquise de Merteuil and the Vicomte de Valmont, who together engineer the latter's seduction of two beautiful and virtuous young women. When I wrote a couple of years ago (*TAS,* July 1987) about the Broadway production of Christopher Hampton's theatrical adaptation of the novel, I complained about the sitcom-style villainy of the two principals; about the proliferation in their dialogue of mediocre Oscar Wilde-ish epigrams and childishly smutty double-entendres; and about the heavy-handed symbolism of the set, which in one way and another sought to remind us that the days of the pre-Revolutionary French society depicted in the play were numbered.

Directed by Stephen Frears from a screenplay by Hampton and entitled *Dangerous Liaisons,* the movie version of Hampton's play represents something of an improvement on these counts. First, the symbol-ridden set is gone, replaced by palatial location settings that are rendered in thoroughly realistic fashion. Second, some of the puerile smut remains, but it is clearer now that its purpose is not to amuse us but to impress upon us the immaturity of the protagonists. Third, most of the epigrams also remain, but while they seemed the very backbone (to be sure, a very flimsy backbone) of the nerve-rackingly talky play, they feel almost peripheral to the action of this magisterially paced movie. Fourth, since most of the roles are here acted in a less stagy and stylized manner than in the play, and since the camera brings us close enough to see the characters thinking and experiencing and expressing emotion, there is less of a sitcomish feel to the proceedings than there was at the Music Box Theater. Indeed, in tone and rhythm and spirit the movie seems much nearer to Choderos de Laclos's stately, probing, and sardonic 200-year-old novel—with its fundamentally serious interest in the nature of love and evil—than to Hampton's own cheap and frivolous play.

But the movie has its own grave problems, one of them being that the two principal actors—Glenn Close and John Malkovich—are among the most decidedly contemporary, and decidedly *American,* in the business. Neither brings us anywhere near the heart of his character's particular darkness. Glenn Close, a wonderful actress, fakes her way through her part creditably enough. But Malkovich is awful: his delivery, his body language, everything down to the way he drops his two front teeth over his lower lip when he closes his mouth, says *Off-Off-Broadway*. His Vicomte simply oozes sleaze. And he's *supposed* to be sleazy. But he's also supposed to be able to fool lovely, intelligent, and refined young ladies into thinking he *isn't* sleazy, and, beyond that, able to make them fall madly in love with him. Patently, the part calls for someone with great surface charm and attractiveness (it's the kind of role George Sanders used to play), but Malkovich is about as far as you can get, in the Screen Actors Guild directory, from charm and attractiveness, surface or otherwise.

How did such an actor end up in such a role? The answer, I suspect, can be given in two words: Stephen Frears. If Malkovich is the last actor you'd cast as Valmont, Frears—whose work is almost relentlessly preoccupied with the new, the Now—would seem to be the last director you'd hire to shoot a movie like this. To be sure, the themes of *Dangerous Liaisons* are not foreign to him: his films *My Beautiful Laundrette* and *Prick Up Your Ears* offer compelling treatments of decidedly dangerous liaisons in post-World War II London, and reflect a lively concern with the nature of love and evil, resentment and revenge. But Frears's most recent film, the infelicitously titled *Sammy and Rosie Get Laid* (in which we got to see a pudgy Shashi Kapoor coupling sweatily with the unfailingly radiant Claire Bloom), underlines the most lamentable aspects of his work: the obsession with sex and sleaze, the injudicious embrace of anarchy, the flippancy. These weaknesses are not entirely absent from *Dangerous Liaisons*. Though the film ultimately affirms the value of love and the destructiveness of vanity, there are times along the way when it appears to celebrate the Marquise's betrayals and the Vicomte's depredations, and to laugh at Christianity, at the ideal of chastity, and (for that matter) at the eighteenth century.

For the most part, however, Frears's film stands head and shoulders above the Broadway production of Hampton's play. At a time when movie dialogue tends to consist largely of grunts and expletives, and music tracks of raucous noise, this film is at least a pleasure to listen to; and Philippe Rousselot's elegant cinematography makes it eminently watchable. Most of the supporting actors, moreover, are far more convincing than the principals. Michelle Pfeiffer and Uma Thurman, in the roles of the victimized Madame de Tourvel and Cécile Volanges, are not only sublimely beautiful but utterly believable as virtuous eighteenth-century noblewomen; Swoosie Kurtz and Mildred Natwick perform admirably as Cécile's harried *mère* and dotty *grandmère;* and Keanu Reeves, who plays a pure-hearted young gentleman in love with Cécile, has just the right awkward grace and air of innocence. While *Dangerous Liaisons* may not quite equal the sum of its best parts, then, there are some very fine parts here indeed.

VERONICA AND VERA

Heathers
Little Vera

Imagine a John Hughes cast hijacked by David Lynch, and you've got a pretty good idea of the territory covered by *Heathers,* a weird, provocative, and gruesomely witty black comedy directed by Michael Lehmann from a script by Daniel Waters. The setting—rendered in shadowless, chillingly cheery primary colors à la *Blue Velvet*—is Sherwood, Ohio, a veritable 1980s Winesburg, where, at Westerburg High, three rich, beautiful, and snobbish girls named Heather constitute "the most powerful clique in school." Our heroine is their classmate Veronica (Winona Ryder), whom they've admitted into their circle. Veronica is of two minds about the croquet-playing, jock-servicing Heathers: she can't bring herself to drop them, but she's put off by their snottiness and cruelty, and confides to her diary her wish for a "world without Heathers."

Along comes the new kid in town, Jason Dean (Christian Slater), who—for very good reasons, it turns out—is called J. D. Smart, sardonic, and jaded to the *n*th degree, the lean, black-clad motorcyclist has the laid-back manner of James Dean, the ironic drawl of Jack Nicholson, and the *modus operandi* of Jason, the bloodthirsty killer in the *Friday the 13th* movies. He's utterly psycho, and he comes by it fairly: a few years back he watched his mother perish in a building demolition at the hands of his dad, a cheerfully amoral real-estate developer. J. D. shares Veronica's distaste for the Heathers, and proceeds, with her help, to wipe out—in highly entertaining fashion—not only the Heathers' ringleader (kown to all and sundry as Heather #1) but Wednesday's two bullying football heroes, artfully disguising all three deaths as suicides.

The deception works. And how does Westerburg High react to the supposed suicides of its three most popular students? Well, nobody's particularly upset. Since true reverence is foreign to most of these kids—whose attachments are as thin as rolling paper, and who respect nothing but good sex, Top-40 music, and fashionable clothing—the death of another human being has little meaning for them. A male classmate kneels at the coffin of Heather #1 and asks God, in the crudest possible language, how He could have robbed the world of such a hot broad. (Yes, even cruder than that.) In the church—which cinematographer Francis Kenny photographs with a dramatically low-angle, sharply tilted, fisheye-lensed camera in dim, otherworldly light, as if to suggest how alien to these kids are the values this place represents—one of the surviving Heathers smoothes down a stray hair with holy water. And later, when Veronica rifles Heather #1's locker and finds a trendy Swatch wristwatch, one of the surviving Heathers says, "She would've wanted you to have it, Veronica—she always said you couldn't accessorize for shit."

The kids' elders are little better. An ex-hippie teacher—proclaiming sagely that "whether you kill yourself or not is one of the most important decisions a teenager can make"—uses the deaths as an excuse to stage a be-in with full media coverage, and spends a class period asking her students to share their "feelings" about the supposed suicides. ("Are we gonna be tested on this?" one boy asks blandly.) At the funeral for Heather #1, the priest tells his flock that Jesus is "that righteous dude who can solve their problems." (Note the nice irony with which the traditional usage of the word *righteous* is played off against its infinitely more trivial slang usage; I can't recall a film that better underlined the failures of sensibility implicit in much current teen lingo.) And at the double funeral for the macho-jerk football stars—whose cleverly conceived "suicide note," forged by Veronica, makes them out to be homosexual lovers—the quarterback's equally macho dad stands over the coffin and, in perfect Donahue-show style, tells the assembled mourners, "My son was gay, and I love him. I love my gay son." In this little corner of America, sanctimonious pop-psych clichés have all but taken the place of genuine emotions and principles.

Grotesquely exaggerated though its vision of middle-American teendom may be, *Heathers* constitutes a perceptive moral commentary upon a very real phenomenon: a generation of teens whose only common value is "coolness," whose only god is fashion ("Grow up, Heather! Bulimia's so '87"), who take promiscuity for granted, who use the foulest language as a matter of course, and who find the signal achievements of Western culture utterly irrelevant to their lives and concerns. At Westerburg High, the kids read *Moby Dick* for English class (and a paperback copy of Melville's novel pops up totemically throughout the film), but its moral force doesn't stand a chance against, say, the decibel power of the inane rock song "Teenage Suicide: Don't Do It"—a tune, ubiquitous in the film, whose wedding of nihilistic discords and hollow message-mongering is too famliar a part of these kids' cultural diet for them to recognize its absurdity or offensiveness. Nor can these kids count on any moral direction from their parents or teachers, who, in a show of what they consider tolerance, have entirely abandoned their responsibilities in that line.

Fortunately, Westerburg High has a few outposts of decency. There's Betty, the awkward, bespectacled childhood friend—an admitted virgin!—whom Veronica dumped when the Heathers took her up. (The obvious allusion to Betty and Veronica, those emblems of fifties innocence from the old *Archie* comics, may be a bit too cute.) There's also fat, pathetic Martha (Dumptruck) Dunnstock, a favorite target of the Heathers' ridicule, whose actual (but botched) suicide attempt is smirkingly dismissed by Heather #2 as "just another case of a geek trying to imitate the popular people in school and failing miserably." And last but not least, there's Veronica, who, despite her complicity with J. D., has a conscience buried somewhere inside. (In the world of this movie, if it were any closer to the surface it wouldn't be believable.) Having pretended to herself through three murders that J. D. sought only to scare his victims and not to kill them, Veronica finally faces the truth. Or, rather, the truths—namely, that the elimination of Heather #1, far from purging Westerburg High of everything she represents, has succeeded merely in promoting Heather #2 to the role of top bitch that J. D. is, as she tells him, "fucking psychotic" ("You say tomato," he replies genially, "I say tomahto"); and that acts of kindness are finer ammunition against evil than acts of nihilistic destruction. Fundamentally, *Heathers* is the story—the singularly bizarre and hilarious story, to be sure—of the difficult awakening and ultimate triumph of virtue within one girl's soul.

Alas, in its closing sequence the film's uniqueness of theme and tone and situation slips away, and we realize that, on one level anyway, *Heathers* is simply a variation on the *Friday the 13th* movies, in which one teenager after another gets bumped off. And the picture's final moments bring to mind the endings of both *Carrie* and *Halloween*—films of considerably less ambition than this. At its best, however, *Heathers* is a splendid accomplishment—an inimitable combination of the outré and the verisimilar, as darkly funny and perversely serious an American movie as has come along in many a moon.

In many ways, the widely publicized new Soviet film *Little Vera* couldn't be more different from *Heathers*. Its gritty, realistic look and its objurgatory tone are a far cry from *Heathers*'s eerie prettiness and sophisticated japery; its grim setting—the city of Zhdanov, an industry-heavy port on the Sea of Azov—is a world or two away from Sherwood, Ohio. (Indeed, Zhdanov makes Gary, Indiana, look rather charming.)

But in one sense, at least, the two films are strikingly similar. For *Little Vera,* like *Heathers,* centers on an attractive but troubled teenage girl whose plight we're meant to see as symptomatic of her society's failings. Played by Natalya Negoda (who, thanks to the miracle of glasnost, can currently be seen in the nonliterary pages of *Playboy*), the film's eponymous heroine resides in a small, shabby flat with her alcoholic truck-driver dad (Yuri Nazarov) and her complaisant factory-worker mother (Ludmila Zaitzeva). As the film opens, Dad is chewing Vera out: Mom has found an American $20 bill in her purse. How did she come by it? What did they do to deserve a daughter who smokes, parties, has American money, dresses like a slut? (Actually, in her bright red fingernails and blond-streaked bouffant hairdo, Vera looks quite a bit like Nancy Sinatra, circa 1966.) Where's her college acceptance? Where's her ambition? Why can't she be like her older brother, Victor (a Moscow physician)?

Every unhappy family may be unhappy in its own way, but director Vasily Pichul and writer Maria Khmelik (a husband-and-wife team) clearly intend for us to recognize the unhappiness of Vera's clan as emblematic of Russian life in the eighties. Just to round out the family portrait, Vera gets involved with—and eventually engaged to—Sergei (Andrei Sokolov), a good-looking college student whose sloth and lack of purpose rival hers. Invited to meet Mom and Dad, Sergei turns up in Bermuda shorts and departs after five minutes. But before long he moves in, and no sooner has he done so than he begins to needle Dad heartlessly. "You have a real smart-ass here!" Dad snaps at Vera. And Sergei encourages Vera's own formidable smart-ass tendencies: when an aunt sends her an old book called *Good Housekeeping* as a wedding gift, Vera and Sergei ridicule the inscription: "For Vera, the future housewife."

Patently, to these two members of Russia's Lost Generation, traditional Soviet values and ambitions are a joke. When Sergei asks Vera flippantly what her goal is, she quips: "We have a common goal, Sergei, Communism." Vera laughs a lot, but it's a deeply sad laugh whose target would seem to be life itself; it's as if she's laughing at the thought that anyone on earth can take anything seriously. For a time, to be sure, Sergei's company appears to satisfy her; but eventually the directionlessness of their existence together begins to gnaw at her. "This is supposed to be the happiest time of my life," she says, "and I just want to weep. My God, how can we go on like this?" Meanwhile, the tensions at home grow apace; the crisis comes when Dad, in a drunken rage, ventilates Sergei with a kitchen knife. Within a few hours, Sergei's in the hospital, Dad's in danger of arrest, Mom's threatening to perjure herself to save his skin, and Vera—well Vera's caught in the middle.

It's all very vivid and interesting. But not a frame of this movie is particularly fresh. We've seen it all before—the long shots of garbage heaps and junkyards, the close-ups of bubbling pots of tomato sauce and rusty, dripping faucets—in dozens of American and European films, beginning with Italian neorealism and continuing down to such recent grimefests as *A Letter to Brezhnev*. Mainly, what makes *Little Vera* compelling is that's it's not about Rome or Liverpool or Clairton, Pennsylvania; it's about some godforsaken burg in the *Soviet Union*. By *them*. It's got full frontal nudity, and a sex scene, and it shows how primitive Russian hospitals are, and it's candid about Soviet problems with gang violence and alcoholism and AIDS. It depicts a country where mothers bear unwanted babies so they can obtain bigger apartments, where everybody's always reaching for the vodka bottle or deciding to hit the sack because there's nothing else to do. Some of the slams at Mother Russia are astonishing: Dad, finally reconciled to Vera during a seaside picnic, hugs her under the rusted hull of a beached ship—an obvious symbol of the Soviet Empire run aground. In an even more stunning sequence, the camera pans the family's depressingly shabby kitchen while a tinny radio plays the "Internationale."

There is much to admire in this movie: the very fine performances (especially that of Miss Negoda), the sensitive direction, the courage of all concerned. But the critics who have celebrated *Little Vera* as great art (it has won prizes at the Venice, Montreal, and Chicago Film Festivals) would not, I think, be so forgiving of its failings were it the work of an American or English or French production team. One thinks in particular of Khmelik's script; though much of her dialogue (in translation, at least) is clever, even witty, she has altogether too heavy a touch. It's quite enough to see Dad weaving around the flat in a vodka-induced stupor; we hardly need to hear him whine that "no amount of drinking will help with this sort of life." Likewise, we could do without the immoderate irony of a line that occurs more than once: "Cherish the innocence of youth." (Fortunately, the most overblown touch of all has been lost in translation: *Malenkaya Vera,* the Russian-language title of this movie about people who have lost virtually all their faith in the Soviet system, literally means "Little Faith.") Granted, excess of this sort is as Russian as caviar and the KGB, but the proper place for hyperbolic Russian dialogue is in hyperbolic Russian movies (e.g., Eisenstein's *Ivan the Terrible*); in the context of so realistic-looking a movie as *Little Vera,* it stands out like a samovar at a keg party.

MORE DANGEROUS LIAISONS

Scandal

Near the beginning of *Scandal,* the riveting new British film about the Profumo affair of a quarter-century ago, a man and woman stroll the grounds of Cliveden, Lord Astor's sumptuous estate. "It's a world you're born to," says the man—referring, of course, to the British upper-class world to which he has won provisional access, and into which he wants to give her a leg up. "Anyone who wants to enter this world has to be very clever or very beautiful." The speaker is the very clever Dr. Stephen Ward (John Hurt), a vicar's son, high-society osteopath, and "connoisseur of sin" who considers it his vocation to "liberate" working-class beauties into the bedrooms of England's movers and shakers; his companion is the very beautiful Christine Keeler (Joanne Whalley-Kilmer), whom he has plucked out of a burlesque show and whom he—being something of a cross between Henry Higgins and a pimp—has moved into his London townhouse, given a new hair color, and trolled past some very big movers and shakers indeed. Before long, Christine has entered into clandestine affairs with both John Profumo (Ian MacKellan), the secretary for war in the new Macmillan government, and Eugene Ivanov (Jeroen Krabbe), the Soviet naval attaché, and has managed also to link up her best pal from the chorus, the vapid Mandy Rice-Davies (Bridget Fonda), with Stephen's friend and benefactor Lord Astor.

Clearly, these are a couple of lucky bimbos. But it can't last. Why?

Partly because Christine is not your ordinary tart. She has a certain stubborn intelligence (remember, we're talking about *movie characters* here, not the actual people upon whom they're based), a perverse pride; though she's a good-time girl of the first water, it's important to her that, technically speaking, she's not a prostitute, having never taken cash in explicit exchange for sexual favors. If she has a tragic flaw, it is that she actually appears to feel guilty about the way she's used her charms: her attraction to dangerous members of the underclass, for instance, seems a manifestation of an unconscious desire for abasement, punishment, even self-destruction. She's certainly not as enthralled by Profumo's position and wealth as many girls would be; in fact, when he offers to set her up as his mistress in a flat of her own—an achievement that, for most girls in her position, would represent a consummate victory—she refuses to bite, preferring to stay with Stephen, the one man whom she truly loves (and one of the few with whom she's never slept). "He needs me," she explains to Profumo. (On one level, it should be noted, this film is far less about Profumo than about what the publicists might call the "very unusual love story" of Christine and Stephen.) Far from being flattered or moved by her rejection of Profumo's offer, however, Stephen is angered by it; and when a murderously jealous black dude with whom she's become involved shoots a few holes in Stephen's front door, the good doctor sends Christine packing—directly, as it turns out, into the waiting arms of a tabloid reporter, to whom she begins to spill her whole sordid story. Bit by bit, and less (it would appear) out of vengefulness or even greed than out of an irresistible compulsion to confess, Christine brings the whole lot of them down: Profumo, Stephen, Astor, all.

Those who remember the Profumo affair (which didn't make it into the pages of my own chief news source at the time, the *Weekly Reader*) will recall that the scandal unfolded, over a number of months, in a dizzying series of as-told-to newspaper exposés, public apologies, betrayals, court cases, a resignation, and a suicide. All this is drastically telescoped in the film (which, we are told, was originally to have been a four-part television miniseries); the extremely interesting later lives of the scandal's principal players are relegated to brief summaries preceding the closing titles. Like the equally gripping *All the President's Men,* in short, *Scandal* doesn't have a satisfactory dramatic wind-up: it just stops.

To be sure, in order to cover the scandal and its aftermath effectively, the film would have had to be at least twice as long as it is, or would have had to give shorter shrift to the material that it *has* concentrated on—the psychology of the principals, the ways they meet and get to know each other, the feel of their relationships. And for director Michael Caton-Jones and writer Michael Thomas to have chosen the latter route would certainly have been a mistake, since the movie's chief strength, I think, lies in its painstaking, subtly ironic delineation of the characters and their interactions. With the exception of Mandy—the classic blond airhead who, when she appears on the steps of a courthouse after testifying, waves and blows kisses to the crowd like a starlet at a movie premiere—they're all fascinatingly complex.

Profumo, for example—a potential prime minister whose political career is utterly destroyed by the scandal—proves to be sensitive and gentlemanly, a far less randy and more honorable sort than most of the other M.P.'s whom we see up close in this film. And Stephen, for his part, is both morally and sexually ambiguous: carousing with his parliamentary buddies, he rhapsodizes about the delights of promiscuous sex, but never makes a move on Christine—for whom he truly cares and wishes well—and isn't known to be consorting with any other girls. (Nor, despite certain rumors, can he be linked to any particular men.) All four of these principal roles—Christine, Mandy, Stephen, Profumo—are intelligently and vividly acted; the picture is worth seeing a second time simply to appreciate the remarkable way in which these paradoxical characters are captured, made believable, and even rendered sympathetic by the leading actors.

Where *Scandal* is somewhat less successful is in its implicit attempt to make the Profumo affair seem even more significant than it really was. Granted, it was *extremely* significant: it helped topple the Macmillan government, and, like Watergate, may be said to have opened a nation's eyes to various unpleasant (and undying) truths about the moral conduct of many public servants. But Thomas and Caton-Jones aren't satisfied with that; they would appear to want us to read their film—on one level, anyway—as an object lesson in the evils and hypocrisies of the English class system. One feels encouraged, for instance, to take seriously Stephen's image of himself as a crusader against class barriers, to admire him for his efforts in this regard, and to see his downfall as a tragic consequence of his brave challenge to the system. More broadly, the film seems to imply that the Profumo affair—by demonstrating the moral bankruptcy of the ruling classes—

played a major role in the fall of the old England of traditional values, of prosperity and world power, and of government by old-boy Oxbridgeans, and the rise of the anomic, morally jaded, increasingly multi-ethnic Britain of the late sixties and beyond. For the first hour or so, the film's musical score consists largely of Verdi arias and Sinatra and Nat King Cole ballads; then, when the scandal erupts, the score switches suddenly to the Beatles (including, appropriately, "Do You Want to Know a Secret?")—as if to imply that, thanks largely to the Profumo affair, the romantic illusions associated with the pre-rock fare have been banished from England forever. It seems a bit much.

Even the scenes of upper-class depravity in this film have a rather quaint, old-fashioned quality. There's no Caligula in this crowd: in one scene, Stephen throws an intimate "sex party" at which respectable-looking men in Savile Row suits carry on like horny pubescent boys, rolling their eyes at cheap chorines, grabbing at their naughty bits, and giggling over a three-foot-high phallus that serves as the centerpiece of an otherwise elegantly appointed dinner table. The atmosphere is pure frat party. One doesn't doubt for a minute the lustiness of England's upper classes—but could the men who walked Britain's corridors of power in the late fifties and early sixties really have been this puerile, this vulgar? (Conceivably, I suppose; as I say, I was busy reading the *Weekly Reader*.)

And as long as we're asking questions, isn't there something just a bit dishonest about a film that manipulates the viewer into a feeling of sympathy for such people as Christine, Stephen, and Profumo, even as it depicts cops and reporters as uniformly, and uncomplicatedly, crass and corrupt? One has only to glance at certain documents in the history of the Profumo case to realize how much has been omitted, sanitized, distorted in this film. In her memoir *My Life and Lovers,* for instance, Mandy Rice-Davies tells of walking in on Stephen Ward "to find him, for no apparent reason, swinging Christine Keeler's cat round by the tail and laughing as he did so. When I protested, he merely sniggered and tossed the poor creature into the corner of the room." Not even John Hurt, I submit, could make the average moviegoer in 1989 care much for such a person. A puckish but good-hearted sensualist? Fine. But a sadistic cat-swinger? Forget it. (Yes, Miss Rice-Davies may be lying about Ward and the cat—but then that makes *her* something other than the harmless doxy the film would have us believe in.)

Such concerns notwithstanding, however, *Scandal* is on the whole an admirable piece of filmmaking—a shrewd and full-blooded treatment of the sort of fact-based story that has inspired many an inane, one-dimensional movie in recent years. One of the things which make this picture so absorbing—and which make it seem far less sensational and exploitative than it might—is its relentless attention to the moral dimension of its principal characters and their acts; one has the impression that Thomas and Caton-Jones have made it their goal to take a certain set of widely familiar and (on first glance) ethically unambiguous facts and to explore the complicated—and even paradoxical—human truths behind them. Highly dubious though some of their elisions, emphases, and implicit moral verdicts may be, the creators of this film are nonetheless to be congratulated for the seriousness of their approach—and for the thoroughly engrossing film that has resulted.

POETRY IN MOTION

Dead Poets Society
Indiana Jones and the Last Crusade

Dead Poets Society is the kind of movie you want to like. Set in 1959, it's about a group of sensitive, intelligent, teenaged boys at the hundred-year-old Welton School, "the best preparatory school in the United States," whose enthusiastic young English teacher, John Keating (Robin Williams), teaches them not just to appreciate but to *love* poetry. How, you ask? Here's how: on the first day of classes, he steers them into a corridor lined with photographs of earlier Welton graduating classes, and has one of the boys read aloud the first lines of the Robert Herrick poem "To the Virgins, to Make Much of Time" ("Gather ye rosebuds while ye may,/Old time is still a-flying . . ."). "We are food for worms, lads!" Keating declares dramatically, and bids his charges look closely at the faces of the Welton students of a century ago—innocent, hopeful faces not unlike their own. "These boys are now fertilizing daffodils," whispers Keating (himself a Welton alumnus) as the camera examines one of the old photographs in extreme close-up. "Seize the day, boys! Make your lives extraordinary!"

What does all this have to do with poetry? Why, everything, of course. "We don't read and write poetry because it's cute," Keating tells the boys, "we read and write poetry because we're human, and humans feel passion." Passion—that's the ticket! He feeds them a purely Romantic conception of things: the poet as savage, as redskin.

No Alexander Pope on *this* reading list! Keating's hero is Whitman, and he scrawls on the blackboard the famous line from "Song of Myself":"I sound my barbaric yawp over the roofs of the world." Before long, he's got his pupils sounding their own yawps; and when the most unassertive boy in the class, Todd Anderson (Ethan Hawke), proves to be too bashful to compose and read aloud a poem of his own, Keating drags him in front of the class and agitates him into inventing one on the spot. The poem isn't very good, needless to say, but it's peeled straight from the gut, and (as Keating makes clear) that's what counts.

For he certainly doesn't teach his students any other criteria for great poetry (not on screen, at least): there's no class discussion here, no exegesis, no *explication de texte.* Instead he conducts unorthodox exercises: during one class period, he has the boys take turns standing on his desk (so that they can see things from a different perspective); during another, he leads them into a courtyard to try out various idiosyncratic ways of walking (so that they can learn not to be conformists). Throughout these peculiarly conceived lessons, poetry itself is reduced to the role which Philistines have always accorded it, that of rudimentary Source of Inspiration: Keating—hovering busily over his bemused, acquiescent, and increasingly adoring boys like a neurotically possessive mother—tosses off isolated lines from great writers as if they were fortune-cookie maxims or desk-calendar Thoughts for the Day. Thoreau, he exclaims, wrote that "most men lead lives of quiet desperation": don't let that happen to you! He has a boy recite the closing lines of Tennyson's "Ulysses," with their description of "heroic hearts,/Made weak by time and fate, but strong in will/To strive, to seek, to find, and not to yield." The lesson is plain: strive, seek, find, don't yield. Seize the day!

Patently, director Peter Weir (whose previous films include *Gallipoli, The Year of Living Dangerously, Picnic at Hanging Rock,* and *Witness*) and screenwriter Tom Schulman want us to love Keating. To this end, they load the dice grotesquely against the opposition—i.e., the other adults in the movie. First, they give Welton an unbelievably cold and intractable old headmaster who prattles on snobbishly about "tradition" and who is deeply suspicious of Keating and his methods. (Then why, one wonders, did he hire him in the first place?) Second, they give the two most prominent boys, Todd Anderson and Neil Perry (Robert Sean Leonard), frosty and tyrannical dads. Finally, they oufit Keating's class with a textbook entitled *Understanding Poetry* by some scholar named Pritchard, whose introduction solemnly outlines a fatuous pseudo-scientific method for determining a poem's greatness. On the first day of class, Keating orders the boys to tear this introduction out of their books, and passes around the wastepaper basket while fulminating against the "armies of academics" who engage in "measuring poetry." "No matter what anybody tells you," he says, "words in meter *can* change the world!" It's an irritating scene: for one thing, Pritchard's straw-man introduction is too ludicrous to be credible, and Keating's opposition to it absurdly facile; for another, whether intentionally or not, the episode comes off as a rude dig at Cleanth Brooks and Robert Penn Warren, the editors of the classic textbook *Understanding Poetry,* whose intelligent and responsible critical method bears no resemblance to that of the fictitious Dr. Pritchard.

Dead Poets Society has been promoted heavily as a Robin Williams film, but it really isn't, strictly speaking. Though we see Keating transfigure the lives of his students, we aren't given much of a glimpse into *his* life; we don't feel as if we know him, and when fate deals him his hand at the end of the film we haven't got a clue as to what that fate means to him, practically, emotionally, or spiritually. The few personal touches about him feel arbitrary: we're told that he's taught previously in England and that he has a girlfriend in London—none of which has any apparent bearing on the story. There are long stretches of the film in which Keating doesn't even appear, and only a couple of brief moments when we see him apart from his students. It's the boys, in fact, who are at the film's center; Weir focuses not on Keating but on how Keating's way of thinking affects them. Which brings us to the title of the movie: through an old Welton yearbook, the boys learn that Keating once belonged to a mysterious student club called the Dead Poets Society; its members, Keating explains to them nostalgically, were "romantics" who regularly gathered in a cave and read to each other from an anthology called *Five Centuries of Verse.* Intrigued, several of the students secretly revive the society—and, in various ways, act upon Keating's philosophy.

None of these ways, unfortunately, is very interesting. Neil defies his father (who wants him to concentrate on schoolwork) by acting in a local production of *A Midsummer Night's Dream;* a boy named Knox Overstreet screws up the courage to ask a pretty girl out for a date. The story of Neil and his dad, to be sure, has a certain poignancy, and is helped considerably by good performances in challenging roles. Leonard (despite a tendency to overexercise his winsome smile) does a credible job of creating a character whose self-possession dissolves completely in his father's presence; and Kurtwood Smith turns in a forceful performance as the father, who is at once genuinely loving and cruelly inflexible, so determined to see his son become a doctor that he is unwilling, even for a moment, to take the boy's own aspirations seriously. But the father-son conflict feels rather cursory at times, bringing us too close for comfort to TV-movie territory. As for the sequences about Knox and his girl, they're so trite and familiar that they might almost have been edited in from some inane coming-of-age movie set in the late fifties—or, for that matter, from "Happy Days."

Some viewers of *Dead Poets Society* will be reminded of Muriel Spark's 1961 novel *The Prime of Miss Jean Brodie* (which, it will be remembered, was made into a 1969 film starring Maggie Smith). Like Jean Brodie, John Keating is a lonely, self-romanticizing egoist whose classroom style fosters a personality cult (he has the boys call him Captain, a name derived from Whitman's "O Captain, My Captain"—a poem which, incidentally, few true Whitmanians would exalt); as in the case of Jean Brodie, moreover, Keating's manipulation of his students has fatal consequences (which I won't reveal here). But whereas Spark recognized the selfishness of Miss Brodie's motives and the destructiveness of her influence, *Dead Poets Society* makes Keating into an outright hero, a dedicated teacher misunderstood and (ultimately) scapegoated by the establishment.

How callow, how sentimental, this film is about its subject! Weir and company would have us believe that getting young people to care for poetry is just a matter of inculcating a romantic sensibility; but surely anyone who has tried his hand at teaching poetry to high school or college students knows that teenaged boys *already* think like Dylan Thomas and Walt Whitman and Percy Bysshe Shelley; the difficulty is getting them to *read* Thomas and Whitman and Shelley, to understand the poets' work, to recognize the poetry's affinity to their own lives—and, above all, to comprehend why the "barbaric yawp" of Thomas and Whitman and Shelley is more valuable than that of this week's Top-Forty *Billboard* sensation. Nor do you have to encourage teenagers to seize the day: the trick is getting them to think in terms of tomorrow. Certainly, in this age of sex, drugs, rock-and-roll, and other forms of instant gratification, "seize the day" is among the last messages teenagers need to hear—which may be why *Dead Poets Society* is set not in an inner-city high school in 1989 (where a

John Keating would merely be contributing to the reigning chaos) but in a stuffy late-fifties prep school, a numbingly reactionary environment in which teaching methods like Keating's can actually be made to seem plausible and sympathetic.

All of which is a shame, because Robin Williams (who convincingly demonstrated his capabilities as a serious actor in *The World According to Garp*) turns in a splendidly modulated performance as Keating; though he seems always to be on the go—bounding tirelessly about the classroom like a Donald O'Connor, constantly pouncing on one student or another to make a point—his exuberance never gets out of control, and his restraint (when called for) is impressive. If Robert Sean Leonard is very fine, moreover, Ethan Hawke is even finer, making Todd's painful shyness so palpable and touching that one all but squirms along with him; indeed, I can't think of a recent film with more promising work by actors of this age. But their characters' tribulations simply aren't that compelling, and the closer Weir gets to them the less certain he seems about where he wants to direct emphasis; the entire middle part of the film—which abandons Keating for extended periods in order to shuttle back and forth between glimpses of the boys' extracurricular lives—feels directionless, unmoored. Skimpily developed though William's character may be, it is only when he is on screen that the movie has energy, color, and dramatic tension.

Fortunately, all three of these attributes around in *Indiana Jones and the Last Crusade,* the third entry in Steven Spielberg's highly popular action-adventure series. As before, our hero is archeology professor Indiana Jones (Harrison Ford), who—what with his life-or-death chases through Austrian castles, German countryside, and Middle Eastern deserts, and his hair's-breadth escapes from Nazi zeppelins, fast-sinking ships off the Portuguese coast, and blazing, rat-infested Venetian catacombs—spends even less time in the classroom than John Keating. Once again, Indy's on the trail of a religious relic—this time, the Holy Grail, the quest for which leads him, in the year of our Lord 1938, from a genteel American university campus all the way to the exotic republic of Hatay (which would seem to be somewhere between Morocco and Iran).

The Indiana Jones films are, of course, a triumph more of special effects than of screenplay, more of stunt work than of great acting;

what's more, one might justifiably be disturbed by Spielberg's consistently glib appropriation of profound religious images and ideas (which brings to mind his equally slick treatment of war and its casualties in *Empire of the Sun*). But for the most part, *Last Crusade* does exactly what this sort of film should do: it moves along (as did *Raiders of the Lost Ark*) at a breathtaking clip, keeping you on the edge of your seat nearly without letup; and it gives you a hero you can root for, while every so often (but not *too* often) laughing along with you at the implausibility of it all. One thing that's new here is that we get to see our hero with his fussy, abstracted dad (Sean Connery), whose lifelong Grail fixation gets Indy into this mess in the first place. We also get to see Indy as a boy—specifically, a Boy Scout in 1912 Utah—who, in a wittily conceived sequence, leads a corps of bad guys on a chase through a circus train. The part is nicely played by River Phoenix, who projects the same boyish earnestness that Ford does—and the same charming combination of resourcefulness and fallibility, savvy and naivete. All in all, it's an entertaining roller-coaster ride.

THE BARON OF BRIGHTON

Remembering Laurence Olivier

For decades—indeed, since long before many of us were born—it has been a commonplace that Laurence Olivier was the greatest actor of our time. So much of a commonplace has it been, alas, that many of us may well have taken his genius—and his contribution to his art—for granted. To be sure, much of that contribution is forever lost to us: Olivier, who shook off this mortal coil on July 11 at the age of eighty-two, was perhaps most celebrated of all for theatrical performances which few of us were privileged to witness. But, over a period of six decades, he also compiled a sizable body of work on film—sixty-odd movies in all, some of which he did just for the money (and it shows), but many of which are masterpieces, and most of which (thanks to the videotape revolution) we can see again and again.

To peruse Olivier's filmography is to be reminded at once of his humor, his energy, and his remarkable range as a movie actor. Brilliant as he was in his adaptations of *Hamlet, Richard III,* and other Shakespearean plays, he was equally adept at enacting everything from the brooding romantic heroes of Emily Bronte, Jane Austen, and Daphne du Maurier to the whimsical and idiosyncratic titled folk of Evelyn Waugh, Terence Rattigan, and James Costigan. His most splendidly realized movie characters tend to inhabit the extremes of life: he seemed born to play both the most virtuous and the most sinister of characters, the most glorious of national heroes and the most forlorn and shabby of losers. He was especially gifted, too, at capturing protagonists with an enigma, a contradiction, at their hearts; one thinks, for instance, of the bold-yet-melancholy Roman general Crassus in *Spartacus,* and of the savage-yet-gentle stableboy Healthcliff in *Wuthering Heights.*

Though he appeared in a number of films in Britain in the early thirties—among them *Fire Over England* (1936) and *Twenty-One Days* (1939), in both of which he acted opposite his wife-to-be, Vivien Leigh—Olivier first came to international prominence in a trio of classic American films based on romantic English novels. In *Wuthering Heights* (1939)—directed by William Wyler from a script by Ben Hecht and Charles MacArthur—he played Heathcliff to Merle Oberon's Catherine, bringing to the part a vigor that bordered on the flamboyant. It was a natural step from Heathcliff to the equally glamorous and enigmatic Maxim de Winter in Alfred Hitchcock's *Rebecca* (1940), based on Daphne du Maurier's best-selling Bronte-ish novel about an ingenuous young bride (Joan Fontaine), her terse, secretive consort, and his vast, gloomy manse. (The screenplay was written by the playwright Robert Sherwood.) And it was another natural step from that film—which won the Academy Award for best picture—to the same year's *Pride and Prejudice* (scripted by Aldous Huxley and Jane Murfin), in which Olivier played the proud Mr. Darcy to Greer Garson's prejudiced Elizabeth Bennet. It's a virtually perfect adaptation, rich and charming and funny—the best possible answer to anyone who claims that a great novel cannot be made into a first-rate movie. If Olivier can be faulted for occasional overacting in *Wuthering Heights* and *Rebecca,* his performance here is essentially flawless. His pairing with Garson is particularly fortuitous; the two leads play splendidly off each other's wit, and the combination of mutual animosity and attraction between them feels wonderfully real.

These films were followed by the less worthy *That Hamilton Woman* (1941), an engaging (if thoroughly routine) World War II-era excursion into historical drama, courtesy of the British producer-director Alexander Korda; this would-be morale-booster cast Olivier as yet another romantic hero, the difference being that the romantic hero in this instance was the national icon Lord Nelson. (Vivien Leigh played Nelson's mistress, Lady Hamilton.) And Olivier impersonated a second national icon in his last major wartime movie, *Henry V* (1944). The earliest of Olivier's Shakespearean adaptations and his first directorial effort, the film is a tour de force almost in spite of itself; fussy, stately, stylized, and almost too richly hued, it hovers awfully close (in tone and aspect) to Michael Powell and Emeric Pressburger's luxuriant, borderline-campy *The Red Shoes* (1948) and *The Life and Death of Colonel Blimp* (1943), but is saved by its intelligence, its patent earnestness of intent, and its director's manifest reverence for the text at hand. The film, indeed, set a standard by which Shakespearean adaptations have been judged ever since. Its patriotic pageantry gave way to the more Spartan *Hamlet* (1948), which won the Academy Award for best picture (and for Olivier as best actor); filmed in black and white, on an austere, expressionistic, almost Bergman-like set consisting mostly of mist-enshrouded stone, Olivier's version of the "story of a man who could not make up his mind" (as he identifies it in a prefatory Wellesian voice-over) features a highly fluid camera and voice-over soliloquies, omits several characters and speeches, and seems designed to make the Bard coherent and captivating to the average moviegoer. The wondrous thing is that the film actually does so without seriously compromising the play; and Olivier's vigorous, athletic Hamlet—a Dane as full of life as he is haunted by death—is well-nigh unforgettable. (One can hardly believe he was over forty at the time.)

From first-rate renderings of Shakespeare, Olivier proceeded (unwisely, perhaps) to a third-rate adaptation of Theodore Dreiser. *Carrie* (1952)—directed by William Wyler from a mediocre script by Ruth and Augustus Goetz—turned Dreiser's biting naturalistic novel *Sister Carrie* into a routinely bland Hollywood tear-jerker with top production values and a modestly talented star (Jennifer Jones) in the title role. As Hurstwood, the affluent Chicago restaurateur whose fortunes plummet as his beloved Carrie prospers, Olivier all but wipes everyone else off the screen; he offers us a genuine tragic character in the midst of much unconvincing pathos.

He is equally commanding in the lighter but far more successful *The Prince and the Showgirl* (1958), which he directed from a very funny, charming, and wittily constructed screenplay by Terence Rattigan, then the reigning master of well-made middlebrow English drama. (Rattigan based the script on his stage play *The Sleeping Princess,* in which Olivier had recently appeared with Vivien Leigh.) Olivier turns in one of his richest comic performances as a cold, choleric middle-European aristocrat, the Regent of Carpathia, who, in London for the coronation of King George V, finds himself involved with a giddy, sentimental American dancer named Elsie Marina

(Marilyn Monroe). *Spartacus* (1960), meanwhile, offers a somewhat different patrician-and-peasant contraposition: in this provocative epic about the slave revolt of 73 B.C., based on Howard Fast's sentimental-Marxist novel and directed by Stanley Kubrick from a most skillful script by Dalton Trumbo, Olivier brings not only great authority but an exceptional poignancy to the character of Crassus, the urbane, corrupt Roman general and dictator whom the film consistently contrasts with Kirk Douglas's true-blue, unrefined slave general.

Is *The Entertainer* still considered as wonderful as it was in 1960? This tears-of-a-clown piece about a down-at-the-heels vaudeville comic, Archie Rice, has always struck me as dull, facile, and stagy, the protagonist's seedy pathos as ultimately pointless; Olivier's spirited performance seems wasted on the one-note script (which was based on the acclaimed play by Angry Young Man John Osborne). His ability to portray a pitiful loser is far more movingly displayed in *Term of Trial* (1962), in which he appears as a sensitive and literate secondary-school teacher in a gray, working-class English town, one of whose students (Sarah Miles) has falsely accused him of sexual molestation. (The carnal wife of this cerebral pedagogue is played by Simone Signoret.) Written and directed by Peter Glenville, the film is a gripping, intensely disturbing morality tale, and Olivier's portrayal of the teacher—a virtuous man trapped in moral circumstances wherein his worst enemy is his own virtue, and the only means of his ultimate salvation a lie—is deeply credible and affecting.

In his last two decades, Olivier seemed to show up more frequently than ever in films, though the vehicles themselves were often mediocre and the parts mere cameos. He served as little more than high-class adornment, for instance, in such high-gloss spectacles as *The Shoes of the Fisherman* (1968) and *Nicholas and Alexandra* (1971), and was hardly challenged by his part as a murderous mystery novelist in the lightweight thriller *Sleuth* (1972); while George Roy Hill's *A Little Romance* (1978) was quite charming, moreover, one grew rather uneasy at the sight of Olivier (in the insubstantial role of a petty con man, Julius Edmond Santorin) providing support to a couple of less-than-brilliant child actors. And of course the very idea of Olivier in Harold Robbins's *The Betsy* (1977), or as Neil Diamond's father in a remake of *The Jazz Singer* (1981), was enough to induce nausea.

Many of his movie assignments of recent years, indeed, required Olivier to be little more than old, colorful, and cantankerous (one thinks, for instance, of the television movies "A Voyage Round My

Father" and "The Ebony Tower"). But he was made good use of—and was very funny—as an Edwardian barrister in James Costigan's Rattigan-like television drama "Love Among the Ruins" (1974), and managed to make a three-dimensional character out of William Goldman's ruthless Nazi dentist, Christian Szell, in John Schlesinger's *Marathon Man* (1976). (His performance, two years later, as a Holocaust survivor and Nazi hunter in the rather shabby *Boys from Brazil* was considerably less impressive.) And it was a joy to watch him in the television miniseries *Brideshead Revisited* (1981)—though one suspected that Waugh's suave, cosmopolitan Lord Marchmain was hardly a stretch for Lord Olivier.

The inferior roles, needless to say, were a waste of his time and ours. But given a halfway decent part, Olivier was almost invariably mesmerizing. Even his deathbed scene in *Brideshead*—the character feeble, gasping, nearly immobile—has fire; even a gloomy character like Heathcliff, in his most controlled, inward moments, excudes an unsettling forcefulness. Yet none of this force, this fire, seemed ingenuine: indeed, in his intensity Olivier generally appeared, if anything, *realer* than the more subdued performers around him, more vital, more acquainted with passion, with evil, with the night. One was, to be sure, often aware of Olivier's acting—yet it was not the way one is aware of some Strasbergian's plodding Methodism; one was conscious of it, rather, in the way that one is conscious of a writer like Joyce or Nabokov even as one is thoroughly absorbed in his fiction. Somehow, with Olivier, the illusion of reality coexisted happily with one's delighted awareness of the maestro's artistry. Take him for all in all, we shall not see his like again.

IN WOODY'S SHADOW

Parenthood
When Harry Met Sally

You might call *Parenthood* a middle-class, Midwestern variation on Woody Allen's *Hannah and Her Sisters*. Like *Hannah*, it's a family portrait—an alternately funny and poignant story of the ups and downs, over a period of a couple of years, in the life of an extended American family of the '80s. But whereas Allen gave us a colorful Manhattan clan composed largely of art-world and show-biz types, director Ron Howard and writers Lowell Ganz and Babaloo (yes, Babaloo) Mandel give us a seemingly more ordinary St. Louis family called the Buckmans. And whereas Allen focused on love and romance—both within and outside of marriage—Howard's emphasis is on parents and their children.

Indeed, the Buckmans have so many parent-child problems to deal with that you may need a scorecard to keep it all straight. Try to follow this: businessman Gil (Steve Martin) and his wife, Karen (Mary Steenburgen), have three kids, including a nine-year-old son, Kevin, who's so high-strung that he needs psychiatric treatment. Gil's divorced sister (Dianne Wiest) is the mother of two troubled youths—an intractable pubescent named Gary, who rents porno movies and keeps a padlock on his bedroom door, and a bright high-schooler named Julie (Martha Plimpton) who insists on consorting with an immature lad named Tod (Keanu Reeves). Meanwhile, Gil's younger sister, a schoolteacher named Susan, has an overzealous Yuppie husband, Nathan (Rick Moranis), who insists on teaching advanced subjects to their toddler daughter, Patty, so that she'll gain a competitive edge on her future classmates.

Got that? There's more. Gil's a loving and attentive father, you see, and it's largely because he's always wanted very much to be a better dad than his own father (Jason Robards, Jr.) was. Not that Buckman *père* wasn't a decent guy; it's just that he's a fun-loving type who never got the hang of fatherhood. Besides, he's always found Gil a bit of a square; he prefers younger son Larry (Tom Hulce), an ever-broke, never-employed nomad who's fond of get-rich-quick schemes and who, after several years' absence, shows up at a family gathering with a seven-year-old mulatto son named Cool. Add to this Gil's mom, his grandma, and assorted others, and it's amazing that you can even remember who's who, let alone care about any of them.

But you *do* care about them—some of them, anyway. The acting has a lot to do with it. Steve Martin, in particular, is remarkable—hilarious one moment, tender the next, and always consistent, credible, and perfectly modulated. Watching him agonize so convincingly over his son's emotional problems makes it hard to believe that this is the man who used to dance on "Saturday Night Live" with an arrow through his head. Yet his performance suggests that, however serious an actor he becomes, he'll never make the mistake of entirely submerging his comic self, the way Mary Tyler Moore and Carol Burnett seem to think they have to do when giving Serious Performances; indeed, at certain points in *Parenthood*, Martin makes excellent and altogether fitting raids on his comic bag of tricks.

Wiest is splendid too, as ever, though she sometimes seems to be reprising her role in *Hannah and Her Sisters*; loveless, stubborn, and neurotic, her character here is as touchingly sincere and as comically maladroit at motherhood as her counterpart in *Hannah* was at relationships. Steenburgen and Reeves (who appeared previously in *River's Edge*) are also especially fine; and the boy who plays Kevin—a big and difficult role, which calls for all sorts of pathetic displays and mood shifts—doesn't make a false move. It's the sort of performance that only a very sensitive director could get out of a kid (and doubtless Howard's own experience as a child actor made a difference here, too).

Indeed, the acting is so marvelously effective, on the whole, that it takes a while to realize how bogus the whole thing is. I mean, this is a big family composed almost entirely of *really nice people.* They have very lovely homes, good jobs, and plenty of time for the kids. They have problems, yes, but they're not *terrible* problems—no terminal illnesses, no teenagers hooked on crack—and virtually all are resolved by the end of the movie, in some cases quite improbably. As for Larry, the solitary exception to the rule of family niceness, he's a classic black sheep, a stereotype in every way (and a too-neat contrast to Gil), whose continuing ability to charm the pants off his dad isn't quite believable.

For all this, the film's a hell of a lot less synthetic-feeling than, say, *Terms of Endearment.* And if it's contrived in its broad outlines, it's authentic in many of its particulars. The one really staggering misstep comes at the very ending, which is set in a maternity ward, and which is so inanely, gratuitously sentimental that it would make Frank Capra wince. It's one of those *ending* endings, which ties up too many story lines too quickly, too glibly, and too improbably for comfort; and the picture that it offers of perfect family harmony and of difficulties overcome by love and patience contradicts the whole point of the movie—namely, that family life is by its nature fraught with predicaments which have no easy solutions.

This is, to be sure, a hard sort of film to find an ending for: it's a character piece, crowded with stories but lacking in a dominant plot line, and there's no ideal, natural conclusion to such a picture. But the one Ganz and Mandel have come up with is all wrong; its unrelenting mawkishness betrays the whole tone of the film, whose saving grace is that it doesn't lean on its emotion and consistently leavens sentiment with humor. Howard and his scriptwriters could have taken a lesson from Woody Allen: compare the final moments of *Parenthood* to the closing dinner-party sequence in *Hannah* (especially the very last part, when Allen and Wiest talk before a mirror). Both sequences have similar purposes, but Allen's is wittier, subtler, and far more effective (which is to say, far more affecting). For myself, if I ever watch *Parenthood* on videotape, I'll turn the TV off after the charming and funny penultimate sequence (set at a school play), which does all the summing-up required, and which Howard would have been well advised to end with.

As for Rob Reiner, I'd advise him to shake off Woody Allen altogether. More than a decade ago—back when we all still thought of him as the Meathead on "All in the Family" (and, by the way, when Ron Howard was still Richie Cunningham on "Happy Days")—Reiner wrote, directed, and starred in one of the worst TV movies of all time. It was called *More Than Friends* and it owed a great deal to *Annie Hall*, which had come out only a year or so earlier. Reiner borrowed with great care but little understanding: he appropriated a plot point here, a detail of character there, and emphasized the metropolitan *mise en scène* in a big way. But he seemed not to understand that these elements had no intrinsic significance, that they were just manifestations of Woody Allen's sensibility, his singular way of looking at life and love. And sensibility was precisely what *More Than Friends* lacked—that, and a feel for the New York streets on which the film was set. At its core, that early effort of Reiner's was fake, empty—a collection of meaningless gestures.

Reiner went on, of course, to make some of the most winsome movies of the past few years—the first (*This Is Spinal Tap*) a side-splitting fake "rockumentary" about a crummy rock-and-roll band on tour, the second (*Stand By Me*) a poignant story about the friendship of four pubescent small-town boys, the third (*The Princess Bride*) a charming comedy-fantasy about storybook lovers, villains, and pirates. No other new director of this decade has created a more solid and respectable body of work; at a time when even better-than-average Hollywood movies often have a slick assembly-line style and point of view, his films have an uncommon quality of character, wit, and gentleness, a pronounced and distinctive humanity. Like Howard, moreover (and like his ex-wife and *More Than Friends* co-star Penny Marshall, who directed last year's *Big*), Reiner has proven himself especially good with children; he seems to respect them, to care about them, to understand the way their minds operate.

But how is he with adults? *When Harry Met Sally* . . . is Reiner's first feature film that's exclusively for and about grown-ups, and it doesn't say much for Reiner's abilities in this line. On the contrary, it demonstrates that Reiner still has a thing for Woody Allen, that his view of adult relationships is no more sophisticated than it was when he made *More Than Friends*, and that he might be better off sticking to kid stories.

Either that, or developing an interest in adults who act more like adults. For Harry Burns (Billy Crystal), the hero of Reiner's new film, is the most juvenile of men. He's the sort whose life with males revolves around sports and whose life with females revolves around sex; who believes firmly that what every man thinks, after intercourse, is "How long do I have to lie here and hold her before I can get up and go home?"; who is constantly turning to his girlfriend and saying things like "I had a dream—we're making love and the Olympic judges are watching"; and who informs her that "there are two kinds of women, high maintenance and low maintenance," and that she's the former.

Yech! The idea here, obviously, is that Harry's supposed to be obnoxious yet brashly appealing. As it works out, however, he's just obnoxious. And yet the very pretty and fastidious Sally Albright (Meg Ryan), who meets him three times over the course of ten years and who at first finds him unbearable, ends up head over heels. Go figure. You'd bet your life that a man wrote this script—a man very much like Harry, naturally. But you'd be wrong: it's by Nora Ephron, the author of *Heartburn* and ex-wife of Carl Bernstein. Could a woman really have created such an odious romantic hero? It seems incredible. Yet think about it for a minute, and it begins to make sense: any woman who married Carl Bernstein *would* find Harry Burns appealing.

Besides, Ephron didn't work alone. Reiner reportedly had a big hand in shaping the script; the story of Harry and Sally is said to be based on his experiences after divorcing Penny Marshall, and Ephron felt the character was so close to Reiner that he should play the role himself. It was Reiner, too, who hatched the film's jejune thesis, which is stated by Harry early on: "Men and women can never be friends because the sex part always gets in the way." (When you see a proposition like this being taken seriously by a scriptwriter, you know you're in trouble.) This thesis notwithstanding, however, Harry and Sally *do* become friends after meeting for the third time. ("Great!" Harry says with his usual charm. "A woman friend!") But you don't buy it for a minute: there's not enough chemistry between these two to make a friendship seem likely, let alone a love affair.

The whole contraption, in fact, feels synthetic. We're told that Harry's a political consultant and that Sally's a *Daily News* reporter, but we don't see either of them at work. They don't even *talk* about work. (For all the difference that it makes, he might be a construction foreman and she a ballerina.) We don't know anything about their families or upbringing, and their friends, ex-spouses, and other lovers are little more than stick-figure plot functionaries. Even Harry's best friend, Jess (Bruno Kirby), and Sally's best friend, Marie (Carrie Fisher), are stubbornly one-dimensional (though the actors do their best to breathe life into them). What's more, Harry and Sally have so many diametrically opposite personality traits—all of them blatantly spelled out in the film's opening scenes—that they can't possibly seem anything but false: he's passionate, she's practical; he's sloppy, she's neat (he calls her "Miss Hospital Corners"); he's into munchies, she won't eat between meals; he'll sleep with any woman that's breathing, she won't go to bed with a man she doesn't love; he thinks a lot about death, she doesn't.

Or at least he *says* he thinks a lot about death, though nothing in his behavior suggests it. That's the difference, of course, between Woody Allen and Rob Reiner: when a Woody Allen character says he thinks a lot about death, you *know* he does. When Harry says he thinks a lot about death, you know that Rob Reiner thinks a lot about Woody Allen. And does he ever! The settings here are vintage Allen: Central Park, the Metropolitan Museum, a bookstore. But the action and dialogue are mainstream yuppie: when Sally meets Harry in Shakespeare & Co., he's in the Personal Growth section; at the museum, he hangs around the Temple of Dendur with her and does bad shtick: "I have a theory that Egyptian hieroglyphics are really an ancient comic strip about a character named Sphinxie." Ugh. Like Allen and Mariel Hemingway in *Manhattan*, they lie in bed and watch *Casablanca* together. ("Best last line of a movie ever," he says, as if it weren't the received opinion on the subject.) And toward the end of the movie, just as in *Manhattan*, our hero, suddenly realizing how much he loves our heroine, sprints across town while a bouncy Gershwin tune plays on the soundtrack, and winds up in a doorway, facing her, breathing heavily. (The difference is that whereas Allen used "Strike Up the Band" for the sprint and "But Not For Me" for the subdued follow-up, Reiner plays a weird, peppy arrangement of "But Not For Me" under the run: for anyone who knows the song, it's a disconcerting choice.)

That's not the only musical echo. The soundtrack contains several songs Allen has used: "It Had To Be You" (from *Annie Hall*), "Love Is Here To Stay" as well as "But Not For Me" (*Manhattan*), "Isn't It Romantic" and "Where or When" (*Hannah*). Yes, they're all wonderful songs, and, yes, it's satisfying to see a new movie whose score doesn't consist of the hideous discords of some top-40 rock group. But given the hundreds of standard ballads by Gershwin, Arlen, Rodgers, et al., to choose from, why did Reiner pick these? Certainly it wasn't a matter of their being just the right tunes for his purposes; most of them seem almost arbitrarily assigned to their respective scenes. Music is, in fact, employed quite crudely here: if, in *Hannah*, Allen delicately underlined the seasonal changes by means of music and atmospheric shots, Reiner hits us over the head with songs like "Autumn In New York" and "Winter Wonderland" and with postcard views of (among other things) the Rockefeller Center Christmas tree.

There's one further curious facet of this film that needs to be mentioned. From the opening credits, Reiner cuts to a Diane Arbus-like two-shot of an elderly couple, who face the camera and tell us how they met. (In *Annie Hall*, Allen cut from the credits to a similar close-up of himself.) They're the first of several such couples who appear at intervals in the film, all telling us similar stories. Why? Hard to say; maybe Reiner and his scriptwriter, Nora Ephron, felt this gimmick would make the story of Harry and Sally seem more real, more universal. Or maybe they were making parodic references to the intercalated bits in *Reds*, wherein a host of oldsters reminisced about the real John Reed and Louise Bryant. Or maybe Reiner is just addicted to structural clutter: he burdened *Spinal Tap* with a gratuitous introductory segment starring himself as the "rockumentary's" producer; he encumbered *Stand By Me* with an unnecessary nostalgic voice-over by Richard Dreyfuss; and he almost sank *The Princess Bride* by interpolating several action-stalling scenes in which Peter Falk—as an old man reading the story to his grandson—answered the child's comments.

Why does Reiner imitate Woody Allen so slavishly? Partly, I'm sure, for the same reason that Allen, in his weaker films (e.g., *Interiors*), goes overboard emulating Bergman; he admires the man's work. But one also has the feeling that Reiner, so comfortable in the realm of storybook fantasy, farce, and boyhood, is ill at ease in the territory of this film—adult romance—and, like a smart but un-self-confident kid copying a book report out of an encyclopedia, felt a need to lean strongly on a recognized authority. One can only hope that, in films to come, Reiner will cultivate his own distinctive manner of looking at grown-up life and love—or else will find his way back to the sort of movie he's made with such splendid proficiency in the past.

SEX AND CANDY

sex, lies, and videotape
Uncle Buck

Steven Soderbergh, the 26-year-old writer-director of *sex, lies, and videotape* (lower-case letters, please), has never been to film school. And it shows: the slick, style-over-substance look and the glib, assembly-line sensibility that typify movies by today's film-school alumni are nowhere in evidence here; while technically unimpeachable, Soderbergh's debut picture also glows with a refreshing distinctiveness of tone, a fine quirkiness of imagination, and a gratifying sensitivity to details of character and atmosphere. As for the story, Soderbergh has put together what is essentially (like Edward Albee's *Who's Afraid of Virginia Woolf?* or Noel Coward's *Private Lives*) a witty, provocative, and fastidiously crafted four-character play, has set it in Baton Rouge, Louisiana, and has cast it with an attractive quartet of gifted, thirtyish performers.

The least likable of the four characters is John Mullaney (Peter Gallagher), a slimy, fast-track, red-suspender-wearing yuppie lawyer, whose boredom with his sweet and beautiful but oddly naive and sexually impassive wife, Ann (Andie MacDowell), has led him into a sleazy, clandestine affair with her wanton sister, Cynthia (Laura San Giacomo), a seductive artist who tends bar. Enter John's old college buddy, Graham (James Spader), a sensitive, laid-back, underachieving drifter who floats into town and inadvertently lures both of John's women into his orbit.

How does Graham do this? Well, Ann's drawn to him out of empathy; she's touched by his shabby, solitary existence, his dread of commitment, his desire to live in his car rather than in an apartment because "I like having the one key." And she's touched, too, by his sexual plight: as he confesses to her (on the day after their first meeting, no less), he's psychologically impotent, unable to make it with women. The sex-happy Cynthia, for her part, is fascinated by Graham's inventive, if aberrant, means of achieving release: during the last several years, he's talked a number of women into sitting on his couch, staring into the lens of his videotape camera, and outlining their erotic histories in graphic detail. He has the tapes neatly labeled, by name and date, and views them regularly in private. This turns him on in a big way.

Which—when Ann finds out about it—turns her *off* in a big way. But in fact both Ann's conviction that "sex is overrated" and Graham's video fetish exemplify a shared fear of intimacy; if character, sex, and circumstance have interacted in such a way as to make John and Cynthia unusually randy, the same forces have operated together in the cases of Graham and Ann to the opposite effect. Not to put too fine a point on it, Ann and Graham are birds of a feather, and one of the questions the film implicitly poses is whether they'll try (and, if so, manage) to burst the bars of their respective cages and fly off together.

Needless to say, this is quite a neurotic foursome, who in raw summary may not sound much different from the bizarre, empty-headed Southerners that populate the plays and movies of Beth Henley (*Crimes of the Heart, Nobody's Fool*). Much to his credit, however, Soderbergh steers completely clear of Henley territory: compared to her goofy stereotypes, his characters are living, breathing people, whom we soon find ourselves caring about (or, in the case of John, despising). It's a testament to Soderbergh's skill, moreover, that he manages to introduce all four of them in apt, memorable, and funny ways—and to establish their relationships and conflicts—before the movie's first ten minutes are up. The entire film, as a matter of fact, is marked by an admirable precision and economy of word and gesture. It takes only two brief, flawlessly delivered lines of dialogue, for instance, to convey the purely utilitarian, businesslike nature of John's liaison with Cynthia: after a midday roll in the hay, they don't part with a kiss, a romantic word, or a lingering look, but with a mechanical request by one to "drive safely" and the other's sneering reply of "Yeah, right."

It's not until the last half-hour or so, when Graham's videotape fixation takes center stage, that the movie falters. Nor is it his videotape fixation, *per se,* so much as it is his ardent, cryptic, and protracted account of its etiology—which he delivers in an awkward, unprepared-for scene with Ann—that throws this hitherto exquisitely poised film off balance. All at once, the focus shifts unaccountably, motivations seem to enter out of left field (nine years ago, Graham reveals, he was deeply hurt by a girl named Elizabeth), and an apparently vital thematic nexus (between love and lying) is introduced but not clearly enough explained. During Graham's speech, one has the uncomfortable feeling that Soderbergh, who all along has kept a seemly distance from his characters, is suddenly embarrassingly close to one of them; that the speech, which does not work well dramatically, exists primarily for other than objective dramatic purposes; and that Graham's predicament has a far more profound meaning for the writer-director than he has succeeded in communicating to his audience.

One feels, to speak plainly, as if it's not Graham but Soderbergh himself who's crying out in pain and confusion over the traumas and betrayals of youth. Suddenly, during this scene, one recalls how very young, after all, the film's writer-director is. And one's disappointment is compounded by the film's pedestrian and overly tidy wrap-up, which betrays both the movie's distinctiveness and its sense of verity.

Yet for most of its length, *sex, lies, and videotape* is an intelligent and remarkably compelling piece of work. Notwithstanding the failure of his big scene, Spader mostly does a very fine job. And the other actors are commendable without qualification: Ann, who might have come across as either a tic-ridden dingbat or a locker-room joke (the sex goddess with no interest in sex), is invested by Andie MacDowell with charm and dignity; Laura San Giacomo succeeds at the difficult job of making the truculent, devious Cynthia sympathetic; and Peter Gallagher, down to his last gesture, gets John exactly right. This is, Gallagher makes clear, a man who will never be able to understand sexual relations beyond the level of macho conquest and intramural competitiveness. These are top-notch performances, and none of them would have been achieved without a superior director. Steven Soderbergh is unquestionably a young man with a future; one hopes that the studios, instead of putting him to work making glossy big-budget movies that are indistinguishable from everybody else's, will give him the freedom to follow his own line of development.

Cross *Mary Poppins* with the old Cary Grant movie *Houseboat,* stir in a bit of *The Seven Little Foys* and *Little Miss Marker,* and you've got *Uncle Buck.* Well, sort of. Written and directed by John Hughes, the uncontested master of inane teen comedy-drama (*Sixteen Candles, The Breakfast Club, Ferris Bueller's Day Off*), *Uncle Buck* is the silly, derivative, but exceedingly amusing story of Buck Russell (John Candy), an undependable, quasi-shady (but goodhearted) bachelor who lives in a shabby walk-up in downtown Chicago, drives a dilapidated car that violates the emissions standards for a Boeing 747, bowls, smokes cigars, swills beer, fixes parking tickets, and bets on the ponies. Somewhere in there he makes a living. Oh, and he's got a fiancee (Amy Madigan)—a tough (but also goodhearted) dame whom Buck, like Nathan Detroit in *Guys and Dolls,* has been stringing along for years. The owner of a tire store, she wants Buck to straighten out, settle down, and work for her. And he's finally agreed to do so when an emergency late-night call comes from his brother, an upper-middle-class executive type who lives in the suburbs. A family illness, the brother says, requires him and his wife to be away for several days; black-sheep Buck is needed to take care of the kids.

So Buck heads for the suburbs. His brother has done such a good job of keeping him at arm's length that the two younger kids, a little boy named Miles (Macaulay Culkin) and a little girl named Maisie (Gaby Hoffman), don't even know they *have* an uncle. They take to Buck readily enough, however; it's their 15-year-old sister, Thea (Jean Kelly), who despises him on sight. But then—neglected as she is by her career-happy mother, and upset by the family's recent move from St. Louis—Thea despises everyone, including herself. She's so desperate for love, in fact, that she's about to go all the way with her creepy boyfriend, Bug—something that Buck, who doesn't share her parents' strictly laissez faire approach to these things, makes it his personal goal to prevent.

How? By any means possible, as it turns out: threatening the boy with an ax, advancing on him menacingly with a power tool, tying him up and stuffing him in the trunk. And this isn't the only problem Buck handles in his unique way. Called in by the school principal for a conference about Maisie's disciplinary problems, Buck soon loses his cool with the woman—a severe, exacting monster—and chews her out as only a Chicago racetrack regular could. Likewise, when a clown hired for Miles's birthday party shows up drunk and surly, Buck decks him in no-nonsense fashion. And—believe it or not—it's all hilarious.

What makes it so, of course, is Candy. An actor who was even remotely credible as a small-time racketeer—a Harry Dean Stanton, say, or a Robert Duvall—would scare the hell out of you in such a part. Not Candy. Paradoxically, he's ideal for the role precisely because he's so wrong for it. In his hands, Buck doesn't come across as ruthless and insensitive but as guileless and well-intentioned—he wants to do right by these kids, and axes and power tools and knockout punches are the only language he speaks. Likewise, when he cooks Maisie an ample breakfast of scrambled eggs and onions that even a starved linebacker couldn't finish—or when he packs an unopened tin of sardines in Miles's lunchbox—it's not because he doesn't care about the kids but because he doesn't know what's appropriate to the situation.

The movie takes a while to hit its stride. The opening scenes, which introduce the kids and their parents, are highly unpromising; Dad and Mom are vapid and witlessly acted, and when they leave (not to return till the closing sequence), one is thrilled to see them go. (The mother is particularly annoying; her face seems frozen in a grimace and at times she seems to think she's Glenda Jackson doing Ibsen.) Even Candy's first appearance—in a restaurant-table chat with his girlfriend that sets up their relationship—is static, colorless, unrevealing. But in Candy's second scene, everything clicks; jolted awake by his brother's phone call, Buck claps his hands loudly to turn on a lamp (he's got one of those "Clapper" devices) and Hughes cuts to a street shot to show lights going on all over the block. It's a funny gag, and from this point onward the humor (such as it is) stays dependably on track. (Indeed, this would've been perfect as Buck's introductory scene; the fiancée situation could quite easily have been set up afterward.)

This is not to suggest that Hughes's script and direction are anything more than competent. His main achievements are (a) not trying to make Buck "lovable," as is the dire fate of many comedians who appear in movies with kids, and (b) not getting too serious about the plot (i.e., dissolute uncle helps transform demoralized family, and vice-versa). Given even this middling material, however, Candy makes it work uproariously. Anyone who sees *Uncle Buck* will not soon forget, among other things, the sight of our extremely stout hero trying to make use of the tiny rest-room facilities in a grade school (an episode which Candy fans may recognize as a variation on the jockey-phone-booth bit in last year's *Who's Harry Crumb?*). His wonderful execution of this and similar bits suggests that Candy, with enough of the right material, could give the late, great Jackie Gleason a run for his money. Certainly he's one of the two or three funniest men in movies today, and this picture—though not quite worthy of his talents—is his best vehicle yet.

BETTE DAVIS, R.I.P.

Remembering Bette Davis

To view, in quick succession, a half dozen or so of the movies that Bette Davis made during what we may call her Golden Age—during the decade, in other words, between the late 1930s and the late 1940s—can be a rather startling experience. One is surprised, for one thing, to realize how exceedingly narrow an acting range Davis possessed. Like her contemporary Katharine Hepburn (whose striking looks she always envied), Davis specialized in "independent" women; but the characters and stories that she burned into our memories are far less varied than those for which Hepburn did similar honors. While Hepburn, for instance, moved smoothly—and without losing any of her authority and allure and presence—from screwball comedy (*Bringing Up Baby*) to sophisticated comedy (*The Philadelphia Story*) to Tennessee Williams (*Suddenly Last Summer*) to Eugene O'Neill (*Long Day's Journey Into Night*), Davis excelled only within a strictly confined territory. The queen of the so-called women's picture, she specialized in melodramatic heroines who were either outrageously blunt and headstrong or pathetically meek and self-sacrificing or some remarkable combination of the two.

To be sure, she performed capably enough in an urbane romantic farce like *It's Love I'm After* (1937), in which she played half of a jealous, competitive Lunt-and-Fontanne-type Broadway acting team (Leslie Howard played the other half)—but from a 52-year distance she seems oddly misplaced in the role. Her talent is there, but *she* isn't—or, perhaps one should say, her distinctive personal magnetism isn't. It's as if somebody forgot to turn on all the lights. And without those lights on, the talent seems astonishingly run-of-the-mill.

But if one is surprised by the narrowness of Davis's range, one is surprised, too, to notice how masterfully she worked within that range, how skilled she was at making each of her heroines utterly distinctive. For, though they're mostly variations on a handful of familiar types, there's no mistaking Davis's most renowned heroines for one another. They even carry themselves differently: the spinster schoolteacher Miss Moffat in *The Corn Is Green* (1945) treads firmly and resolutely, without a wasted motion, while the spinster heiress Charlotte Vale in *Now, Voyager* (1942) strolls with a graceful sweep, vivacious and self-confident; belle-of-the-ball Fanny Skeffington in *Mr. Skeffington* (1944) glides coquettishly, while belle-of-the-ball Julie Marston in *Jezebel* (1938) moves with every step as if she's trying to pull away from someone's grasp.

One is struck, too, by how contrived the stories of Davis's best films are. They're full of people going blind, of letters that destroy people's lives, of mothers who keep their motherhood secret over decades (with, needless to say, disastrous results). In not one but two movies—*A Stolen Life* (1946) and *Dead Ringer* (1964)—Davis plays twin sisters, one of whom loves the other's husband and (after her death) masquerades as her in order to possess her husband. Implausible transformations abound (making possible a tour-de-force Davis switch from meek to headstrong or vice-versa): in *Dark Victory* (1939), the frivolous, fun-loving heiress Judith Traherne learns she's suffering from a fatal brain tumor, and (after marrying her doctor) dies with selfless stoicism; in *Now, Voyager,* the shy, sexless, mother-dominated Back Bay heiress Charlotte Vale is changed by a psychiatrist (Claude Rains) and by a married man named Jerry Durrance (Paul Henreid), whom she meets and falls in love with on a South American cruise, into a model of poise, conviviality, and romantic passion; and in *Mr. Skeffington,* the shallow, self-indulgent belle Fanny Skeffington is given a chance to redeem herself as a loving helpmeet when diphtheria robs her of her extraordinary beauty (and of her legion of admirers), and fate brings to her doorstep the still-adoring but now penniless ex-husband (Claude Rains) whom she cruelly neglected throughout their marriage, and who has (conveniently) lost his sight and therefore will always see her as beautiful. (Got that?)

There's no getting around the fact that these are soap-opera stories about soap-opera characters. At the same time, however, one is struck by how engrossing these films remain a half-century later, by how sympathetic Davis's heroines are, how compelling their often inane predicaments seem. To watch Davis's best movies is to be fortified in one's judgment that they are decidedly not art—but it is also to come away with the conviction that nobody else in the history of the medium has ever been connected with a series of films that so superbly embody the idea of pure screen entertainment. Granted, there is a camp element to these pictures: watching *Now, Voyager,* one smiles at the famous business with the cigarettes (as you may remember, Henreid lights two of them in his mouth, hands one to Davis, and they blow smoke into each other's faces while staring deeply into each other's eyes; this happens *at least* three times); watching *Mr. Skeffington,* one laughs at the idea of Bette Davis being the most ravishing woman in New York.[1] But at the same time one is hooked; these stories grab one's attention in the opening moments and don't let go until the final credits.

It was not ever thus. Arriving in Hollywood in 1930, Davis began her movie career with a string of thirty-odd pictures, mostly quite forgettable, in many of which her roles were extremely small. Throughout this period, she played tough, even shady types: gangsters' widows, lowlife flirts, hard-boiled nightclub hostesses. Among her few plum roles was that of the crass, licentious waitress, Mildred Rogers, to Leslie Howard's sensitive, lovesick medical student in the widely admired but rather dull *Of Human Bondage* (1934). A year later came *Dangerous,* which won Davis the first of two Academy Awards, and which inspired one reviewer to comment that "Bette Davis would probably have been burned as a witch if she had lived two or three hundred years ago. She gives the curious feeling of being charged with power which can find no ordinary outlet."

That power found its first major outlet in *Jezebel* (1938), for which Davis won her second Oscar. Julie Marston—the antebellum Southern belle whose neurotic willfulness destroys her hopes of romantic happiness—was the first of many remarkably intense, passionate heroines. Julie was succeeded, in *The Old Maid* (1939), by Charlotte Lovell, a Civil War-era Philadelphia woman who allows her child,

[1]One must add, however, that Davis leaves the distinct impression that she's laughing, too; part of the point of the movie is that Fanny is an absurd creature, and part of its achievement is that it manages to make her at once a joke and an object of pathos.

born out of wedlock, to be raised by her vengeful cousin Delia (Miriam Hopkins); unable to acknowledge her parenthood as she watches the child grow to maturity, Charlotte turns from a sweet young woman into an embittered, misanthropic old spinster.

Charlotte was hardly Davis's only old maid. Indeed, while she played very few mothers, Davis portrayed quite a few spinsters (including—twice—the most eminent one in all history, Queen Elizabeth I). Many of these spinsters are women who—to borrow a phrase from Davis's eponymous character in *The Nanny* (1965)—take care of "other people's children": Charlotte in *The Old Maid* runs a nursery school; Lilly Moffat in *The Corn Is Green* (1945) is a schoolteacher in a Welsh mining town who, at the end of the film, agrees to raise her prize student's bastard child while he attends Oxford on a scholarship; Henriette Deluzy in *All This, and Heaven Too* (1940) is a governess and later a schoolteacher; Charlotte Vale in *Now, Voyager* takes Jerry's troubled daughter Tina into her house and mothers her.

Part of the strategy in such movies, of course, is to win our sympathy for heroines who are big on sacrifice and who, as Henriette says, "must be content with picking up a few crumbs of happiness from other people's tables." When Henriette's employer, the Duc de Praslin (Charles Boyer), with whom she shares a deep but unconsummated love, asks about the lack of fulfillment in her life, she replies: "I have the children and even though they're not mine I sometimes imagine they are." Charlotte Vale responds in like fashion when Jerry poses her a similar question: "When Tina said she wanted to come home and stay with me it was like a miracle happening—like having your child, a part of you—and I even allowed myself to indulge in the fancy that both of us loving her and doing what was best for her together would make her seem actually like our child after a while . . ."

These are women for whom devotion to children is, in large part, a form of sublimation; they approach young people not with a mother's equipoise but with the outsized ardor of women who lack any alternative object of passion. Consequently, they're ideal characters for Davis, who was a natural at embodying fervent devotion, a not-so-natural at quiet fidelity. It's not surprising that in those few films in which Davis does play a quietly loving mother—in *Watch on the Rhine* (1943), for example—she seems oddly passive and unconvincing as such. She is far more believable when playing an indifferent mother like Fanny Skeffington, or a substitute mother like Charlotte

Vale or Maggie Patterson in *The Great Lie* (1941), or a mother, like Charlotte Lovell, who is made vicious by her inability to tell her daughter that she *is* her daughter and not her niece; certainly one of the most memorable mother-daughter relationships in any of Davis's films is that in *The Little Foxes* (1941) between her ruthless, tyrannical Regina Giddens—as monstrous a character as ever filled a movie screen—and Teresa Wright's meek, defenseless Alexandra. (Davis plays an equally despotic matriarch, incidentally, in the bizarre 1968 film *The Anniversary*.)

As her performance in a role like Regina Gibbens demonstrates, Davis believed unapologetically that motion-picture characters should be at once lifelike and bigger than life. And at her best, she was capable of giving an appearance of magnitude and depth—and even of intelligence—to characters whose actual lack of dimension would, in other hands, have been painfully manifest. But an actress who aims always for bigger-than-life performances must exercise consistent and rigorous self-control to avoid becoming merely flamboyant, garish, histrionic; and it is no secret that Davis did not always succeed entirely in this regard. Even in her finest performances she could not completely avoid gratuitous mannerisms and moments of hamminess; it is no coincidence, surely, that this actress, who at times reminded one a bit too forcefully that she was indeed acting, played more than her share of actresses, from Joyce Heath in *Dangerous* and Joyce Arden in *It's Love I'm After* to Margaret Elliott in *The Star* (1952) and Baby Jane Hudson in the incredibly goofy *Whatever Happened to Baby Jane?* (1961).

Self-control, alas, apparently became increasingly hard for Davis. After the late 1940s she grew more and more prone to self-parody, seemingly reveling in her broad trademark gestures, and sometimes offering little more by way of a performance than stiff comportment, tart and halting line readings, and periodic rolling of those protuberant Bette Davis eyes. (Then again, most of her vehicles of the past couple of decades were tawdry TV movies and gruesome horror flicks with titles like *Scream, Pretty Peggy*, none of which deserved any better from her.) It is no coincidence that her best work after the late 1940s—in *All About Eve* (1950)—was in the role of a stage actress, Margo Channing, who had a decidedly theatrical manner, and that part of the reason for the success of Davis's other most celebrated later role, in *Baby Jane*, was that the film provided a sound dramatic context for extreme immoderation on her part. As for her wonderfully restrained performance in *The Nanny*—a first-rate Hitchcock-style thriller about an unobtrusive English governess bent on murder—it seems almost miraculous, coming as it did between the grisly *Hush . . . Hush, Sweet Charlotte* (1964) and *The Anniversary,* for both of which Davis pulled out a great many more stops than was probably advisable.

Yet what makes Bette Davis worth remembering is not the failings of her weakest work but the high caliber of her strongest. At her best, she mesmerized, lending a semblance of urgency to material that might otherwise (as a reviewer suggested of *Dark Victory*) be dismissed as "emotional claptrap." In *Now, Voyager, The Old Maid, Mr. Skeffington,* and half a dozen other movies she leaves us a collection of supremely captivating diversions that, for what they have managed for so long to do so well, have rarely been surpassed.

DOPES ON DOPE

Drugstore Cowboy

Finally, a movie whose characters we can all identify with. Twenty-six-year-old Bob Hughes (Matt Dillion), the eponymous hero of *Drugstore Cowboy,* is a full-time dope fiend. So are his wife, Dianne (Kelly Lynch), his sidekick, Rick (James Le Gross), and Rick's girlfriend, Nadine (Heather Graham). It's 1971, and these four adorable kids live together in Portland, Oregon, where—since none of them holds down a job—they spend their days jabbing hypodermic needles into their arms and ripping off local pharmacies. A scene early in the movie illustrates their *modus operandi:* Nadine distracts the druggist and his customers by faking an epileptic seizure near the doorway; meanwhile, Bob slips nimbly behind the prescription counter and empties a drawer full of controlled substances; Dianne helps keep attention away from the counter, and on the way out steals a paperback copy of *Love Story* from a rack (she's the literary one); and Rick drives the getaway car. Bob's so eager to get his fix that he starts shooting up on the way home. As he explains in retrospective voice-over, dope delivered him from the unpredictability of life: "Most people don't know what's going to happen next. But a dope fiend's got a pretty good idea. All you have to do is read the labels on the little bottles." And what happened next, when he shot up, was invariably glorious: "Everything took on the rosy hue of unlimited success. As long as it lasted, life was beautiful."

And, for a while, to Bob and company, the beauty of this drug-engendered escape from reality seems well worth all the trouble of knocking over Rexall's and getting hassled by the fuzz. These kids have *fun* being junkies. They play games. For example, when two plainclothesmen stake out their second-floor pad from a ladder, Bob tells a neighbor that one of the cops is a peeping tom, and the neighbor—who, quite conveniently, proves to be the neighborhood maniac—blows the lawman away with a rifle. Cute, no? It's not till Bob and his friends leave Portland for a cross-country drive that things turn sour. Bob almost gets caught breaking into a hospital pharmacy; Nadine—who has deliberately flouted the extraordinarily superstitious Bob's injunction against putting a hat on a bed—dies of an overdose. Suddenly Bob does an about-face: he wants to stop doing drugs. Dianne and Rick think he's crazy, and won't have anything to do with it. So Bob returns alone to Portland, takes a monotonous factory job, rents a grim little apartment, and goes on a 21-day methadone program.

Too bad. For up till Nadine's death the movie has a certain gritty, disturbing power. The characters feel real, the action darkly compelling: though director Gus Van Sant and his co-writer Dan Yost hardly overload the film with plot, they know something about dramatic shape and pacing, and they're gifted with a genuine—if aberrant—wit. (Well, *somebody* is; perhaps it's James Fogle, the Washington State jailbird from whose unpublished, largely autobiographical novel this picture was adapted.) But once Bob returns to Portland the whole contraption falls apart. His transformation doesn't convince for a second. Nor does his explanation help matters much: as he tells Dianne, he was so freaked out by Nadine's death that he vowed he'd kick the habit if only God or the Devil or Whoever Was Up There helped him get safely through the ordeal of disposing of her body. He stuck to the vow, you see, because he's so superstitious; and he's so superstitious (it's implied) because he was brought up a pious Catholic. But this just doesn't work dramatically, for neither Bob's immoderate superstition nor his Catholicism is ever made to seem a truly integral part of his character; from the moment that it's introduced, the superstition comes off as a feeble joke on the part of the filmmakers, a wacky quirk of character that doesn't quite click into place, while the Catholicism is barely established at all.

Nor do the filmmakers seem to have a clear idea what they're doing in this latter part of the film; the scenes—Bob at work, Bob at an ex-junkie rap session, and so forth—follow each other in a meaningless jumble. And a *dull* jumble, for while the lawless, amoral, drug-addicted Bob of the earlier part of the film is at least interesting to watch, the drug-free Bob is downright boring. The movie flounders badly, then, until its dramatically unsatisfying conclusion—a conclusion whose impact derives entirely from a graphically depicted act of violence, and whose intended irony falls completely flat because it presumes a level of sympathy for Bob, on the part of the audience, that is utterly inconceivable.

And that's a big problem with *Drugstore Cowboy:* Bob is completely, undividedly, and utterly unsympathetic. This young man who doesn't give a moment's thought to anyone else (including the members of his make shift "family"), and for whose perfect insensitivity the filmmakers don't even try to hint at a coherent motivation, is impossible to care about. Not only does he lack a single redeeming feature; aside from his superstition, his encyclopedic knowledge of narcotics, and his apparent indifference to sex (quoth Dianne: "Bob's just like a rabbit: in and out, and no nonsense—and that goes for a lot more than a hospital pharmacy"), there isn't much of a character here. Nor do we have any sense of what drove him to drugs in the first place, aside from the aforementioned fact that they made life beautiful. It's part of the implicit argument of this movie, indeed, that drugs *do* make life seem beautiful, that in order to treat the subject of drug addiction realistically a filmmaker must begin by owning up to this fact, and that if there *is* a reason why you can't stick with drugs forever it's surely not that they fail to live up to their rep or that the obligatory criminality might eventually make you feel remorseful. Which is also part of the problem with this film: Bob doesn't quit drugs because he comes to realize that it's wrong for him to be robbing pharmacies, sponging off society, getting cops shot up, breaking his poor mother's heart, and so forth; nor does he quit because he wants to do himself a favor. Rather, he quits because of an asinine superstition. (As he puts it: "I like drugs. I like the whole life-style. But it just didn't work out.") His reversal is thus both dramatically inert and ethically meaningless.

The moral bankruptcy of the film is underlined by the presence in the later Portland sequences of the elderly Beat novelist William S. Burroughs (*Naked Lunch, Junky*). Burroughs plays Tom Murphy, a ruminative, soft-spoken ex-priest who is "the most notorious dope fiend on the Coast" and whom Bob (a former altar boy) has known since his childhood. It's a disturbing bit of casting. What, one must ask, is Burroughs doing here? He's arguably the most despicable creature in the history of American letters (if you don't know why, next time you're in a bookstore grab Ted Morgan's 1988 biography of him, *Literary Outlaw,* and open it to any page), and the filmmakers obviously expect us to recognize him and to identify him with his character. But why? Why place this vile, unscrupulous old monster in the role of a gentle sage to whom Bob says, "You should've been a philosopher"? Are Van Sant and company suggesting that they want their film to be seen as a cinematic counterpart to Burroughs's appalling, amoral, egocentric novels? Certainly some of the film's "wisdom" (e.g., "You can buck the system, but you can't buck the deep forces that lie beneath the surface") sounds suspiciously like the kind of fatuously anarchic and penny-ante mystical nonsense that Burroughs serves up in his books.

The movie has a weird tone, one that combines a TV movie-style earnestness about drug addiction with an irreverent, absurdist waggery about the subject. The film tries to get you to laugh at all sorts of things, at the wacky as well as the grisly—at, for instance, Rick's unremitting literalmindedness; at Bob's perverse superstitiousness; at the way Bob's runaway dog (in one of several brief, goofy, extraneous flashbacks) leads the police to his door after a crime; at the sight of that undercover cop being shot by that rifle-toting neighbor; at the way Bob, walking into a room to find Nadine dead, barks, "Who left this hat on the bed?"; at Father Tom's pious gratitude for Bob's stash ("God bless you, my son, may you go to heaven") and his blunt dismissal of certain items contained therein ("This is for squares—never touch the stuff"). Sometimes you do find yourself laughing—and sometimes you find yourself a bit stunned at everyone else's amusement.

Yet these touches of comedy seem frequently to be at odds with the film's non-comedic aims. One laughs not because the filmmakers have humorously illuminated some aspect of the movie's theme or of its protagonists, but because they've interjected a piece of action or a line of dialogue so extreme in its stupidity, its evil, or its ludicrousness that it serves to remind one—to one's great relief—either (a) that this is just a *movie,* and not reality, or (b) that these characters are so inane and despicable that their fate is not worth getting anxious about. If the Coen brothers (*Blood Simple, Raising Arizona*) are better than Van Sant at mocking the vapid and malevolent, it's because the Coens' jests are more sharply and insistently focused (it's always clear whom they're satirizing and why) and because their satire is given spirit and purpose by a keen, if highly idiosyncratic, moral faculty; in *Drugstore Cowboy*, by contrast, the gags pop up when least expected, and tend (in the "tradition" of Burroughs and his fellow Beats) to be pretentiously and pointlessly nihilistic. The Coens' well-aimed ridicule distances them morally from their characters; Van Sant's scattershot japery makes him seem a veritable accomplice in his characters' anarchic malfeasance.

I don't mean to suggest that the film doesn't have some noteworthy assets. Whether because he has developed remarkably as an actor or because he has been allowed here to play a character who is shallow and inarticulate enough not to strain him beyond his limits, Matt Dillon is generally convincing as Bob. Le Gross likewise rings true as the dense and tractable Rick. James Remar, for his part, is very fine as a tenacious Portland cop named Gentry who takes a provocative but ultimately implausible interest in Bob. (Whether the attraction is sexual, or whether Gentry—the very embodiment of law and order—envies Bob's rebelliousness, remains ambiguous.) For the most part, moreover, Robert Yeoman's photography is at once exquisite and appropriately naturalistic—though his terse, surrealistic representations of Bob's drug-induced euphoria feel clumsy and curiously old-fashioned.

The film offers, then, a vivid close-up view of the world it surveys. Yet its perspective on that world is more than a bit cockeyed. You get the feeling that the filmmakers think there's something potent and honest and unsentimental about their morally neutral, self-centered vision of life, about the fact that Bob—for all he goes through—comes away with little in the way of moral insight ("It's this f—ing life," he says in his valedictory voice-over speech; "you never know what's going to happen next"), and about the irony that Bob's final downfall, after all his years of selfishness, is a direct consequence of the only two generous acts one sees him performing in the entire picture.

Yet, for all its toughness, the film is not free of a certain Beat-style sentimentality. For one thing, the picture opens with a tenderly nostalgic vocal arrangement of the wonderful standard "For All We Know," the romanticism of which may well be intended ironically, though it doesn't come off that way. For another thing, Bob and

Dianne, despite their heavy use of narcotics, are as pretty as can be, and look young for their ages to boot. This film would've been a lot more respectable a work of realism if Van Sant had dared to put people in the title roles who *looked* like 26-year-old drug addicts.

MANHATTAN MELODRAMA, BAYOU BANTER

Crimes and Misdemeanors
Steel Magnolias

Woody Allen's *Crimes and Misdemeanors* begins with a black-tie banquet at which Judah Rosenthal (Martin Landau), a sixtyish, affluent, distinguished-looking New York ophthalmologist, is being saluted for his fundraising efforts on behalf of a new hospital wing. It's not long before you know you're in Woody Allen territory: when a colleague raises a toast, he hails Judah as a man who can tell you the name of "the best hotel in Moscow, the best restaurant in Paris, the best recording of a particular Mozart symphony." This gauche, unintentionally daffy equation of great art and *la dolce vita* is vintage Allen; Judah—the public Judah, anyway—is plainly Allen's idea of what every man would like to be. And the best thing he has going for him, it would seem, is his long and happy marriage to the lovely Miriam (Claire Bloom).

Yet, as it develops, everything's not coming up roses for the Rosenthals. Unbeknownst to Miriam, Judah's been having an affair for over two years with a dumpy middle-aged stewardess named Dolores Paley (Anjelica Huston). This unstable dame is threatening to tattle not only to Miriam but to the hospital authorities (into whose funds, it appears, Judah unwisely dipped a while back when he was having cash-flow problems). Judah's in a quandary: as he explains to his patient Ben (Sam Waterston), a rabbi who's gradually losing his eyesight, Miriam would never forgive him for having an affair. What to do? To his horror, he's tempted to call his lowlife brother Jack (Jerry Orbach)—who knows how to arrange a rub-out and has no qualms about doing so.

Meanwhile, another marriage—between Ben's aloof, cranky sister Wendy (Joanna Gleason) and her filmmaker husband Clifford (Woody Allen)—is also on the ropes. Clifford's a specialist in pious, low-budget documentaries on acid rain and toxic waste, and Wendy can't help comparing his pathetic career highlights (e.g., honorable mention in a Cincinnati documentary film festival) with the glorious achievements of her brother Lester (Alan Alda), a rich sitcom producer with "a closet full of Emmys." In what seems a last-ditch attempt to turn Clifford around, Wendy arranges for him to do a profile of Lester for a public-TV series; yet Clifford's more interested in getting the series' associate producer, Halley Reed (Mia Farrow), with whom he finds himself becoming infatuated, to back his work-in-progress on the elderly philosopher Louis Levy (Martin Bergmann). Thus we have two protagonists, *Doppelgängern* of sorts, each of them a Jewish man lured by the attractions of a gentile woman into a solemn moral predicament. The questions before us: Will Judah order a hit on Dolores? Will Clifford desert Wendy in short order and hit on Halley?

Plainly, love and death remain Allen's major themes. (Indeed, the title *Crimes and Misdemeanors* might be seen as something of a variation on the title *Love and Death,* with the emphasis this time being not on emotional abstraction but on morally meaningful action: the misdemeanor being adultery, the crime murder.) This is not the first time, moreover, that Allen has placed tenuously connected plots alongside each other: *Hannah and Her Sisters* is the most notable previous example. But the stories in that film fit together in a way that the stories of Judah and Clifford don't. Their connection feels entirely theoretical; they may reflect Allen's enchantment with a single set of ideas, but they don't strike one as authentic components of a single vision.

And *ideas* is the operative word here. While waiting to find out what Judah and Clifford will do, we listen in on lots of Philosophy 101 chitchat. Judah, we learn, finds the world "harsh and empty of values and pitiless"; Ben counters that it manifests a "moral structure and higher power." Clifford and Halley exchange similarly weighty remarks. This sort of stilted, ponderous give-and-take has made for awkward moments in Allen's movies ever since *Annie Hall,* but he usually gets through them fast enough to avoid major damage. *Interiors* and *September* were exceptions; so, alas, is *Crimes and Misdemeanors.* Contributing to the devastation is Allen's most fully orchestrated attempt yet at symbolism, wherein everybody in the picture makes constant references to eyes, blindness, vision, and the like, all of which are meant to allude to a frequently quoted remark by Judah's late father, a rabbi (seen in flashback), to the effect that "the eyes of God are on us always." This pattern of symbolic references is grotesquely overdone and thoroughly mechanical, a textbook example of symbolism-by-the-textbook.

But then virtually all of Allen's post-*Love and Death* movies have been blemished, to some degree, by his intellectual and artistic pretensions. If the strongest of them were nonetheless redeemed by their engaging stories, their sympathetic (or, at least, credible) characters, and (above all) their humor, such is not the case here. Throughout *Crimes and Misdemeanors,* one feels strangely distant from the characters, many of whom conform too tidily to Allen prototypes. Lester, for example, is a vapid retread of the Tony Roberts character in *Annie Hall;* Levy (whose big surprise later in the picture is no surprise at all if you've seen *La Dolce Vita*) recalls the aging artist played by Max Von Sydow in *Hannah and Her Sisters.* (Levy is, incidentally, the only character in any of Allen's films whose spoutings on love, death, God, and the meaning of life rise consistently above the sophomoric; it's dismaying, then, to discover that Bergmann—who is, in real life, a Manhattan psychiatrist—improvised most of his own stuff.) Woody Allen is, as ever, Woody Allen, but here, more than usually, he counts on our previous acquaintance with and presumed affection for him to give his character dimension and empathy.

Nor are the situations particularly fresh. As a friend of mine commented, "I wish I had a nickel for every scene in a Woody Allen movie where he proposes marriage to somebody in Central Park." Certainly some of Allen's pet ideas and motifs have worn dangerously thin: the notion of a grown-up protagonist peeking in on an agonizing dinner-table scene of his childhood; the stiff, devout name-dropping of bygone artists, composers, and poets (and of that supreme temple of learning, Columbia University); the celebration of innocence, in the form of children; the celebration of movies as both reality's mirror and its escape hatch; and the celebration of artistry—as invariably personified by Woody Allen—over commercial claptrap. Many of the film's subsidiary characters, moreover, tend to be contrived (Ben with his emblematic blindness; Judah's father with his handy aphorisms), and many of the motivations dubious. (Would Judah really have gotten entangled with a dreary harridan like Dolores? And would his fear of Miriam's wrath really cause him to contemplate murder?)

What damages the film more than anything, however, is its posture toward Judah's and Clifford's respective transgressions. Murder is in the air here, but the ultimate sin in Allen's world is plainly not homicide but fornication. Whereas Judah's debates over whether to have Delores slaughtered are relatively brief, mannerly, and low-key (coming off as little more than *pro forma*), Clifford's hysterical carryings-on about Halley seem interminable. Truth to tell, Allen is far more captivated by the misdemeanor of sexual dalliance than by the high crime of murder. Underneath all the gags, his is a harsh Old Testament world in which the Jewish husband is sinner and the infidel woman the occasion of sin; Judah and Clifford lust after shiksas in the same way they lust after (respectively) high and pop Western culture. (It seems no coincidence that Judah's favorite composer is Schubert—an Austrian!—and that Clifford is seen viewing a movie with the definitive Wasp title of *Mr. and Mrs. Smith.*) But Allen's apparent newfound esteem for Jehovah feels slick, insincere; though his message is presumably that, in order to behave decently, we must believe God's eyes are on us, he doesn't convince us for a minute that it's a lack of religious conviction that makes possible Judah and Clifford's ethical waverings. (He doesn't even convince us that this is what *he* believes.) *Crimes and Misdemeanors* pays homage to the Almighty, in short, in the same superficial way that earlier Allen films have paid homage to Bergman and Fellini.

Robert Harling's play *Steel Magnolias,* which can currently be seen at the Lucille Lortel Theater in New York, is a two-act, four-scene, six-character hen session set in a Chinquapin, Louisiana, beauty parlor. The men are all offstage, and a miserable lot they are: Truvy, the bighearted, self-styled "glamour technician," has a spouse who lies around all day and sponges off her; Annelle, her bashful assistant, has just been deserted by a husband who's wanted on drug charges; Ouiser, a wealthy, cantankerous regular patron, has been so embittered by two lousy marriages that she shows affection only to her mangy dog; M'Lynn, another regular, is married to a goofball who spends every spare moment shooting at birds and beasts; and as the play opens, M'Lynn's daughter, Shelby, is about to wed a selfish young lawyer.

The point is clear: men are thoughtless, childish, irresponsible—and they're not even the one thing they're supposed to be, *strong*. When M'Lynn's family suffers a crisis, her mate folds up helplessly, and to her surprise she's the one who hangs tough. They're *all* tough, these delicate flowers of Dixie (thus, of course, the title). And they're funny, too: the catty crosstalk is consistently entertaining. The only problem, aside from the creaky exposition and uneven acting, is that the characters often remind one less of Southern belles than of the boys in Mort Crowley's *The Boys in the Band:* Harling's humor, in other words, can be extremely campy, and one comes across locutions, references, and touches of sensibility here that seem to have less to do with small-town Louisiana womanhood than with the milieu of the thoroughfare—namely, Christopher Street in Greenwich Village—on which the Lucille Lortel Theater is situated. If Tennessee Williams had written *The Women,* it might've come out something like this.

Directed by Herbert Ross from a script by Harling, the movie version of *Steel Magnolias* stays close to the text of the play (though some of the more caustic lines about men and religion have been omitted) while opening up the action quite effectively. The cast is a mixed bag: Dolly Parton is splendidly right for Truvy, whose motto is "There's no such thing as natural beauty," and Olympia Dukakis does a perfect job as Clairee, the rich, gracious, quip-happy widow of the town's longtime mayor. But the neat little part of Annelle is wasted on Daryl Hannah (Flannery O'Connor would've understood this role, but Daryl doesn't), and Julia *(Mystic Pizza)* Roberts barely makes an impression as Shelby.

The big disappointment is Sally Field, who fails to have a single natural moment as M'Lynn, her accent wandering all over the place (but then, so did those in *Gone With the Wind:* bad Southern accents are a proud tradition of Hollywood movies) and her Big Scene toward the end of the movie coming across as little more than a bid for a third Oscar. (You keep expecting her to look into the camera and wail: "Do you still like me?") The sad part is that it's a good, solid role; one would've liked to see Tess Harper, Christine Lahti, or Jessica Lange take a stab at it. As for Shirley MacLaine, she's dreadfully miscast as Ouiser, and her presence makes one realize how similar this story is to her schlocky *Terms of Endearment,* the main difference being that the eccentric, misanthropic, fanatically possessive mother of that movie splits in two here, into the eccentric, misanthropic Ouiser and the fanatically possessive mother M'Lynn.

One wonders why the producers of *Steel Magnolias* bothered to drag this predominantly Yankee cast down bayou way: though it was shot in the author's hometown of Natchitoches, the film only intermittently captures the flavor of the Deep South. For instance, though Harling has fleshed out the *dramatis personae* with a few males (including Tom Skerritt as M'Lynn's husband), the only black person I remember seeing in the whole picture was an affluent-looking guest at Shelby's wedding. Not since Mayberry, on the old "Andy Griffith Show," has anyone committed to celluloid a more thoroughly caucasian Southern burg. (I'm not quota-mongering, you understand; I'm just saying this odd deficiency robs the movie of realism.) It would've helped, too, if instead of opting for the usual big-budget glossy-realistic cinematography, the filmmakers had gone for photography that was just a bit more stylized (or, at least, nearer to the look of *sex, lies, and videotape,* which captured Louisiana nicely without hitting you over the head with atmosphere). And rather than commission the syrupy standard Movie Music that has been provided by Georges Delerue *(Jules et Jim, Julia, A Little Romance),* they might've done better to slap together a score out of the sort of country-and-western tunes that Harling's play uses as a bridge.

But the film is in many respects an improvement over the two-acter. By adding a few scenes that take place in a hospital, and by transferring much of the beauty-parlor action to M'Lynn's house (and, in the climactic sequence, to a cemetery), Harding lends credibility to the catastrophe at the center of his story, making it—as well as the beauty parlor—seem less of a structural artifice than it does in the play. A number of other big new sequences, furthermore—among them Shelby's wedding, a Christmas festival, and a riverside Easter get-together—are fitting and funny, even if the sight gags (e.g., a wedding cake with gray frosting in the shape of an armadillo) do fall a tad too often into the category of Southern tawdry-grotesque, Beth Henley division. On the whole, indeed, notwithstanding all its imperfections, *Steel Magnolias* is well worth seeing; quite simply, it's a top-notch amusement—a genuinely diverting movie at a time when funny film comedy can seem as rare as magnolias in January.

EGO TRIPS

Roger and Me
Henry V
Enemies: A Love Story

Michael Moore is lucky: he was born in one of America's most economically depressed cities, Flint, Michigan. I say lucky because Moore has now, with his documentary *Roger and Me,* become famous off his hometown's misfortunes. He's become just as famous, in fact, as his nemesis Roger Smith, longtime chairman of General Motors and the Roger of Moore's title, who helped send Flint's economy into a tailspin, a few years back, when he and his board began closing plants there and opening new ones in Mexico. Moore's film portrays Smith as a distant, impassive, and amorally calculating CEO; painstakingly contrasted with him throughout is Moore, who depicts himself as an earnest, hapless little schmo, the David to Roger's Goliath (and the proud son of a sometime GM worker), who wants nothing more than to speak to Roger and bring him to Flint, where GM was founded, so that Roger can see the harm he's caused and take action to restore prosperity.

Moore is, however, no camera-toting Common Man. On the contrary, as the film never acknowledges, he's a notorious figure in Flint. Yes, Moore does mention his past editorship of the *Flint Voice* (the local equivalent to New York's *Village Voice*); what he fails to tell us is what a high-profile editor he was, renowned for his leftist zealotry and tireless self-aggrandizement. He tells us, too, about the editorial job he held briefly in San Francisco, from which he was fired for (he implies) being too much of a renegade; what he fails to tell us is that the job was with the far-left *Mother Jones,* whose editors reportedly found him too radical even for them.

Shorn of this political history, however, and disguised as a Capra-esque Everyman whose lifelong trust in corporate paternalism has been shaken to its roots by Roger Smith's perfidy, Moore is not too radical for anybody. Certainly, if the audience with which I saw *Roger and Me* is any indication, Moore is winning the yuppie crowd over with his comedy—which is no wonder, for his sense of humor is as mean-spirited and condescending as David Letterman's. Time and again, Moore invites us to laugh at poor folks because they're still benighted enough to believe that The System will save them. And he jeers endlessly at the bourgeoisie, cutting (in a typical sequence) from a scene in which a poor Flint family is being evicted for nonpayment of rent to a scene in which he interviews some elderly lady golfers at a local course. We're supposed to laugh at the foolish answers they give to his questions about the poor, supposed to see them as heartless for golfing when people are being thrown out of their homes. But it's Moore who's heartless, ambushing seemingly decent folks, implicitly indicting them as co-conspirators with GM simply because they can afford to golf, and editing his footage in such a way as to make even their modest pleasures seem brutally insensitive.

Like Letterman, too, Moore gets a lot of mileage out of ridiculing vapid showbiz figures. A favorite conceit throughout the film is that some visiting celebrity—Pat Boone, Anita Bryant, Bob Eubanks, Miss Michigan—has come to "save" Flint; Moore interviews each of these celebrities, and we are invited to laugh at their ignorance of Flint's economic problems (as if we were all that familiar with them an hour earlier!) and at their simpleminded instant optimism about the city's economy, an optimism which contrasts sharply with the scenes of boarded-up houses and abandoned auto plants that Moore has been showing us. But Moore's attention to these celebs gives new meaning to the phrase "easy target." And didn't we tire of laughing at Pat Boone and Anita Bryant years ago?

More than once while watching *Roger and Me,* I was reminded of Ross McElwee and his documentary *Sherman's March.* Just as McElwee (a Georgian) squeezed easy laughs out of the Southern commonfolk on whom he trained his camera, so Moore has gotten comedy mileage out of Flint locals; just as McElwee made a running gag of his nominal interest in General Sherman, so Moore has made a running gag of his less-than-serious attempt to wangle an interview with Roger Smith; and just as McElwee (an egomaniac in hapless schmo's clothing) put himself at the center of his film, so Moore has made himself the hero of *Roger and Me*. (Like McElwee, incidentally, Moore managed to get his hands on government money: *Roger and Me* was partly funded by the Michigan Council on the Arts.)

There's no question but that Roger Smith made decisions that hurt Flint, and the worst of all—in the view of a friend of mine from Flint who attended the movie with me—wasn't even mentioned in the film: an entire residential neighborhood was razed so GM could build a plant it soon abandoned. But there are aspects to the situation that Moore deliberately ignores. "What really ruined Flint," my friend said after the movie, "was that the UAW got too strong and made increasingly ridiculous demands on an industry that was losing ground to the Japanese. Of course GM went to Mexico: thanks to the UAW, it couldn't *afford* to have cars made in Flint anymore. By the time the UAW's power waned, it was too late for Flint."

These are points that Moore allows no one to make in his film. Patently, he doesn't want to deal with complicated truths, especially those that might weaken his case against GM. Thus, he describes GM repeatedly as "the richest company in the world"—as if there were at its disposal an unlimited supply of funds that it could (if so inclined) dole out to Flint's poor for ever and ever—but he never mentions the precipitous decline in the company's market share during the seventies and eighties. Likewise, Moore habitually implies cause-and-effect connections that may or may not actually obtain: my Flint friend asserted, for instance, that the deterioration of Flint's downtown had less to do with GM's pullout than with the opening of a new shopping center—the Genesee Valley Mall—on the outskirts of town.

Needless to say, Moore's attack on corporate callousness is profoundly disingenuous: he, of all people, knows how business operates. He's the very definition of an operator: *Roger and Me* exploits Flint as surely as GM ever did, and Moore is certainly as arrogant as any CEO. His ego trip of a film has become a success not because it sheds light on a significant and complex predicament (it doesn't), but because it entertains its audience—at the expense of an unfortunate city and its residents—while allowing it to feel both virtuous and superior; to put things a bit differently, Moore makes his viewers feel sensitive to the problems of Flint even as he panders to their insensitivity. Indeed, the only person not laughing, in the Manhattan theater where I saw the picture, seemed to be my friend from Flint. "Flint didn't need this," he said, shaking his head, as we left. No, but Michael Moore did.

In America, when egocentric would-be *auteurs* want to be famous, they make pugnacious documentaries; over in England, they do Shakespeare. Meet Kenneth Branagh, the 30-year-old director, star, and adapter of the brand-new, slimmed-down screen version of *Henry V.* The homely Branagh, who has in recent years won himself a reputation as the reigning boy wonder of the British stage, proves to be a commanding actor and a fluent director; his film moves quite smoothly, and (despite his apparent attempt to counter the pageantry of Olivier's 1945 film with explicit scenes of battlefield carnage) has some magnificent sequences. But it also has the overall feel of a *Reader's Digest* condensed book, or even—leaping, as it does, from Big Scene to Big Scene, with all the Dull Parts neatly excised—of a long, long trailer. Or perhaps it should more properly be compared to one of those videotapes that actors put together to showcase their talents for casting agents: for the fact is that Branagh's camera concentrates so intensely on Branagh that the drama, as such, suffers. Henry's Big Speeches, after all, are intended not just as histrionics but as calls to action; yet when Branagh cuts to the faces of his listeners at Harfleur or Agincourt, the tattered extras don't seem to have been told how to react: the expressions on their faces seem to be saying, variously, "What an actor!" "What a time to make a speech!" and "Gee, why's he speaking in iambic pentameter?" Yes, when the speeches are over the soldiers behave as if somebody's lit a fire under them, and proceed to fight heroically; but one misses a sense of vital connection between them and their king.

Branagh appears, in short, to see Shakespeare less as drama than as an occasion for dazzling solo turns. This might explain why, despite his severe abridgment of Shakespeare's text, he has chosen to interpolate several dramatically extraneous scenes from the *Henry IV* plays, all of them featuring Henry's highly colorful erstwhile friend, Sir John Falstaff (Robbie Coltrane), who doesn't appear anywhere in the pre-Branagh text of *Henry V.* Branagh's relative indifference to dramatic requirements might also explain his failure—which has been noted by many critics—to account for the victory at Agincourt of the drastically outnumbered English.

There is, to be sure, much to admire here: the sense of period, which is for the most part meticulous (in the age of Joe Papp, of course, one is grateful for any Shakespeare production that does not feature helicopters or nineteenth-century German military uniforms); Paul Scofield's grand performance as the French king; and the funny, charming, and marvelously natural scenes involving the princess Katherine (Emma Thompson). Yet at times the film strays dangerously close to Monty Python territory. During the Agincourt sequence, for instance, Branagh cuts at least three times to what looks like the very same shot of a sky ludicrously crowded with arrows; at another point, when Henry declares "We are in God's hand," it begins to rain *immediately;* and throughout the movie, the abrupt appearances, whether in a castle or on a battlefield, of the film's one-man chorus (Derek Jacobi) in twentieth-century garb bring to mind the similarly clad roving narrator of *Monty Python and the Holy Grail.* The film's sense of period, moreover, is harmed by Branagh's prissy coiffure, which (thanks to his many lingering close-ups of himself) we find ourselves staring at again and again.

The film's sense of period is also violated—and in far more injurious fashion—by its musical score. For one thing, it's often much too loud: more than once, when Branagh or some other actor is shouting out the climactic lines of a speech, one has the impression that he is doing so in order to be heard over the orchestra. But most of all, the score is mind-bogglingly terrible—hackneyed, vulgar, and (in its aggressive, penny-ante pseudo-romanticism) flagrantly anachronistic. Wherever it intrudes, the sense of period that the other elements of the film have striven for so mightily is completely vanquished; at times, indeed, you'd think the sappy, schlocky music had been borrowed from one of those panoramic, surround-screen movies of the Grand Canyon, the Mississippi River, and so forth that they show at Disneyland. Even the majestic "Non nobis domine," which is sung by an apparently mixed chorus (another anachronism) over an extensive tracking shot of Henry trudging across the corpse-strewn Agincourt battlefield, is badly handled; it's so overdone—the chorus would seem to be of Mormon Tabernacle Choir proportions, and the anthem too elaborately arranged—that it all but overwhelms the on-screen action. (One is reminded of the self-consciously theatrical first-act finale of *Reds,* with its triple-fortissimo deployment of the "Internationale.") I've never known bad music (and good music, badly employed) to damage a major film as extensively as it has this one, and it's simply a sign, I think, of rampant rock-era tone-deafness that the so-called educated public has applauded *Henry V* without so much as noticing how awful and unsuitable its score is.

It's New York in 1949, and Herman Broder (Ron Silver), a struggling young Jewish immigrant ghostwriter for a rich rabbi (Alan King), has a bizarre domestic crisis: having shuttled regularly, for some time, between his simple, devoted second wife, Yadwiga (Margaret Sophie Stein), the Polish Catholic house servant who saved him from the Nazis and with whom he lives in Coney Island, and his beautiful, lusty Jewish mistress, Masha (Lena Olin), a fellow Holocaust survivor with whom he shares a flat in the Bronx and who is pressuring him to marry her, he suddenly finds himself confronted with Tamara (Anjelica Huston), his shrewd, sardonic first wife, whom he believed dead in the war but who has now come to live on the Lower East Side and work in a religious-articles store.

What to do? Based on the novel by Isaac Bashevis Singer (which was published in English in 1972) and directed by Paul Mazursky from a script he wrote with Roger L. Simon, *Enemies: A Love Story* is the hugely entertaining, richly human tale of a *schlemiel* who is as irresponsible as he is indecisive and of the three remarkable women with whom he rides the Wonder Wheel of life. He's a man whose very ordinariness and lack of imagination have helped to steer him into extraordinarily profane circumstances—who, paradoxically, ends up a trigamist less because of his temerity than because of his timidity, less through lewdness than through a misguided sense of decency. It's a beautifully shaped film, with a rare sense of story, character, and place (and an entirely appropriate musical score by Maurice Jarre); the consistent matter-of-factness with which it contemplates Herman's increasingly outrageous situation is perfect, as is its scrupulously sustained balance of gentleness and irony. And while all the actors are fine, Miss Huston's wise, droll, and thoroughly authentic performance is a standout; the surgical precision and seeming effortlessness with which she delineates this complex, singular woman are breathtaking. Watching her bring Tamara to life, one wonders if Meryl Streep could have played the role half as well.

BLACK AND WHITE IN COLOR

Glory
Driving Miss Daisy

For weeks now, a movie theater near my home has been playing *Glory,* the much-lauded movie about the 54th Massachusetts Infantry, the first black regiment in the Civil War. The movie is doing very good business there, and much of the credit should doubtless go to the New York City Board of Education: for whenever I walk by that theater at noon or thereabouts on a weekday, I find myself in a crowd of high school students, mostly black, who are waiting to see the picture. Yep, you heard right: at a time when American schools—especially those in the inner cities—are graduating kids who can't read, write, or find the United States on a map, teachers (in New York City, at least) are hauling their classes to the movies during school hours.

Presumably, the idea behind these midday movie-theater trips is to use *Glory* as an educational tool—to make history come alive for students, and to give the black kids pride in their heritage. There's nothing wrong with these goals, I suppose, although (a) making history come alive for kids is hardly of any use if they don't also learn the *facts* of history and come to understand them, and (b) pride in something over which one has no control—whether it's one's sex, race, ethnic background, or national origin—seems to me a less meaningful commodity than it's sometimes cracked up to be.

Or maybe New York's high school teachers have been reading

Hendrik Hertzberg, who in a recent issue of the *New Republic* wrote passionately about the experience of seeing *Glory* in "the cozy screening room of the Motion Picture Association of America." Hertzberg came away convinced that *Glory*, by illustrating "that the Civil War was a revolutionary war, that black soldiers were freedom fighters in that war; and that they were all the more heroic because they not only fought but had to fight to fight . . . could do more to alleviate the alienation of young blacks from the 'mainstream' than any amount of . . . curricular victimology."

The other day, in an attempt to test Hertzberg's theory, I went to see *Glory* at a little past noon on a weekday. It was not an affair to warm a Hertzberg's heart. When Trip (Denzel Washington), a truculent ex-slave, began to deliver the movie's obligatory and improbable Big Speech, in which he expressed a prescient skepticism about postbellum race relations and proclaimed stirringly that he was fighting not for the white man's Union but for himself, the high school kids who were seated all around me grew bored and rambunctious, and jabbered noisily among themselves. When Trip tormented his fellow soldier Thomas (André Braugher), an intelligent, Emerson-reading Bostonian, the kids hooted delightedly, showing no empathy whatsoever for Thomas's poignant, acutely ironic position as a privileged member of society who has relinquished his cherished freedom only to find himself in the company of fellow blacks who seem thoroughly alien to him. And the kids laughed, too, when the seemingly hard-hearted Trip stood up, on the eve of battle, and, choking back tears, told his fellow soldiers that he loved them.

The only portions of the movie that drew as enthusiastic a response as the pre-movie soft-drink commercial—in which an eminent basketball player leaped up and, to the cheers and applause of the entire audience, slamdunked a six-pack of Coke into a treehouse—were the hideously graphic battle sequences. The kids savored these episodes; they relished every thrust of a bayonet, every bullet in a chest, every exploding shell, every flying limb. It didn't seem to matter to them who was being sliced and diced, or for what cause, so long as there was a generous display of blood and guts. Plainly, they hadn't enjoyed anything so much since *Rambo*. (To be sure, there were demurrers. When the movie ended, a girl sitting near me shook her head at all the carnage. "I *hate* this kind of movie!" she declared.)

If I've gone on so extensively about the audience reaction to *Glory*, it's because this film has been acclaimed—not only by Hertzberg, but by many well-meaning white liberals—for something other than its artistic or entertainment value; they've celebrated it largely because, like Hertzberg, they figure it must be inspiring to blacks, especially to disaffected young members of the "underclass." But popular culture is not going to save these kids. On the contrary, it's part of the problem: these kids' lives, as a rule, are already tragically circumscribed by rap music and slasher movies and MTV, by aggressive sounds and images with little or no thought content. Far from making them think, a movie like *Glory,* with all its grisly combat sequences, is experienced by them as simply one more raucous, belligerent, visceral event.

This is not to say that *Glory* is without merit. It *is* true, however, that the only surprising thing about this film is how thoroughly unsurprising it is: the characters, the conflicts, the big scenes are all exactly what you'd expect. In addition to Washington's Angry Young Slave and Braugher's Genteel Negro, the 54th contains one Wise Old Trooper (Morgan Freeman) and one Good-Natured Innocent (Jihmi Kennedy). The 24-year-old leader of the regiment, Colonel Robert Gould Shaw (Matthew Broderick), whose parents are longtime abolitionists, is uncomplicatedly earnest and upstanding—a regular little Eagle Scout—and the obstacles he has to overcome are predictable: the jeers of white soldiers (which, of course, turn into cheers by film's end), the unwillingness of a narrow-minded supply officer to provide his men with shoes, the disinclination of the War Department to send black troops into battle.

There is, moreover, an oddly mechanical, low-voltage quality to the way the film's writer, Kevin Jarre, and its director, Edward Zwick, set up and resolve these conflicts. Indeed, if it weren't for the wonderfully staged and highly charged battle sequences, one might confuse *Glory* with one of those solemn, plodding biographical dramas, with titles like "Galileo: A Man and His Telescope," that you run across now and then on educational TV. Certainly the film's worst failing is that Shaw—thanks, largely, to Broderick's lack of range, presence, and moral weight—never grows as a character; and the film itself, excessively mindful of its Good Intentions, too often shares his empty earnestness.

The film's other major roles, by contrast, are remarkably well served by the performers. Schematically routine though their parts may be, Washington, Braugher, Kennedy, and (especially) Freeman all turn in riveting, beautifully shaped performances, lending depth and nuance to characters that might easily have been rendered as caricatures. And Freddie Francis's cinematography makes striking use of light and mist and shadow without being either too overpowering or inappropriately pretty. (The camerawork often reminds one of Francis's equally impressive work in *The French Lieutenant's Woman.*) Just one question: Why is this movie called *Glory?* The whole point, I should think, is that these soldiers are *not* fighting for glory; they're fighting for a cause.

Driving Miss Daisy, the Oscar-nominated film which has been adapted by Alfred Uhry from his play and directed by Bruce Beresford, is as gentle as *Glory* is brutal. The story couldn't be simpler: it's the late 1940s in Atlanta, and a feisty, seventyish Jewish widow, Mrs. Daisy Werthan (Jessica Tandy), has reached the point at which she can't drive anymore. Over her objections, her son Boolie (Dan Aykroyd), who runs the lucrative family cotton mills, hires her a wise, easygoing black chauffeur named Hoke Colburn (Morgan Freeman). Miss Daisy resents Hoke, and for a while refuses to get in the car with him; when she finally does relent, she nags him mercilessly about his driving. Gradually, however, she comes to like and respect him, and to rely upon his companionship; and over the years (for Miss Daisy and Hoke stay together for a quarter of a century) a genuine affection develops between them.

And that's pretty much it. There are no surprises, no sensational turning points, no grand sentimental scenes: along with Beresford's *Tender Mercies* (1982), this has got to be one of the most spare, understated movies ever made. Like *Tender Mercies,* however, *Driving Miss Daisy* is miraculously affecting—and I *mean* miraculously; for though it moves modestly and unhurriedly from episode to episode, taking care that every word and gesture comes across as utterly natural and unmagnified, it packs an unprepared-for punch at the end that does seem rather magical. It's a textbook demonstration of the fact that, even in the most notoriously immoderate of all genres, less *can* be more, and that—given an honest, humane, and intelligent script, a company of dexterous and discerning actors, and a sensitive, compassionate director with a first-rate eye for illuminating detail—a film's paucity of incident can be more than compensated for by a credible and captivating richness of character.

And what unforgettable characters they are. Tandy brings to her performance as Miss Daisy the same capacity for tight-lipped toughness that, forty-five years ago, made her such a magnificently shrewish spouse to the long-suffering Gregory Peck in *The Valley of Decision*. But Miss Daisy is no shrew. She is, rather, an outsider in her society, a thoroughgoing Southern lady who nonetheless, simply because she's Jewish, will never seem *completely* Southern to her fellow born-and-bred Atlantans; she's also a rich woman who can't ever forget that she was born poor. This is not to say that she is ashamed of her erstwhile poverty, or that she—like Florine, her snobbish, social-climbing Georgia-JAP daughter-in-law—tries to hide her Jewishness. Far from it. But her exotic status *has* made her vigilant and wary and distrustful; she's on guard in a way that the good-natured Boolie, who was born into wealth, is not. If she's grown a tough hide, it's because she's felt a need for it.

Hoke has strength, too. And he has pride—*real* pride, the sort that's grounded in a quiet and amply justified sense of self-worth, that makes moral distinctions but doesn't lash out at each perceived slight, that's able to recognize and forgive human frailties for what they are. (This is true, too, of Rawlins, Freeman's otherwise very different character in *Glory*.) Hoke is also blessed with a marvelous sense of humor; he laughs readily, finding amusement where he can, laughing less at Miss Daisy, per se, than at the ironies and absurdities of life itself. If toughness is Miss Daisy's weapon against the pain of exclusion, laughter is his.

Both Tandy and Freeman are splendid actors—but we already knew that. The eye-opener here is Dan Aykroyd. Having floundered, in recent years, in one insipid comedy after another, the sometime Blues Brother proves himself here to be a very fine light character actor in the Jack Carson mold; he suits the film perfectly. So, for that matter, do Hans Zimmer's jaunty, goodnatured score and Peter James's radiant photography. And the exemplary costumes and art direction do a phenomenal job of making one feel as if this *is* pre-Peachtree Center Atlanta.

Two small criticisms. First, the movie's focus tilts toward Miss Daisy—and reasonably so, since Hoke is the constant here, and she's the variable. But one does wish one knew as much about Hoke as about her. Second, there's a short scene, about midway through the film, whose implications are unfortunate. During an excursion to Mobile in the 1950s, Hoke and Miss Daisy pull over for lunch, and are confronted by two patrolmen who demand to see their papers.

Asked what kind of a name Werthan is, Miss Daisy explains that it's of German extraction. The car drives off, and one lawman quips: "An old nigger and an old Jew woman taking off down the road together—that is one sorry sight."

Bigot or not, would an Alabama highway cop really have said such a thing? Would he have pegged Miss Daisy as a Jew? And, if so, would he have considered the spectacle of her, Hoke, and their huge, shiny car a "sorry sight"? It seems unlikely. (If anything, he'd be envious.) What's truly dismaying about this scene, though, is that since these two cops are the most prominent gentile Caucasians in the movie, their encounter with Miss Daisy and Hoke appears to imply that affluent Jews are black people's natural allies against ignorant, less well-to-do white Protestant Southerners; and this implication, to my mind, is unfair to the many white Protestant Southerners who, despite their often deeply ingrained notion that political equality for blacks would represent a threat to their own precarious socioeconomic position, have helped in the last few decades to make the South (in the eyes of many observers) a less racially polarized place than, say, New York City.

But the highway episode runs counter to everything else in *Driving Miss Daisy*. For one of the most commendable things about the film is that, its concern with race relations notwithstanding, it recognizes that where the ethical constitution of ordinary people is concerned, nothing is (if you'll excuse the expression) black and white. When it comes to the question of race, the characters contradict and deceive themselves just as in real life. Take the Martin Luther King dinner sequence. In 1966, King comes to Atlanta to speak at a gala fund-raising dinner to which Boolie and Miss Daisy have purchased tickets. Though Boolie claims to admire King, he decides not to attend because he's worried how his fellow businessmen will react; Miss Daisy, also a declared King fan, chides Boolie for not going, but balks at his sincere proposal (hardly that of a redneck!) that she take Hoke as her escort; she finally mentions the suggestion to Hoke when the two of them are in her car, headed for the dinner, and does so in an oblique, unintentionally insulting way, provoking a rare outburst of indignation on the part of Hoke, who would clearly like to have been asked. The unpleasantness is never resolved. A less intelligent movie would've ended the sequence with all three of them—Miss Daisy, Boolie, and Hoke—at the King dinner, basking in their bold and righteous interracial solidarity, challenging all Atlanta to reproach them. Uhry and Beresford prefer, sensibly, to keep the characters believable—human, not saintly.

Indeed, while the gradually shifting tone of the relationship between Miss Daisy and Hoke can be seen as a metaphor for the developing relations between the races in the South from the forties to the seventies, the filmmakers don't press this interpretation upon us. They're smart enough to recognize that the value of *Driving Miss Daisy* lies in its particularity, in the precision with which it attends to the lives and personalities of these two individuals. It's an unapologetically "small" story, the sort that is often swallowed up helplessly on the big screen—and the ultimate testament to its power is that it fills the screen at every moment. In a time of war and space epics, of super heroes and big-budget special effects, it's nice to be able to say that the most profoundly satisfying movie in a long, long while is a quiet, unpretentious story about people and what they can mean to each other—a film about the brief, luminous moments that add up to a life.

MEN AND THEIR VESSELS

The Hunt for Red October
The Handmaid's Tale

Given everything I'd heard about *The Hunt for Red October*, the new film based on Tom Clancy's bestselling novel, I'd expected to be (a) confused to death by the brilliantly complicated plot and (b) blown away by the extraordinary level of suspense. I was wrong on both counts. The movie, directed by John McTiernan from a script by Larry Ferguson and Donald Stewart, proves to be a thoroughly straightforward, sturdy thriller which differs from other films in this genre neither by its brilliance nor by its intricacy but, chiefly, by its production values. I'm not just talking about the much-heralded sequences involving submarines and other military hardware. I'm talking also about such elements as the lighting, which is painstaking (though the film should more properly carry a credit not for lighting but for chiaroscuro), and the sound, which is so impeccably milked that every opening of an envelope, every jangle of a set of keys, seems to offer itself up as a potential aesthetic experience.

It's a big movie, but McTiernan likes getting close to, and lingering over, little things. His camera angles invite us to focus on details we wouldn't ordinarily pay much attention to: the flag button on a Soviet diplomat's lapel, the coffee cup on a Kremlin bureaucrat's desk. But a bit of this meticulousness goes a long way, and after a few minutes one finds oneself thinking that it's all rather *too* fussy, that the potential for human drama is practically stifled by a welter of minutiae, that the characters are getting lost amid all the nicely rendered particulars. The lighting is especially distracting: so many submarine-interior scenes are lit mainly by the dramatic red glow of the navigational equipment that one gets to wondering why the crewmen don't spend their spare time developing pictures. In one such scene, the reflected red light forms a hideous shape on a man's face which reminds one very much of Gorbachev's birthmark, and for a couple of minutes one sits in the theater munching popcorn and wondering: Hmmm, could this be a *symbol*? You know, presaging glasnost, and all that?

For it *is* a historical movie, set in the dark, early-80s days of Konstantin Chernenko. (Remember Chernenko?) Here's the story: the Soviets, in an attempt to enhance their first-strike nuclear capability, have built a submarine, the *Red October*, with a propulsion system so quiet that American sonar can't detect its presence. Just as the world trembled at Sputnik, declares a Kremlin lackey, so the world "will tremble again at the sound of our silence." What the Kremlin doesn't know is that Captain Marko Ramius (Sean Connery), who has been put in charge of the sub, is eager to vacate the Evil Empire, and has chosen as his officers other would-be defectors; when Ramius, who has taken the *Red October* out on its maiden run, informs the Kremlin of his intention to turn the ship's highly advanced technology over to the United States, his superiors initiate a search-and-destroy mission.

Meanwhile, everybody on our side is completely in the dark about what's going on, except, of course, for one guy: the spunky young Britain-based CIA analyst Jack Ryan (Alec Baldwin). Singlehandedly, Ryan ascertains that the Soviets have developed this amazing sub; singlehandedly, he figures out that Ramius is heading our way not because he's gone crazy and wants to bomb New York (as the Soviets have told U.S. officials) but because he aims to defect; singlehandedly, he divines how Ramius plans to carry off this scheme; singlehandedly, he talks White House officials into buying his argument and helping Ramius out; and singlehandedly, he has himself dropped by helicopter onto the American attack submarine *Dallas* and—but I don't want to ruin it for you. Let's just say that without Jack Ryan we'd all probably be plunged into World War Three.

Needless to say, *Hunt* is a man's film. *Top Gun* gave us the warplane-as-phallus; this movie gives us, well, subs. "Jesus, that's a big sucker," says an American when he gets his first look at the *Red October*. When Bart Mancuso (Scott Glenn), the *Dallas*'s wary captain (who's inclined to think Ramius a warmonger, not a defector), lets his ship's location be known to the Soviet sub, he says, "Well, we've unzipped our flies." What would Bruno Bettelheim have said about all this? McTiernan has said that *Hunt* is about how Ryan "learns to stand up and be a man among men," and one gets the idea, watching the film, that something of this sort is indeed supposed to be happening. But it doesn't work: all the characters in *Hunt* are plot functionaries, and they stay plot functionaries. One never feels as if one knows any of them. This hurts in the case of Ryan, and it hurts even more in the case of Ramius, whose motivation for deserting his country is hinted at but never made real.

If *The Hunt for Red October* constitutes a solid, two-hour chunk of male fantasy, *The Handmaid's Tale*, based on the novel by Margaret Atwood and scripted by Harold Pinter (Mr. Silent Propulsion System himself), offers a distaff nightmare. At least so its advertisements brag: "One woman's story. Every woman's fear." Directed by Volker Schlondorff, *The Handmaid's Tale* gives us a feminist dystopia, a Women's Lib version of *1984*. "Once upon a time in the recent future," we read in the opening explanatory note, "a country went wrong. The country was the Republic of Gilead." Then we watch a young couple and their small daughter trudge through a snow-filled forest in an attempt to sneak across an international boundary. Their plan misfires: the husband is shot dead by border guards, the daughter is seized, and the wife, a librarian named Kate (played by Natasha Richardson, who bears an amazing resemblance to the slender-faced, frizzy-haired, dewy-eyed Miss Atwood), is taken into custody. It's not long before we realize that Gilead is America—an America, to be specific, of the near-future, in which an anti-feminist revolution has brought to power a ruthless autocracy that takes its notions of sex, marriage, and justice straight from the Old Testament—and that the country to which Kate and her family hoped to escape was (where else?) Miss Atwood's icy homeland to the north.

The film acquaints us with the wacky folkways of Gilead by taking us, step by step, through Kate's new life. Since, unlike ninety-nine out of a hundred women in Gilead, she is fertile and free of venereal infection, Kate is sent to a re-education camp of sorts where she sleeps on a gymnasium floor with several dozen other fertile young women and is harangued endlessly by a pretty, wholesome-looking instructress named Aunt Lydia (Victoria Tennant). The revolution, Aunt Lydia informs her charges, was triggered by the proliferation of "lazy women, sluts" who, failing to respect their bodies as "temples of purity" and to recognize fertility as a "precious gift," advocated such evils as abortion, birth control, and artificial insemination. In the Republic of Gilead, such women are summarily executed. In Gilead, it's understood that while men can't be expected to keep it clean, women are different: "We have self-control, dignity." A woman's duty is to bear a man's children; and in Gilead, if his wife can't do the job, the state—taking its cue from Genesis 30, in which Jacob's barren wife Rachel invites him to impregnate her handmaid Bilhah—provides him with a woman who can.

That's where Kate and the other fecund females come in. "You're going to be handmaids," Aunt Lydia tells them. "You're going to serve God and your country." They're given official handmaid garb: bright red habits and veils. They're taught to grovel. ("You're not an equal, you're a handmaid: that is your role in life.") They learn a new doxology (all together now, to the tune of "Old One-Hundredth"): "Remove our anger, cleanse our will;/And leave us empty to be filled." And they're given assignments. Kate, as it happens, is assigned to a couple of VIPs: the Commander (Robert Duvall), an army officer who is in charge of security for the entire state, and his wife, Serena Joy (Faye Dunaway). Kate lives in their lovely suburban home and, whenever the Commander wishes, participates in the "ceremony," a weird, impersonal fertilization ritual in which the Commander, Serena, and Kate (now renamed Offred) all take part.

Naturally, Kate doesn't dig this new life. Sex with the Commander is *icky*. Besides, as months pass without a pregnancy, it becomes clear to her that he's sterile. If she doesn't have a baby, she knows, it will officially be her fault, and she'll be dispatched to the "colonies" (apparently some sort of gulag). But what can she do? She can't run away: the city in which the Commander and Serena live is heavily militarized, with armed checkpoints all over the place, and if she tries to escape she'll be killed. At Serena's suggestion she copulates behind the Commander's back with his young driver, Nick (Aidan Quinn), even though it's a capital crime. Meanwhile, behind Serena's back, the Commander has frank, intimate tête-à-têtes with Kate. It seems only a matter of time before somebody in the household finds her out, gets angry, and turns her in. Or will somebody—Nick, her friend Moira

(Elizabeth McGovern), or perhaps a sympathetic neighborhood handmaid—help her escape?

If this all sounds ridiculous, it is. But it's *wonderfully* ridiculous. It's ridiculous in the way that solemnly paranoid movies always are. At first, to be sure, one is irritated by this film's inanity, its vulgar religion-bashing, its thoroughgoing political correctness. How much braver, wittier, and more to the point it would have been, one thinks, for Atwood, Pinter, and company to depict a future America in which men are incarcerated for calling eighteen-year-old females girls rather than women, for finding attractive women more attractive than unattractive women, and for getting excited by naughty photographs in magazines.

Such, as I say, is one's initial reaction to *The Handmaid's Tale*. But after the first half-hour or so, one realizes that this picture is simply too ridiculous to stay angry at, and one actually relaxes and starts to enjoy the damn thing. For—assuming one is capable of suspending one's philosophical antagonism along with one's disbelief—there's a lot to enjoy here. To watch *The Handmaid's Tale* is to climb for a couple of hours into the cranium of a canny feminist with a fantastic imagination, and it's a real adventure. Atwood has worked out Gilead's whole social system—everything from grocery-shopping protocol and the role of television to birthing rites and rituals of punishment—and it's fun to watch it all unfold. There's something genuinely spooky, too, about the stylish, well-bred Gilead housewives in their standard-issue uniforms—blue dress, pearls, and blue pillbox hats—who make the women in *The Stepford Wives* look like Jane Fonda in *Barbarella*; as in *The Stepford Wives*, and as in *Rosemary's Baby* and *The Invasion of the Body Snatchers*, much of the dramatic impact of this film derives from an association of the thoroughly outlandish and creepy with the familiar and domestic. Here, as in those films, there's a real undercurrent of terror: set aside the silly politics, in fact, and the suspense easily surpasses that in *The Hunt for Red October*.

One reason for this is first-rate acting. Dunaway—who brings to her part a breathtaking intensity—is the standout: the minute we see her as Serena, we know she can't be trusted. Underneath the Gilead-housewife sweetness and light, she radiates looniness, resentment, malevolence: it is plain that she desperately wants a baby, and it is also plain that she will be desperately hostile toward the handmaid who furnishes her with one. As for Duvall, he makes the Commander arrestingly ambiguous. On the one hand, he seems sincere when he argues that pre-revolutionary America "was in a mess," torn apart by black, gay, and women's pressure groups, and had to be cleaned up: "Nobody really knew how to feel anything anymore: respect, reverence, values." On the other hand, he likes being around the feisty Kate and enjoys being beaten by her in cards and Scrabble; he keeps a stash of forbidden old magazines like *Vogue* and *Cosmopolitan*; and he patronizes an underground nightclub where other high officials of Gilead dance with bimbos ("Jezebels") in black tights and excessive makeup. The Commander is virile, sanctimonious, horny, humane, and hypocritical, and somehow Duvall makes the combination believable.

Yet for all the richness of Dunaway and Duvall's performances, neither of their characters pays off as one expects them to; ultimately, both actors' efforts seem largely wasted. As for Natasha Richardson, she falls a tad short of making Kate thoroughly coherent and sympathetic. Much of the time she just doesn't strike one as a woman who has lost her husband and child; in particular, her concern for her daughter—whose whereabouts she doesn't know—seems to materialize on those occasions when the script calls for it and then to disappear. She never quite comes into focus: if at times she's impertinent, at other times she comes off as torpid, apathetic. One of the movie's primary flaws, indeed, is that for all its feminism, its heroine is a largely passive character whose one definitive act in the whole movie seems rash and pointless, and who—in a final irony that may or may not be intentional—relies on men for her deliverance. No Tom Clancy hero, she.

COMMONPLACE COMEDY

Pretty Woman
Nuns on the Run
I Love You to Death

The first thing you should know about *Pretty Woman* is that it was directed by Garry ("Laverne and Shirley") Marshall, a man who became famous back in the seventies for doing the impossible—namely, lowering the intellectual level of the television sitcom. In the early eighties, Marshall switched genres and began churning out mildly successful big-screen comedies: *Young Doctors in Love, The Flamingo Kid, Nothing in Common.* Now the nineties are here, and so is Marshall's biggest hit ever, *Pretty Woman,* a romantic comedy (written by J. F. Lawton) which will do nothing to tarnish Marshall's reputation as a schlockmeister *par excellence.* Critics have described it as a fairy tale, and I guess it is, if you can imagine the brothers Grimm confabbing poolside at the Beverly Hills Hotel with a gaggle of box-office-obsessed Touchstone execs. For *Pretty Woman* is the very model of the slick, formulaic contemporary star vehicle, the sort of glossy, diverting, outrageously synthetic picture that nobody involved could possibly take seriously but that almost everybody involved is sure will pack them in at the multiplexes; it's the sort of picture whose every last line feels as if it has been test-marketed.

To describe it in publicist's terms, *Pretty Woman* is a Cinderella story for the nineties. Our Prince Charming is Edward Lewis (Richard Gere), a handsome, divorced, and exceedingly busy New York tycoon whose mistress has just left him because she finds herself speaking to his secretary more than she does to him. Our Cinderella is Vivian (Julia Roberts), a young L.A. streetwalker from Milledgeville, Georgia. But Vivian's not just any streetwalker: she's improbably beautiful, sweet-natured, wholesome-looking. And her street isn't just any street: it's Hollywood Boulevard, where she and her fellow trollops use the names of celebrities on the Walk of Fame to mark their territorial boundaries. (In another director's hands, this detail might have seemed grimly ironic, even witty: in the hands of Garry Marshall, it comes off as a dumb Neil Simonish gag.) Edward and Vivian meet when he, on the first night of a week-long L.A. business trip, makes a wrong turn on his way to Beverly Hills and asks her for directions. She ends up accompanying him back to his hotel, and the twice-burned Edward, wary of serious entanglements, ends up asking her to serve as his paid escort for the week. "I want a professional," he tells her. "I don't want any romantic hassles." Their liaison begins as a simple commercial arrangement; but over the next few days—surprise!—they fall for each other and overcome their mutual unwillingness to "become emotionally involved in business."

Meanwhile, Vivian gets acquainted with Edward's world. We're supposed to laugh when her rakish, revealing attire shocks the hell out of his fellow hotel guests; and we're supposed to feel sorry for her when she's ordered out of a Rodeo Drive clothing store by a snooty saleslady who recognizes in an instant that she doesn't belong. But these episodes are sheer balderdash, based on the fantasy that the guests at top-dollar Beverly Hills hotels, and the shoppers at fancy Rodeo Drive emporia, are all tasteful patricians, socialites of the sort that used to be played by Lucile Watson. The truth is quite the opposite: these establishments are patronized largely by gauche, overpaid show-biz types and their dependents, many of whom not only dress but talk and behave very much like cheap hookers. Anyone strolling into a Rodeo Drive boutique clothed the way Vivian is at the beginning of *Pretty Woman* would probably be taken for a rock star and treated like royalty. (Indeed, compared to the outfits that some actresses wear to the Oscars, Vivian's streetwalking attire looks downright demure.)

Then there's Vivian's big cultural experience. One evening, Edward flies her by private jet to San Francisco, where she see her first opera—and proves her sensitivity, of course, by weeping all the way through. Watching this scene, one wonders how much Garry Marshall would've wept if someone had forced him to score *Pretty Woman* with serious music instead of with insipid hard rock. This movie pretends to honor great music, but like the character in Woody Allen's *Crimes and Misdemeanors* who equates an awareness of Mozart with a knowledge of European hotels, it's merely acknowledging great music as an essential component of a high-class, luxurious life.

But Marshall is, in fact, better at depicting the luxurious than the not-so-luxurious life. The point of the movie's opening sequence is to underline the squalor of Vivian's existence—a simple enough proposition, one would think, given the seediness of downtown Hollywood. But Marshall can't bring himself to show things as they really are. He makes Vivian's flat (which is supposed to be shabby) look pretty. He makes the bar where she and her friends hang out (and which is supposed to be grubby) look pretty. Even when the body of one of Vivian's colleagues turns up in a local dumpster, everything in sight is clean and colorful and radiant. Next to Marshall, Steven Spielberg is an Italian neo-realist.

If, in spite of all this, *Pretty Woman* is entertaining to watch, it's mostly because Julia Roberts is adorable—especially when she smiles, which is virtually all the time. You can almost hear Marshall behind the camera, saying, "Smile, honey! Smile at the customers!" He's plainly trying to turn her into a new Audrey Hepburn: her wide, sparkling smile is very much like Hepburn's, and the dresses she buys on Rodeo Drive strongly suggest the Givenchy fashions Hepburn made famous. There are moments, too, when the storyline of *Pretty Woman* recalls, variously, *Sabrina, Funny Face, Breakfast at Tiffany's*, and *My Fair Lady*. (One is also reminded occasionally of Marilyn Monroe in *The Prince and the Showgirl*.) There's even a scene in which Vivian watches the closing moments of *Charade* on TV. Woody Allen often pays homage to Bergman and Fellini; is *Pretty Woman* Garry Marshall's homage to Stanley Donen?

You've probably got to be either British or Catholic, or both, to respond fully to the humor of *Nuns on the Run*. It's the story of Brian (Eric Idle) and Charlie (Robbie Coltrane), two English bank robbers who, finding that the criminal life isn't what it used to be, decide to go straight—straight, that is, to Rio de Janeiro. (I guess they haven't heard that Rio isn't what it used to be, either.) So they quit their gang and head for Heathrow with two suitcases full of money stolen from a drug-pushing Asian syndicate. But their car runs out of gas, and—

with the cops, the Asian mobsters, and their own former confederates on their tails—Brian and Charlie are forced to hole up in a London convent, disguised as nuns.

The results are—well—mildly amusing. Writer-director Jonathan Lynn tries to jazz things up by using funky, pseudo-Wellesian camera angles, and editor David Martin does his part by cutting briskly between scenes. But these strike one as contrived, ineffectual attempts to inject energy into what is essentially a tired piece of work. Lynn has taken a silly but not unpromising premise—it's pretty much the same as that of *Some Like It Hot,* one of the funniest film comedies ever—and has come up with a succession of terribly unimaginative complications. (Eric Idle's romance with a girl named Faith is particularly tiresome.) Michael Garfath's camerawork, moreover, is astonishingly drab; and despite Martin's abrupt interscene cutting, the cuts within the scenes themselves are rather sluggish: at times the movie looks like a rough cut, and one finds oneself wishing one had an editing maching handy.

Lawrence Kasdan directs with a witless and slightly plodding earnestness, with a hand that's a bit too heavy for his material. Sometimes this style pays off: it made many people take *Body Heat* and *The Big Chill* more seriously than they deserved. In the black comedy *I Love You to Death,* however, Kasdan's style largely works against the designs of John Kostmayer's screenplay. The only word for the script is *zany,* but rather than start the zaniness off at full throttle, Kostmayer builds up to it adroitly, scene by scene. Kasdan's job, as director, is to prepare us for the madness to come, to cue us in as to what we're expected to make of the motley collection of characters we've been presented with: Joey (Kevin Kline), a happy-go-lucky Italian pizza man in Tacoma, Washington, who, in the opening church-confessional scene, tries to remember exactly how many times in the past two weeks he's committed adultery; Rosalie (Tracey Ullman), his devoted wife, who's so obtuse she doesn't realize he's been two-timing her left and right until she sees him necking in the public library; Devo (River Phoenix), the soft-spoken young New Age waiter in Joey's pizzeria, who loves Rosalie, knows Joey's a rat, and wants her to give the guy his walking papers; and Nadia (Joan Plowright, a.k.a. Lady Olivier), Rosalie's live-in Yugoslavian mother, an inveterate *National Enquirer* reader who can't stand Joey and is willing to do anything to get him out of her daughter's life.

At least in the opening scenes, however, the clash between these potentially farcical characters and Kasdan's sober direction is merely baffling. On the one hand, Kline renders Joey in a broad, burlesque manner (he goes around singing "Non Dimenticar" and saying things like "I'm a man, I gotta lotta hormones in my body") that seems wholly indebted to the character of Father Guido Sarducci on the old "Saturday Night Live." On the other hand, Kasdan solemnly soaks up the local color and focuses in on such naturalistic (if amusing) details as the awful, sickly-yellow paintings of the Pope, Christ, JFK, and Sinatra on the wall of Joey's pizza parlor. Initially, then, the overall feel is that of a homely, relatively realistic domestic comedy on the order of *Mystic Pizza,* and it makes one wonder why Kline's performance is such a caricature. (Try to imagine *Raising Arizona,* say, directed by Arthur Hiller.)

The tone doesn't really click into place, in fact—and Kline's exaggerated performance doesn't begin to make sense—until a pair of dense, spaced-out druggies named Harlan (William Hurt) and Marlon (Keanu Reeves) come on the scene. Rosalie, you see, having finally discovered Joey's infidelities, has decided she wants him dead; but several attempts on Joey's life—by Rosalie herself, by Nadia, by Devo, and by an amateur hit man from the Old Country—fail to do the job. Finally, in desperation, Devo brings in Harlan and Marlon to help out. Hurt and Reeves (the latter of whom has a ring in his nose, a razor haircut, and a tattoo of a marijuana leaf on his neck) are hilarious, and when they're on screen, responding in matter-of-fact, dimwitted fashion to the most outrageous goings-on, everything seems to come together. "They look like drug addicts," Rosalie whispers to Devo after he introduces Harlan and Marlon. "They *are* drug addicts," Devo replies. "I don't like having drug addicts in my house," she complains. "Don't think of them as drug addicts," Devo suggests. "Think of them as killers."

This last line epitomizes the wacky tone that Kasdan takes so long to find his way to. Not that Kasdan is entirely at fault here: Kostmayer himself is responsible for one of the picture's major liabilities, a running gag (though one with Serious Thematic Implications, natch) about America. The Old Country hit man, for instance, disguises himself with a Lincoln mask and swings at Joey with a baseball bat (a symbol, we're reminded, of the National Pastime). Likewise, when

Harlan is about to shoot Joey in the heart and can't recall which side it's on, he remembers that the Pledge of Allegiance is said with one's right hand on one's heart, and proceeds, with Marlon's help, to recite—in a perfect deadpan not unlike that of which Kasdan made extensive use in *The Accidental Tourist*—a funny, fractured pledge that incorporates elements of the Lord's Prayer and ends with the words "deliver us from freedom." Finally, there's Marlon's line: "If we're gonna waste the dude, we gotta get paid for it. That's the American way."

As in *Blue Velvet* and *Heathers,* the implication throughout *I Love You to Death* is that this absurd tale of violence (which is based, believe it or not, on a true story) reflects some larger truth about America. But what about the fact that Joey, Rosalie, and Nadia are all European immigrants? Well, Joey is given a line that's apparently supposed to smooth over this little inconsistency: America, he reminds us, was discovered by one Italian and named after another. This hardly takes care of the problem, though. For the leading characters' chief motivating traits—Joey's unthinking combination of Catholic piety and extreme promiscuity, and Rosalie's quickness to turn from servility to murderousness—strike one not as American at all, but as the manifestations of an Old World peasant mentality. Yet even to make such criticisms, I suppose, is to take a film like *I Love You to Death* more seriously than it deserves.

CANNES ARTISTS

The 1990 Cannes Film Festival

Thursday, May 10

This is it: I'm on the plane from New York to Paris, traveling several thousand miles to watch movies for a week.

The Cannes Film Festival is now in its forty-third year, and its prestige has never been greater. To be sure, the festival (which this year runs twelve days) is notorious for rewarding pretension, impenetrability, and gloominess, and for looking warily upon the sanguine, the accessible, the popular; as an editor of France's *Studio* magazine writes, "It is a place where the films that please the public are systematically suspect." In a genre still dominated by America, Cannes is something of an enemy fortress, a stronghold of defiance against Hollywood ways and means. Yes, some stateside movies have won Cannes's top award, the Palme d'Or; but they tend to be movies that offer a dark, seditious vision of American society. Consider the U.S. winners of the last twenty years: *M*A*S*H; Taxi Driver; Apocalypse Now; Missing; Paris, Texas; sex, lies, and videotape.* Though most of these are worthy films, the list confirms an unmistakable pattern of rewarding U.S. films for being bleak and subversive.

Yet one can't easily dismiss an institution that routinely presents work by the planet's most distinguished directors. This year, alas, there are a few such films that I won't get to see: I'll be arriving several hours too late for the opening picture, Akira Kurosawa's *Dreams,* and leaving several days too early to catch new movies by Godard, Fellini, and David Lynch. But no matter: there'll be plenty to see.

In fact, there'll be altogether too much. As I peruse the list of screenings (or "séances") in *Le Monde,* it all seems quite baroque. First there are the nineteen "official selections" in competition for prizes. Among these are three apiece from France and the U.S., two apiece from Italy and the Soviet Union, and one apiece from Great Britain, Czechoslovakia, Poland, China, Japan, Colombia, and Burkina Faso. In addition, there are nine non-competing films that are also considered "official selections." Then there are four "parallel" series, which, though associated with the Festival International du Film, have their own selection committees and juries. These series were founded in the early sixties and afterward, supposedly to exhibit work by filmmakers who are young or "different'" or working in obscure corners of the globe; the films in these series that represent directorial debuts are eligible for a prize called the Camera d'Or (which in 1984 went to Jim Jarmusch for *Stranger than Paradise*). This year, the series called "La Semaine International de la Critique" ("Critics' Week") offers seven movies; "La Quinzaine des Realisatures" ("Directors' Fortnight") offers twenty; "Perspectives du Cinéma Français," seven; "Un Certain Regard," seventeen. Then there are several short films. Total: over eighty movies shown under the auspices of the FIF or one of its wings. Add to that the dozens of other films shown in other venues, mainly to prospective distributors, and you've got a veritable torrent of celluloid.

From Paris I fly to Nice, then proceed to Cannes by minibus. The Festival employee at the wheel drives at breakneck speed—upwards of 120 kilometers per hour—as if rushing a shipment of life-saving medicine to a disaster area.

Friday, May 11

Cannes is beautiful, despite the hundreds of billboards promoting everyone from Costa Gavras to Arnold Schwarzenegger. The lavish bayfront Palais des Festivals, nerve center of the city, looms like a cathedral. At 8:30 a.m. to the immense Grand Auditorium Lumière at the Palais to see the new Clint Eastwood movie, *White Hunter, Black Heart.* What a shock. The movie has its virtues, but the performance by Eastwood—who also directed and produced—is not among them.

As a flamboyant 1950s film director named John Wilson, he's awful. During the first few minutes I keep wondering: Why is he acting as if he can't act? Then I realize: maybe he *can't* act—not in this kind of role, anyway. Meaning, that is, in a talky role that requires him to be something he's not. Peter Viertel (who co-wrote with James Bridges and Burt Kennedy) based his original novel on his experience as a script-polisher for John Huston on *The African Queen*. Here, as in Viertel's novel, Wilson becomes obsessed, soon after arriving in Africa to make the film, with the desire to kill an elephant. Thanks to this obsession, the shoot is held up, its finances imperiled, people's lives endangered: yet Wilson refuses to behave responsibly.

Not a bad idea for a movie. But the scriptwriters have miscalculated: rather than adapt their protagonist to Eastwood's laconic style, they have chosen to give him reams of garrulous, Huston-like dialogue. And—equally unwisely—Eastwood has chosen to imitate Huston's characteristic inflections and physical mannerisms, which are miles from his own natural ones. The result is one of the most unsuccessful attempts I've ever seen by a major star to stretch his range.

To make matters worse, the scriptwriters invariably drive home their points in lumbering, one-by-one fashion. Various scenes exist for the sole purpose of showing (a) how much Wilson hates anti-Semitism, (b) how much he hates racism, (c) how much of a ladies' man he is, (d) how much of a man's man he is, (e) how gutsy he is, (f) how much he loves to play practical jokes, (g) how much he loves to shock people, (h) how little he cares about money. As he tells Pete Verill (Jeff Fahey), the sensible, Nick Carraway-like Viertel character, he doesn't think of himself as being in show business, but rather considers himself "a lousy little god" who creates his own worlds without a thought of box-office potential: "To write a movie you must forget that anyone's ever going to see it." Movies, he says, should always reduce life to its fundamental terms: love and death, good and evil.

Eastwood—who, though American and popular, is revered by many European cinéastes as a master of symbolically resonant simplicity—plainly shares most of his character's views; it is clear that he intended this film to be about the elemental mystery of a heroic soul's attraction to sin. But the film falters not only because of Eastwood's acting but because Wilson is simply not the heroic soul that Eastwood thinks he is. Simply put, he's an arrogant, self-dramatizing big shot whom people regard as "bigger than life" because his fame, wealth, and host of tolerant hangers-on make it easy for him to gratify his every asinine impulse. To be sure, in a moment of anger, Pete does call Wilson "the most egocentric, irresponsible son of a bitch I've ever met"; but too often this movie doesn't go along with him, and insists on finding deep spiritual significance in what is merely a celebrity's self-indulgence. At the post-screening press conference, Eastwood savers that he didn't base his performance on Huston (!) and says he shares Wilson's disdain for Hollywood's cautiousness. (*Quel rebelle!*) He discusses Zimbabwe, where the picture was filmed: "You'd never know there'd been a war there. The people were very up." And he fields questions. A Swedish woman complains about the film's females; Eastwood cites his feminist credentials. Another journalist asks if the film's message is partly environmental; Eastwood says that, yes, thanks to environmentalism, Viertel's story has taken on new meaning. This pleases him. It seems to please the press, too: that the movie has a trendy political angle apparently makes for more interesting copy.

In the afternoon I sit through twenty minutes of John Waters's campy *Cry Baby*. Set in a 1950s high school, it's a retread of *Hairspray* without the redeeming presence of Divine: if the earlier movie was dopily funny, this one is just dopey. A delinquent (Johnny Depp) falls for a rich girl (Amy Locane). Now and then he sheds a single tear. This, I gather, is meant to be hilarious. I don't get it. Nor do I understand why this frivolous movie is at Cannes, supposedly a showcase for serious cinema. I suspect it's because Waters mocks the U.S. bourgeoisie and its glory days, and exalts poor folks over rich bigots. Doesn't it matter that his social views are simpleminded and slickly expressed, that his jokes have no wit or moral bite, that he glories in the tawdry and trashy?

At 8:00 p.m., a very different pack of juvenile delinquents. *Rodrigo D: No Futuro* is a Colombian movie about lower-class Medellin teens for whom crime and drugs are a part of daily life and gainful employment and sexual fidelity are alien concepts. With its grittily realistic photography and cast of real-live Medellin JDs, the film feels evocative and authentic. But when it comes to making sociological points (his main goal here), director Victor Manuel Gaviria's touch is about as subtle as that of the heavy-metal music these kids adore. He doesn't move far enough beyond documentary into art: the script (by Gaviria and two others) meanders, repeats itself, and is ultimately boring. One is put off, too, by the press kit's exploitation of the fact that three kids who appear in the film have since died violently.

A quick circuit through the exhibition hall at the Palais. Every film outfit you can name, from Miramax to Sovexportfilms, has a berth here. I'm reminded that Cannes is mostly about people coming from all over the world to unload distribution rights to spaghetti westerns and Kung Fu movies.

Saturday, May 12

If *White Hunter, Black Heart* was inspired by John Huston, *Artificial Paradise*—directed by the Yugoslav Karpo Godina and written by Branko Vucicevix—concerns the early life of director Fritz Lang. Like Lang's pictures, it's heavy on stylization: every so often, the actors in realistically rendered scenes will suddenly strike melodramtic poses, deliver their lines in stilted fashion, or die theatrically. It's as if Godina wants to remind us of film's artificiality, its ritualistic function. One character, a magician, keeps saying "hocus-pocus"; the movie continually reminds us of its own magical quality, of the power of film's hocus-pocus to enrich one's conception of the nature of reality.

At one point, Lang (played with wit and authority by Jurgen Morche) asserts that it's foolish to go into the past because "time disorients." Certainly this movie does its best to disorient: its episodes, unchronologically arranged, reach back into Lang's youth and are linked only by the device of a middle-aged Lang, newly arrived in Los Angeles in 1935, relating his biography to a young admirer. These episodes emphasize bizarre and tragic turns in his friends' lives, most of which we're not prepared for. It's an arresting, if not quite coherent, piece of work which, like the Eastwood film, presses upon us its disapproval of Hollywood. Indeed, the endings of both films involve a pointedly ironic implication that true film artistry derives from complex spiritual experience of a sort that cannot flourish within the U.S. studio system. This shared attitude doubtless helps explain the attraction of these two films to those who make the selections here: increasingly, it's clear that nothing appeals to the powers at Cannes quite like a put-down of Hollywood.

Press conference for *Rodrigo D.* Gaviria asserts that the Medellin teens in his movie are "heroes, not criminals" and calls the police "political whores." Nobody challenges him or requests an explanation: radical-sounding statements are taken for granted here. Gaviria says his movie is about the "war" between the kids and the cops—but if there had been more "war" in the picture and less desultory criminality (with no cops in sight), it would have been a lot more dramatically gripping. Two of his "heroes," by the way, flank Gaviria on the dais, and the look in their eyes is frightening: sullen, glazed, unblinking. Mid-conference, one of them gets up and bums a cigarette off somebody offstage. The other has a better idea what's expected of him: "All my friends are dead," he says woodenly. The press seems to love the idea that three actors have died violently; one reporter wants to know all the details, and everyone eagerly takes them down.

In the evening, some welcome comic relief: a screening of Gabriele Salvatores's *Turne,* a sort of Italian counterpart to Doris Dorrie's *Men.* It's about two friends, actors in a troupe that's touring Italy with *The Cherry Orchard.* Federico (Fabrizio Bentivoglio) is aloof and self-absorbed, a melancholic type whose abandonment by his lover Vittoria (Laura Morante) drives him to despair. His only foundation is his friendship with the earthy, extroverted Dario (Diego Abatantuono)—who, unbeknownst to him, has taken up with Vittoria. It's all quite funny (especially a running gag about Federico's inability to remember his lines), though Federico remains something of a closed book throughout and though the film's five writers couldn't come up with an ending; rather than build to a riotous finale, it tapers off, running out of ideas and energy.

Afterwards, I join the huddled masses outside the Palais and look on while hundreds of formally attired *mesdames et messieurs* mount the red-carpeted stairs of the Grand Auditorium Lumière to watch, God help them, *Rodrigo D.* There is a uniformed honor guard, and classical music is playing. Who are these tuxedoed glitterati? Some are obviously American filmmakers, Tokyo movie merchants. Others look far too young, and have that distinct Riviera look: dainty, olive-skinned, *raffiné.* This elegant display could not be more removed from the press screenings, which begin every morning at 8:30 and for which we all show up in T-shirts and shorts. How bizarre that all these dinner-jacketed sophisticates should be lining up for a film celebrating Colombian street gangs.

Sunday, May 13

In the Morning, Alan Parker's *Come See the Paradise.* What to make of this U.S.-based British writer-director? *Shoot the Moon,* about a crumbling marriage between Albert Finney and Diane Keaton, was (despite the boom mike that hung down into several shots) satisfying, because Parker stuck close to home. He's done offbeat films about kids: *Bugsy Malone, Fame, Birdy, Angel Heart.* But his big hits were two political dramas: *Midnight Express* (1977), about an American teen in a Turkish pen, and *Mississippi Burning* (1988), about civil rights workers and Dixie racists. In both movies, Parker assailed social wrongs on which virtually no one would disagree with him—but he used those wrongs as a basis for glib attacks on American mores and on the U.S. political system.

He's up to much the same thing in *Paradise,* a well-edited, too-pretty movie set on the West Coast during the thirties and forties. Jack McGurn (Dennis Quaid), an Irish-born union organizer (without a trace of brogue), marries Lily Kawamura (Tamlyn Tomita), a second-generation Japanese-American, only to be separated from her after Pearl Harbor by her consignment to an internment camp. Everything is spelled out. We know Jack has principles because somebody says "You've got principles." We know Jack adores Lily not because there's chemistry between them (there isn't) but because he keeps telling her so: "They can break both my arms and legs and it could never hurt me as much as losing you, Lily. You have a happiness inside of you that makes you so beautiful, as if you had a little bag of magic that only you could dip into." Yet we don't see her magic, and don't see Jack responding to it. Nonetheless, as if to insist on their passion, Randy Edelman's musical score swells up soppily at each of their dozen-odd parting and reunion scenes. Equally insistent is Michael Seresin's romantic, softly lit photography. (Seresin never misses a chance to shoot the lovers in the vicinity of a sunbeam penetrating a haze of dust.)

At times, the movie recalls an aggressively sentimental AT&T commercial. And one of the things it sentimentalizes is Depression-era leftist radicalism—as if the whole experience of the thirties (and of 1989) hadn't taught us anything. It's a puerile movie, and it makes one conclude that if Parker's kid pictures are better than his political films, it's because he has a childlike mentality. His politics are at the level of protest music lyrics (it's no surprise that he directed *Pink Floyd: The Wall*); he manifestly understands history in terms of sentimental-liberal clichés. It puts *Paradise* in perspective to see it in Provence, where fifty years ago the Vichy government was helping ship Jews off to camps—and not detention camps, either.

Interestingly, at the post-screening press conference, Parker pretty much admits his puerility—and does so with an odd populistic pride: "I'm pretty happy with how simpleminded I am." He says that *Paradise* is "much softer in attitude than some of my previous films"—and he's right; he's tempered his shrillness. ("I'm getting older and more subtle," he suggests.) As Eastwood claims not to have imitated Huston, so Parker insists that "I don't intentionally make controversial films." Yet he congratulates himself on them: "Most American directors are not interested in a movie with some political backbone. I'm different from them because I'm not an American, and can step outside a situation and see it with a little more clarity."

The questions are predictable. "How much do you feel constrained by commercial pressures?" someone asks Parker. The three Japanese-American actors on the panel are asked whether there is an "increase in xenophobia in America toward Asian-American actors." (It's obvious none of them knows what xenophobia means, but they try to answer anyway.) Another reporter wonders if the film is meant as an indirect comment on today's "economic racism" against the Japanese. (Parker: "No.") The man from *Variety* begins his question: "Given the arch-conservative climate in America right now . . ." And a European wonders why the "racist scenes are somewhat weak"—meaning that Parker doesn't show enough violent acts against Japanese-Americans. Parker's reply: there *weren't* that many such acts. Compared to the press, he comes off as a voice of sanity and moderation.

In the afternoon twenty-six small planes circle over the Bay of Cannes, towing a set of banners announcing that anyone interested in distribution rights to *Superman: The New Movie* should head for the Carlton, suite 643. Why not just call it *Superman V?* Because then everyone would be reminded what bombs *III* and *IV* were.

Later, a cryptic 18-minute Soviet film, *Inoi* by Sergei Masloboichtchikov. (Try to fit *that* on a marquee.) It's recognizably Russian in its grimness: the weather is gray, and the protagonist is in prison, harassed by a grotesque fellow inmate. The glasnost difference? The star is strikingly handsome, and is shot throughout (often barechested) in fashion-magazine poses, with lighting and photography to match. GQ goes to the Gulag.

After *Inoi,* a surprisingly polished Czechoslovakian comedy, *Cas Sluhu,* whose French title is *Le Temps des Larbins.* (I look up *larbin:* "flunky.") Like *Turne,* it's a study in romantic fixation and betrayal. Dumped by her beau, a neurotic young Prague woman named Dana

(Ivana Chylkova) cajoles a friend's docile boyfriend, Milan (Karel Roden), into marriage. She ends up living very well, with a maid, a car, and a regular schedule of dinner parties. Yet she's unsatisfied—and thoroughly ungrateful to Milan, whom she tortures with sadistic mind games and ultimately betrays. It's a fine film—its tone just right, its psychology convincing. And Miss Chylkova is first-rate: though her character might have come off as completely unsympathetic, she makes one pity Dana even as one laughs at her frantic, flagrant selfishness. It's a part you could see a young Shirley MacLaine playing.

Monday, May 14

At 8:30 a.m. to Bertrand Tavernier's *Daddy Nostalgie.* The story is simple: after a heart attack, the elderly Daddy (Dirk Bogarde), English by birth, returns from the hospital to his Côte d'Azur villa and his tight-lipped French wife, Miche (Odette Laure), to whom he complains: "You never speak English to me anymore." Knowing that his days are numbered, his middle-aged daughter Carolyn (Jane Birkin), a screenwriter, comes down from Paris for a few days. The film chronicles her visit with intelligence and compassion, splendidly capturing the rhythms of the family's lives and the textures of their relationships. (It's appropriate that we see Daddy reading *To the Lighthouse,* a novel that does much the same thing for another seaside family.)

Daddy and Carolyn make an interesting pair. He exudes a tired, gentle elegance, rather reminding one of Herbert Marshall in a Somerset Maugham movie. Carolyn is high-strung, easily hurt, and fearful of responsibility; she has a child's desperate need to know whether Daddy still loves her mother (the household bilingualism serves as an apt symbol of their marital near-estrangement), and her memory of his neglect during her childhood still stings. "I don't give a damn about your great beautiful life," Carolyn snaps when he waxes nostalgic. "It's a beautiful selfish life." Yet mostly they're simpatico. Daddy observes that they share "a great talent for life," and warns her that "the sweetness of life is terribly perishable." She tells him he was a "ghastly" father, but adds: "You make me laugh—and dream."

A promising setup. But Tavernier (*A Sunday in the Country, Round Midnight*) doesn't do enough with it. After a certain point the film doesn't go anywhere or change pitch; there's simply not enough drama. The particulars, too, often seem arbitrary. Daddy shows

Carolyn a villa (in Cannes!) and tells her a story about it; it's a nice scene, but doesn't resonate with anything else or advance the plot. The film closes with one of my favorite songs, "These Foolish Things," and the rendition by Birkin's untrained voice has an extremely sweet quality. But its use here is thoroughly sentimental: Tavernier is trying to force a degree and kind of emotion on the film that it hasn't earned—and, for that matter, hasn't seemed to be aiming for.

Flaws notwithstanding, though, I'd see *Daddy Nostalgie* again in a minute. It's a human film—honest, wise, serious. Denis Lenoir's cinematography is breathtaking; the beautiful soft lighting and muted orange-and-blue Côte d'Azur palette are utterly appropriate to the film's gentle, pensive tone. And the performances are marvelously sensitive and discerning: Jane Birkin, who's familiar to French audiences but almost unknown in the U.S., is very touching as the brittle, ardent Carolyn; Dirk Bogarde does a masterly job of capturing Daddy's sad, remote dignity, his spiritual and physical fragility, his matter-of-fact egoism and his quiet air of regret.

The press conference for *Daddy Nostalgie* proves to be the most literate and lively thus far, and the most free of political cant. The movie's ensemble feeling carries over. Tavernier says it's about a failure who "discovers through his daughter what he's lost." But this seems to be claiming too much.

At 2:30 to the English director Ken Murray's *1871*. Ghastly. I walk out after about a half hour, and I'm not the first to do so.

Tuesday, May 15

Reading Cannes pieces in several French publications, I notice that the word *americain* generally carries with it an automatic sneer. Interesting footnote: Maurice Huleu, reviewing *Daddy Nostalgie* in *Nice-Matin,* writes that Bogarde is "right out of a Somerset Maugham novel."

Today's morning film: *Night Sun,* a remarkable work directed by Paolo and Vittorio Taviana, whose *Padre Padrone* won the Palme d'Or in 1977. The new film, based on Tolstoy's story "Father Sergius," concerns a virtuous young baron (Julian Sands) who, upon learning that his fiancée was the czar's mistress, becomes a monk, then a hermit. He struggles against fleshly temptations; yet in his proud aloofness he is guilty of vanity, learning ultimately that service to God demands not isolation from but involvement with mankind. Ironically, the movie itself keeps a certain distance from its subject.

Yet it's a thoughtful film, dignified and deliberate; there's a nice symmetry, too, to the trinity of temptresses (Nastassja Kinski, Charlotte Gainsbourg, Patricia Millardet) whose brushes with Sergius drive him, step by step, from human contact. Appropriately, the color is lush, the lighting radiant, the camerawork stately (no jerky movements, no abrupt cuts): the Tavianis render church, palace, and nature alike as holy places, as if to repudiate Sergius's Spartan outlook, his concentration on otherworldly things. At the press conference afterwards, the Tavianis justly describe the film as a brief for "religion without religiosity," for faith in what takes place between people, for recognition of the miracle of love and the mystery in all things. Funny to hear all this talk of faith and love and humility while photographers crowd the dais, shoving past each other to get a good shot of Nastassja Kinski.

Later, at a sidewalk cafe, I overhear three Ivy Leaguers. Turns out they're earning college credit by attending screenings here.

Wednesday, May 16

On the flight back to New York I plunk down my twenty francs and watch *Back to the Future, Part Two*. Its production values make, say, *Rodrigo D.* look primitive. Yet, compared to films like *Daddy Nostalgie* and *Night Sun,* how slick it seems, how spiritually hollow—all special effects and no human content to speak of. Are the French right, then, about American movies? No, not so long as a *Driving Miss Daisy* can get made and become a hit. This thought comforts me. I fall asleep about half an hour into the picture and awaken to find the window shades up and the sun streaming in.

Further Thoughts

What Ever Happened to Doris Day?

It happened all at once—or so, at least, it seemed to me at the time. Throughout my tender years, the movies as I knew them had been summed up in the single glorious and inviolate image of Doris Day. Yes, there were the wondrous, sentimental Disney cartoons, the most memorable of them being *Bambi* and *Lady and the Tramp* (both of which my mother dutifully took me to see in re-release); there were the predictably dopey live-action Disney movies with such cutesy titles as *The Absent-Minded Professor* and *That Darn Cat;* and there was *The Wizard of Oz,* which (like everyone else my age) I watched every year on CBS—but these were movies for *kids,* a distinction that we all understood at an early age. On the more grown-up end of the scale, there was (till 1962, anyway) Marilyn Monroe—but Norman Mailer hadn't yet gotten around to explaining to us her Cosmic Significance, and in any case my mother didn't take me to see Marilyn. She took me to see Doris.

To be sure, Doris frequently went under the name of Julie Andrews or Debbie Reynolds, and sometimes she even dyed her hair, acted a bit more genteel, and called herself Audrey Hepburn. But it was always Doris, perky and well-bred and wholesome, appealing but not coarsely seductive, often cosmopolitan but never rich or snooty, who personified the movies for me; it was Doris who sanguinely inhabited that respected territory between good-time girl and old maid (for the movies in those days made it clear to us that it was pitiful, if not disastrous, for a woman to be either), Doris who expertly fended off advances, in one congenial sex comedy after another, from the likes of Clark Gable, Gary Grant, and Rock Hudson (for the movies made it clear, too, that all men were by nature wolves, unless there was something wrong with them), Doris who elegantly and entertainingly managed the game of courtship in such a way that she would inevitably, at the end of the picture, win that man, that home, that wedding ring (for the movies made it clear that it was every woman's task to maneuver a good man into a marriage he may not have sought—which was, after all, for his own good as well as hers). And it was Doris, too, who time and again played the perfect middle-class American wife and mother—a doctor's wife (what else?) who'd sacrificed her singing career for husband and family in *The Man Who Knew Too Much* (1956); another doctor's wife who (again for husband and family) gave up her job as a TV-commercial pitchwoman in *The Thrill of It All* (1963).

Then, all at once—or, as I say, so it seemed to the late-baby-boom child that I was—everything was different. Suddenly Elizabeth Taylor was getting a lot of attention for braying dirty words in *Who's Afraid of Virginia Woolf?* (1966). Suddenly there were movies—foreign movies, *Danish* movies—playing in our local theater that took love-making a good deal further than the ardent looks and merry badinage that passed between Doris and Rock in the first movie my mother had ever taken me to, *Pillow Talk* (1959). I didn't know much, at the time, about the events that formed the background to these developments—among them, the rise of TV and the concomitant collapse of the studio system in Hollywood; the influence of Italian neo-realism and of the French *nouvelle vague*, alongside whose finer fruits many of the products of Doris and company suddenly looked timid and synthetic; the slow disintegration of the once-mighty censorial power of what had been called first the Hays Office and then the Breen Office (whose code had insisted, among other things, that even husband-and-wife characters couldn't share a bed, and that wrongdoing must always be punished by the last reel); the watershed event that was Maggie McNamara's employment of the formerly *verboten* word "virgin" in Otto Preminger's *The Moon is Blue* way back in 1953. Nor did I realize that Doris herself had been the queen regnant of a transitional epoch in American motion pictures, that the remarkable combination of charm, wit, obsessively sophomoric naughtiness, and mawkish moralizing that had characterized so many of her pictures reflected a Hollywood in somewhat muddled passage from one way of rendering the world to another. Indeed, it took one further event—the rise to majority of the baby boomers—to bring an end to the muddle and to deliver American movies to a New World's not-so-bright shores.

Landfall came with *The Graduate.* I for one didn't encounter it till years later when it came to television, but upon its theatrical release in 1967, every teenager I knew went to see it at least once and talked about nothing else for weeks. And it *was* an entertaining picture. But what inspired such extraordinary enthusiasm on the part of these teens? Mostly this: *The Graudate* made a hero of someone close to their own age—a rare thing for an American movie to do in those days—and made dolts of the grown-ups. The movie laughed at the whole *idea* of being a grown-up (a responsible one, anyway), laughed at the whole idea of making a career, of becoming a useful part of The System.

The most famous line in *The Graduate*—perhaps the most famous line in any movie of the Sixties, for that matter—is the one-word bit of career advice given by Murray Hamilton's Southern-California-businessman Mr. Robinson to Dustin Hoffman's just-graduated-from-Harvard Benjamin: "Plastics." The line got a big laugh way back then from the picture's baby-boom audience, and it continues to get big laughs every time a couple of hundred baby boomers pack into a revival house to see the movie again. And in context, the line *is* sort of amusing. But not *that* amusing. The laugh's supposed to be on Mr. Robinson for pronouncing the word in such a reverential whisper: imagine thinking about plastics this way, imagine consecrating your life to it! But what, one must ask, has Benjamin got planned that's so much better? Sure, he's brilliant, or so we're told—but what sign does he show of it? He never says or does or creates anything brilliant. He floats in the family swimming pool. He responds with numb condescension to the compliments of his parents and their friends, all of whom consider him a Golden Boy. He's empty, anomic, uninspired. Who *better* to spend a lifetime in plastics? Besides, plastics was the sort of field in which you could've imagined Doris working in one of her career-gal roles. (After all, she'd worked with computers in *That Touch of Mink,* at a pajama factory in *The Pajama Game,* in advertising in *Lover Come Back.*) And if plastics was good enough for Doris, then why wasn't it good enough for Dustin?

But the army of Prosperity Children who lined up for *The Graduate* didn't see it that way. Endlessly pampered by their Depression-Children parents—by dads who were earning several times more than *their* dads ever had, and by homemaker moms who had diligently read their Dr. Spock—these kids, the most privileged generation in the history of the world, were now in their teens and had begun to feel that movies should not be about people like their folks (who were, in any case, staying home and watching TV most of the time now) but should be for and about *them*. Like Benjamin—and like most young people raised in peace and comfort and abundance—these baby boomers believed fervently in their own importance, believed in their superiority to the bourgeois modalities which had helped make that peace and comfort and abundance possible, and believed, too, that the movies should reflect their own ready-made, glibly seditious attitudes about life, love, and the world around them. Never mind that those attitudes were jejune and narcissitic, and that these kids didn't really know a damn thing about the world around them: *The Graduate* made money. Those kids—rewarding it generously for its implicit endorsement of their *Weltanschauung*—made it the highest-grossing picture since *The Sound of Music* two years earlier. And they made Dustin—no Captain von Trapp, he—a star. A star! America had never seen anything like it. For Dustin wasn't anything like Doris's leading men. He was not only no Captain von Trapp. He was no Gable, no Grant, no Hudson. Dustin was short, Dustin was homely, Dustin didn't know how to dress or make scintillating small talk, Dustin was congenitally awkward and unsuave. But suddenly that didn't seem to matter anymore. Suddenly the movies, as they had been, were fading fast. The reception of pictures like *The Graduate* had helped Hollywood producers to realize that the grown-up audience for theatrical films had diminished dramatically, and that there was therefore a smaller market than ever before for Doris Day-type fare—let alone for the sort of literate comedies and dramas in which actresses like Bette Davis, Katharine Hepburn, Jean Arthur, Irene Dunne, and Rosalind Russel had once starred. No, the target audience for theatrical films now consisted principally of young people—namely, the overpopulated, overindulged, just-edging-out-of-its-minority baby-boom generation, who had more leisure time and pocket money than any previous generation of American youngsters, who were more *aware* of themselves as a generation, and who were unabashedly eager to see themselves celebrated on the screen, their lifestyles glorified, their manners and morals lionized. So it was that a star such as Julie Andrews turned anachronistic overnight—her manner being simply too decorous, her appearance too tidy, and her singing voice too removed in timbre from that insolent Jim Morrison/Janis Joplin raspiness—for the comfort of many baby boomers. And so it was, too, that Doris (herself no Janis Joplin) hastily effected, in 1968, an escape to TV.

And just in time too, for the next year saw not only the return of Dustin in *Midnight Cowboy*—the first A-budget picture to get an X rating, and the first X-rated picture to win an Academy Award for Best Picture of the Year—but also the advent of Peter Fonda and Dennis Hopper in *Easy Rider*. The scuzzy, undomesticated protagonists of these pictures could hardly have been more different from polished gents like Clark Gable and Cary Grant. And that, of course, was the whole idea: these were characters that baby boomers could "identify with." They were "free." They'd "dropped out" of a corrupt society, a *plastic* society. Yet what did they have to offer in its place? "Do your own thing," they said. Yet in these movies, and others like them, they all were doing exactly the same thing—goofing off, abusing controlled substances, wandering aimlessly across America. They claimed to be creating a new society, but they didn't put much serious thought into it. As Ned Rorem wrote at the time, "the freedom of the easy riders is no more self-questioning, no less assembly-line than the conformism of the fifty annual Miss America contestants." Pictures like *Easy Rider* didn't encourage independence on the part of their young viewers; they fostered imitation. They provided baby boomers with a dress code, a vocabulary, a primer of attitudes. And their arrival marked the beginnings of something else, too: a new, distinctly baby-boomer attitude toward movies.

For *Easy Rider* and its ilk weren't primarily out to entertain: weak on story and character and dialogue, they sought rather to embody the vapid slogans of Youth Culture, to epitomize the politically correct generational attitudes toward Life (which, for the baby boomers, generally meant lifestyles), toward Politics and Culture, toward War and Peace. And most baby boomers ate it all up. Had their parents, in Thirties and Forties, ever asked for or been served such shrill, facile fare? Not really. There *had* been stark, socially conscious pictures during the Depression (among them, of course, such estimable movies as *The Grapes of Warth* and *I Am a Fugitive from a Chain Gang*), and during World War II there'd been the occasional flagrant piece of propaganda (such as Lillian Hellman's awful *The North Star*). But for the most part, moviegoers in the Thirties and Forties didn't get or want strident, self-righteous politics or sociology in their movies.

And why *would* they have wanted it? During the Thirties and Forties, the world was a tough place; moviegoers *knew* it was a tough place; they didn't need or want to be lectured about this state of affairs by, of all people, sheltered, affluent Hollywood writers and directors. In times of depression and war, what an affront that would have been! Movies (everybody knew) weren't serious, they were entertainments; life itself was too serious a proposition for movies to be taken seriously as a reflection of it. With the rare exception of a film like *Citizen Kane*—whose artistic ambition and extraordinary merit clearly placed it in another category altogether from the usual deft diversions—serious-minded people didn't take movies *seriously,* as they did literature and the fine arts.

At the same time, however, moviegoers of the Thirties and Forties did expect the movies themselves to take certain things—religion, chastity, and patriotism among them—very seriously. And justly so. For escaping temporarily from one's own life into the world of a movie didn't mean escaping from morality; it didn't mean renouncing, even for a moment, the ethical standards by which one lived that life. Nor did it mean being encouraged to sneer at intelligence, at culture, at the arts. On the contrary, the movies of the Thirties and Forties consistently reflected an understanding that in the real world, real commitment—artistic, social, political, or otherwise—involved not only rhetoric but hard work and sacrifice. Philistine though those movies often were, they at least tended to bow respectfully whenever real art—or, for that matter, real greatness of any kind—came within their purview, erring (as they often did) in the direction not of scorn or ridicule but of a preposterous pietism (toward, for instance, Cornel Wilde's Chopin, Fredric March's Mark Twain, Greer Garson's Madame Curie, Paul Muni's Juarez). In those days, American movies routinely and unapologetically celebrated great men and women and their accomplishments.

Granted, the Thirties and Forties were a time of prudish, reactionary production codes which made it impossible to tackle certain aspects of life honestly, and which—had those codes remained in effect in later decades—would have obstructed the production of some of the better films of recent years (e.g., *After Hours* and *Blue Velvet*). Yet, for all their failings, these codes frequently (if unintentionally) served a constructive purpose: for their very existence obliged writers and directors to find subtler, more elliptical—and therefore often more sophisticated and witty—ways of handling sex, violence, and the like than they might otherwise have chosen to adopt. (Check out the banter, for instance, in such movies as *The Palm Beach Story, His Girl Friday,* and *Mr. Blandings Builds His Dream House.*) Inadvertently, in other words, the censors' edicts strongly enforced the fundamental idea that art often lies in implication, sexual allure in suggestion.

By contrast, the rise to majority of the baby-boomer generation ushered in an era of movies that were bluntly, numbingly literal-minded—movies often free of implication and explicit to the point of witlessness. Though increasingly candid about sex (displaying to us, in the "breakthrough" 1972 film *Last Tango in Paris,* a fat, aging Marlon Brando writhing nakedly atop one Romy Schneider), the movies were robbed of sexiness; while increasingly graphic in their violence (showing us, in the "groundbreaking" 1974 picture *Death Wish,* the unprecedentedly brutal and bloody murder of Hope Lange, who was the very *image* of Doris), they came to depend, in many cases, more on sensationalism than on thoughtfully conceived emotional conflict for their dramatic impact. While movies ceased, moreover, to take such things as religion, chastity, and patriotism very seriously, baby boomers—who have always been good at being shallow about important things and deadly serious about frivolous things—began to take the movies themselves quite seriously indeed.

More and more frequently, as the Sixties shaded into the Seventies, baby boomers went to the movies looking not for dreams but for truths. But they didn't want just *any* truths: they wanted truths that flattered them, that were simple to digest, that didn't challenge their minds or assumptions, that confirmed their sense of their specialness and that confirmed also the corruption of the System, the emptiness of its values, and the awfulness of their parents (who, after all, personified that System, those values). Like so many turn-of-the-century American Naturalistic novelists, moreover, the baby boomers often tended to equate truth with sordidness, with brutality, with inarticulateness. Wit? Fluency? These were forms of oppression. High culture? Anti-democratic. Screenwriters who had written movies for decades found themselves being told, in the 1970s, that their dialogue was "too uptown"—too artful, too polysyllabic. Systematically, movie producers dumbed-down the flicks, purged them of regard for intelligence and sophistication. The handsome bourgeois heroes of earlier decades gave way to homely bohemian anti-heroes; comely, cultured leading men largely evaporated from the scene (their breed continuing to be represent mainly by Redford and Newman), and in their place rose an army of Dustins, Elliott Goulds, Al Pacinos, and Jack Nicolsons. When well-dressed, well-bred, well-spoken, and well-adjusted citizens did surface in movies of the late Sixties and Seventies, it was generally as villains or fools; their very cultivation was understood to brand these men as sinister or silly.

The rules that these movies followed were in their own way as strict as those of the Breen and Hays offices: a hero could be a hooker (like Jon Voight in *Midnight Cowboy* or Jane Fonda in the 1971 *Klute* or Richard Gere in the 1980 *American Gigolo*) but never an artist; he could be a borderline-psychopathic patient in a state mental hospital (like Jack Nicholson in the 1974 *One Flew over the Cuckoo's Nest*) but never a physician or research scientist in the same hospital. If you *did* dare to make a movie about something as hoity-toity as, say, a classical composer, you had to be sure to make a total jerk out of him—as Tom Hulce did with Mozart in *Amadeus* (1984)—or else worry that nobody would like him. Likewise, if you had a character who was identified in any way with the System—say, a senatorial candidate (like Redford in the 1972 *The Candidate*), a detective (Nicholson in the 1974 *Chinatown*), or a CIA agent (Redford in 1975 *Three Days of the Condor*)—you had to be sure that by the end of the picture he was thoroughly disenchanted with the whole shooting match. But it was even better to have as a hero somebody who was completely at odds with the System, however inane (or even insane) his reasons for his opposition, however barbarous his means of enacting it. There had always been movies that made heroes of gentlemen burglars and the like (*Raffles, The Law and the Lady, To Catch a Thief*), but now we were given a spate of pictures celebrating truly murderous, amoral criminals, most prominently *Bonnie and Clyde* (1976) and *The Godfather* (1972).

Even as all these outrageous new ethical guidelines were taking hold in Movieland, baby boomers who'd gone off to college were learning from their hipper humanities professors (many of whom had been specially trained in that brave new discipline known as Popular Culture) that film (not "movies" anymore) was *the* art form of the century—precisely because it was the most *populistic* art form. Its potent accessibility, they explained, was its glory; the fewer barriers a film placed between itself and the Common Man, the better. Yet these profs—and, within a few years (and in far greater numbers), their baby-boom pupils—took to explicating some of the more uncomplicated specimens of this most accessible of genres as if they were as intricately layered with meanings as *Hamlet:* periodicals with titles like *Sight and Sound, Film Literature Quarterly,* and *Cinema Journal* soon littered the academic landscape. And as baby boomers themselves gradually advanced into the august ranks of the pop-culture professoriate, film study came to be taken for granted as a serious intellectual discipline, and its pipe-smoking, tweed-wearing practitioners—who applied their critical gifts to sober, heavily footnoted essays on such subjects as "The 'Liberated' Heroine of Recent Hollywood Films" and "Woody Allen's Comic Use of Gastronomy"—came to be accepted as legitimate educators alongside the professors of classics and history.

What's important here is that those footnote-heavy essays reflected more than just a reaction to academic publish-or-perish pressures: they mirrored a new baby-boomer seriousness about movies. It was a seriousness that was reflected, more prominently, in the writings of Pauline Kael, who, after being hired as a regular film critic by *The New Yorker* in 1967, quickly became to many moviegoing "intellectuals" of the baby-boom generation rather what Edmund Wilson had been to their more literary-minded counterparts of a generation earlier. In her long, intense, often spontaneous-seeming reviews, Kael enthusiastically endorsed off-the-cuff, experimental movies like Robert Altman's *McCabe & Mrs. Miller* (1971), *Thieves Like Us* (1974), and *Nashville* (1975) for their crude vitality, while condemning more literate and accomplished films for their excessive polish and professionalism—thereby lending a profound air of legitimacy to the already widespread baby-boom preference of spontaneity to craft, of the visceral to the intellectual, of the raw to the *raffiné*. The staid columns of *The New Yorker* and the suppleness of her own prose helped to disguise the degree to which Kael's terms of praise and putdown were, in the annals of serious criticism, genuinely grotesque: while Julie Andrews (as Kael declared in a typical critique) was "infuriatingly sane," Nick Nolte was an "ideal screen actor" because of his "rough edges," and Matt Dillon excelled because, having absolutely no acting technique to encumber him, he allowed viewers to "feel they're in direct contact with this luminous kid." Altman, one of her favorite directors, earned this honor by being "recklessly original"; similarly, a movie won her praise for its "likable sloppiness." Reckless, rough, sloppy, uncivilized: in Kael's lexicon, such words became the chief terms of praise.

Though herself no baby boomer, Kael vividly mirrored baby-boomer tastes and assumptions and (in turn) exerted an extraordinary influence upon the ways in which baby boomers, in the Seventies and Eighties, came to think and talk about movies. Kael had a lot to do, in fact, with the widespread repudiation by baby boomers of the distinction between movies and high culture: if there had been a time when one was expected to know something about current poetry, theater, and art in order to be recognized as a serious cultured person, there came a time when all that one had to do was to be able to quote Pauline Kael on the latest James Bond picture. In bestowing the *New Yorker* badge of seriousness upon even the junkiest of pop movies—movies about which, time and again, she wrote in a rhapsodic tone, and at an epic length, that would be more appropriate to a critical discussion of, say, Proust—Kael freed a million upwardly mobile baby boomers from the oppressive notion that they had to know anything about *real* culture to be intellectually respectable. It should be no surprise, then, that Kael served as *the* model for many of the baby-boom generation's most influential movie critics.

How things were changing! Hollywood had always made movies about young people—but never had there been so many, and never had they *glorified* young people so much. Andy Hardy had, after all, always learned his lessons from Judge Hardy, not the other way around. And he'd hardly been looked upon as representative of a generation. *That* was what was different now: the baby boom was the first generation to have movies made about it, as such. And invariably there was less self-criticism in these movies than there was self-celebration. For, cynical and irreverent as baby boomers have always been about everything else, no generation has ever been more brazenly sentimental about itself, about the trashy pop-culture totems of its common childhood, and about its solemnly proclaimed "idealism." Lawrence Kasdan's slick, dishonest *The Big Chill* (1983) gave baby boomers a chance to wax nostalgic about their erstwhile hippiedom—but despite the film's pretense of engagement with ideas about baby-boomerdom, it was essentially an empty orgy of generational self-love and self-congratulation. There was little moral exploration in *The Big Chill,* little attempt to find meaning in the characters' metamorphoses from young rebels into upstanding citizens in their thirties. Mainly, the movie exuded an infantile sense of wonder: "Wow!" it appeared to be saying, "We've turned into grown-ups! And we're *mortal!* Aren't we remarkable!" This shallow picture struck as forceful a note with baby boomers as *Easy Rider* had done fourteen years earlier; and if the earlier movie had seemed to reflect a romantic conceit that baby boomers were the first generation ever to go through puberty and have sex, so *The Big Chill* likewise seemed to reflect an equally romantic conceit that they were the first generation ever to settle down with marriages, houses, careers, and children of their own.

The baby boomers' highly vocal existence had helped induce Hollywood to gear the movies largely toward their sensibilities. But as the Seventies melted into the Eighties, movies increasingly became directed toward an even younger generation—namely, toward the baby boomers' own small sons and daughters. Having abandoned the adult for the teenage audience in the late Sixties, Hollywood turned ten or fifteen years later to the even younger pre-teen market. And these movies were largely the products of baby-boom writers, directors, producers, and studio executives—the products of people who (unlike their counterparts of old) had grown up on TV and talkies and consequently appeared to comprehend life, to a disturbing extent, in rudimentary visual terms.

Accordingly, it was the distinctively filmic virtues that tended to receive the most attention in these movies. Almost invariably, baby-boom moviemakers (many of whom were graduated from film schools) are masters of film technique; but their ability to write (or at least select) good scripts is far less impressive. They don't seem to realize the importance of a well-written script, don't seem to know anything about dramatic construction, don't seem capable of telling good dialogue from bad. The sure grasp of dramaturgical rules that one used to be able to count on in major-studio movies is nowadays largely absent from all but the very best Hollywood films; what's perhaps even harder to find are successful screenwriters who have a feel for language, who can write dialogue as clever and playful and literate as that which Anita Loos, Billy Wilder, Ben Hecht, and Preston Sturges (among many others) once did. It's astonishing: whereas studio chiefs once sought out the talents of the foremost serious novelists and playwrights, nowadays baby boomers who have never even *read* anything serious can enjoy highly successful careers as scriptwriters. And whereas the effectiveness of movies once relied mainly on compelling, well-thought-out, and cleverly written stories about human relationships, it now often depends quite heavily on wide-screen location cinematography, on loud, Dolby-ized rock scores, and on special effects courtesy of International Light & Magic. With the advent of baby-boomer moviemakers, the dramatic content of American movies—and, therefore, the *human* content, the *conceptual* content—has withered drastically.

Consequently one has the impression, at times, that the minds of most baby-boom moviemakers have been expertly trained to process nothing but images. At least one obvious reason, in fact, why these moviemakers so often execute elaborate "hommages" to their celebrated predecessors (a practice pioneered largely by pre-boomer Peter Bogdanovich, born 1939, in such efforts as the 1972 Thirties-style screwball comedy *What's Up Doc*) is that they don't really have sensibilities of their own. When a baby-boomer movie does get political, moreover, what it customarily amounts to is a dose of facile, Politically Correct piety about race, war, gender, Big Business, nuclear power, the environment. Often such movies come accompanied by powerful visceral imagery (e.g., the battle scenes in *Platoon*) and Sixties-peace-movement nostalgia (e.g., Joan Baez singing "Amazing Grace" at the end of *Silkwood*). But they tend to originate less from a genuine sense of political commitment than from a desire, on the moviemakers' part, to assume a fashionable posture of "sensitivity" (which often means insensitivity to thoughtful distinctions); and if they have a clearly defined goal, it would apparently be less to shed light on the human condition than to give baby-boom filmgoers a chance to feel virtuous. Indeed, in an era when concerts, picnics, Hands Across America-type displays, and Sunday-afternoon marches down Fifth Avenue are regarded as serious political acts, attending movies—certain movies, anyway—likewise often qualifies, in enlightened baby-boom circles, as a manifest demonstration of liberal virtue.

Yet baby-boomer liberalism is a frivolous affair. In the average baby-boomer-made film, there's little sense that anything is really worth striving for except fame, sex, money, and athletic victory. One movie after another—among them John Hughes's *Ferris Bueller's Day Off* and Paul Schrader's *Risky Business*—presents, with patent admiration and with only the most superficial irony, a hero who combines a reckless, narcissistic, *Easy Rider*-ish antipathy for bourgeois norms and obligations with a frank appetite for bourgeois comforts. Nor is there much evidence, in contemporary movies, of a curiosity about history (how, after all, *could* history be interesting? *We* weren't there): whereas the Thirties and Forties saw the production of hundreds of historical dramas, hardly any baby-boomer-created movies are set in earlier time periods, unless the protagonist travels there by means of a wacky time machine. Meanwhile, there are comedies galore—generally in the *Meatballs-Stripes-Caddyshack* vein—but little wit; as a rule, their humor is banal and empty and visual, aimed at childish minds, lacking in the charm and cleverness of such typical Thirties and Forties comedies as *Ninotchka, The Women, The Awful Truth,* and *The Philadelphia Story*.

As has been demonstrated by Ron Howard's *Splash* (1984) and *Cocoon* (1985), Rob Reiner's *The Princess Bride* (1987), Robert Zemeckis's *Back to the Future* (1985), and Steven Spielberg's *Close Encounters of the Third Kind* (1977), *Raiders of the Lost Ark* (1981), and *E.T.* (1982), many of the top baby-boom directors have a knack—or at least a penchant—for fantasy and adventure. And some of these movies are truly wonderful of their kind. But some—such as *Gremlins, Goonies, Jaws* and its sequels, and the *Ghostbusters* and *Rocky* series—reach a level of aggressive stupidity, of calculated sameness, that few "A"-budget, major-studio movies of the Thirties and Forties did. When baby-boom moviemakers, moreover, try to do sophisticated romantic comedy or "realistic" drama, the results (*When Harry Met Sally, Empire of the Sun*) tend to be insipid, even embarrassing. You get the feeling that when these folks venture beyond the puerile they're on alien territory. What's more, if the movies of the Thirties and Forties often made heroes out of men and women (Zola, Edison, Lincoln) who had made lasting contributions to mankind, today's movies are more likely to glorify the accomplishments of teenage black belts (*Karate Kid*) and exceptional bartenders (*Cocktail*). On the very rare occasion when high culture does enter into the equation, it's generally extolled for shallow baby-boom-style reasons: in *Dead Poets Society*, for instance, poetry is celebrated not for its beauty but for its ability to improve our lifestyles by spurring us to action (poetry, in other words, is News You Can Use).

Ironically, films of the Thirties and Forties which nobody took seriously at the time are now frequently looked upon by baby boomers as if they were high culture. PBS routinely telecasts Thirties and Forties movies such as *It's a Wonderful Life,* as well as gossipy documentaries about the lives of old movie stars such as Gregory Peck and Spencer Tracy; the promotional copy and introductory materials associated with these telecasts would have us believe that these motion pictures and performers comprise the chief monuments of American civilization. (Yet who doubts that if Peck and Tracy came along now, they'd have to content themselves with careers in dinner theater?)

That Spielberg is, unarguably, *the* movie director of the baby-boom generation is supremely fitting. There's a lot to be said for movies like *Close Encounters* and *E.T.* and *Raiders*. But what all these pictures reflect is an extraordinary indifference to the comic and dramatic possibilities of adult life. That Spielberg chose, for example, to make a hero rather than a laughingstock of the pathologically regressive young husband and father in *Close Encounters* was astonishing enough; that so many baby boomers joined Spielberg in identifying with this character (who was played by Richard Dreyfuss) was truly bizarre. Spielberg's preoccupation, here and in his other big box-office movies, with childhood dreams of outer-space visitors and with preposterous, boyishly imagined fears of derring-do is so romantic and obsessive that it would have unsettled Rousseau. These are children's movies for grown-ups; and their well-nigh unparalleled popularity among baby-boomers makes it clear that baby boomers *want* children's movies. Perhaps even more influential than Spielberg, among fellow baby-boom (and post-boom) directors, is the redoubtable John Hughes, who during the past several years has specialized in inane films about high-school children. These pictures—which include *Pretty in Pink, Sixteen Candles, The Breakfast Club,* and *Ferris Bueller's Day Off*—represent an eerie accomplishment: the work of a man who seems completely (and quite happily) in sync with the mentality of a fifteen-year-old, and who apparently feels no compulsion to bring grown-up ironies or insights (à la *The Catcher in the Rye*) to bear. Hughes is, indeed, a perfect symbol of what would appear—so far, anyway—to be the baby boom's principal cinematic legacy to the generations that follow: namely, a consummate and abiding immaturity.

Novel to Film

The World According to Garp

No film of recent years has received a smaller proportion of the attention and admiration that it deserves, whether from critics or the viewing public, than George Roy Hill's *The World According to Garp*. This amazing film, which is about nothing less than what it means to be human, had the misfortune to be released in a year when everyone in America seems to have forgotten what it means to be human. *Time* named the Computer the "Man of the Year"; the movie public fell in love not with Garp, but with E.T. That humans can be as fascinating as hardware is fast becoming an outdated notion.

The film, scripted by Steve Tesich, is of course based on John Irving's novel about the struggles of T. S. Garp—writer, wrestler, husband, and father—against the brutal destructive forces of life. Garp, in Irving's book, is an all-too-mortal Everyman, at war with the Undertoad, the symbolic embodiment of the omnipotent supernatural entity that lies in wait to crush us all. The book has many funny, happy moments, but as it progresses, things become bleaker and bleaker, and a profound pessimism asserts itself, until by the end there is an overpowering sense of doom. "Life can be sublime," the book tells us, "but it is also unpredictable and cruel." Readers loved the novel for its humor, for its offbeat characters and witty dialogue, for its picaresque format and its quixotic protagonist. Garp, the tilter against windmills, became a cult hero.

Hill's film retains the thematic materials of Irving's book, but goes around and looks at them from the other side. If Irving's theme is "Life can be sublime, but it is also unpredictable and cruel," Hill's theme is "Life can be unpredictable and cruel, but it is also sublime." The reversal makes all the difference. Whereas Irving gives us Garp *vs.* Life, Hill gives us Garp *qua* Life. Or, if you prefer, Garp *in* Life, the way some people are in love. If the novel is cynical, the film is sentimental. But it is a sentiment tied to a comprehensive view of things, and a creative faculty which knows exactly how to mold the materials of *Garp* to the needs of its own somewhat different intentions. Hill, unlike Irving, refuses to see the good and bad aspects of existence as attributes of different entities. The happiness and sadness in life, his film tells us, are intimately connected. They are part of the same whole. Everything is part of everything else; we are all part of each other. Frank Capra's *It's a Wonderful Life* has the same theme, and Hill's film resembles it in many particulars.

Both versions of *Garp* have been interpreted as political statements. Such readings, particularly in the case of the film, miss the point. For Hill's film, even more than Irving's novel, is meant to remind us that we are not mere sociological statistics or partisans of particular ideologies, but people—confused, complicated, here to make the best we can of ourselves, of this world, and of each other between the time we are born and the time we die. The only political statement the film makes is that political statements are limited, that to make a political ideal the center of your life is to deny life. The film tells us that people do not become heroes by dedicating themselves to pure, deathless, precisely formulated ideals, like John Reed or Gandhi. They become heroes by dedicating themselves to Life itself—a Life which is not simply one of evil and destruction, but which is the essence of contradiction: cursed by mortality, yes, but also much blessed, in particular by the human power of creation.

Though it may seem foolish to think of Hill's film in connection with *Ulysses*, perhaps the twentieth century's single greatest work about what it means to be human, about Life, the sublime and the contradictory, I propose to put them together for a while. The film itself seems to suggest this connection. *Ulysses*, in its Modern Library edition, is the book Helen Holm (Mary Beth Hurt), Garp's future wife, is reading when she meets Garp (Robin Williams). Like *Ulysses*, Hill's *Garp* contains elaborate patterns of signification which punctuate this theme of Life as the essence of contradiction. Some of these patterns are borrowed from the novel, and some are not; all, however, are successfully translated into cinematic terms, and are intensified in accordance with Hill's thematic intentions.

One of these patterns we may call the *creation* pattern. It is, to be sure, important in the novel. Sexual reproduction and writing, in Irving's book, are both forms of creation, ways by which human beings may hope to achieve a sort of immortality. At the end of the novel, however, the ultimate power of death is affirmed; Irving's last sentence is, "In the world according to Garp, we are all terminal cases." As I have said, Hill turns things around. In the last scene of the film, the helicopter carrying the mortally wounded Garp rises out of the shot (as Redford's plane rises out of the last shot of *The Great Waldo Pepper*, suggesting his death), and a moment later the baby Garp (with whom the picture began, and about whom more presently) rises into the frame and freezes in mid-air. The sky is bright blue, just as bright and blue as in the film's joyous opening shot; the tone is not defeated but uplifting, the implication not one of extinction but of endurance. In some way, the film suggests, Garp lives on—that baby remains pasted in the sky, gurgling and grinning. We may be mortal in one sense, the film tells us, but we endure, in various ways, nonetheless. We live on in what we leave behind—our writings, our children. Garp, author and father, will survive. Like Joyce, Hill offers us comfort in cycles.

The film is full of comforting reminders of this cyclicality, some from the book, most original with the filmmakers. For example, in the film as in the novel, Garp is named after his dead father—the opening lines of the film make a big point of the identification of one with the other—and his baby daughter is named after her grandmother Jenny Fields (Glenn Close). Toward the end of both film and novel, Garp takes over the coaching job once held by his father-in-law, and, as his mother once did for him, checks out classes for his son Duncan (Nathan Babcock).

The film does more than borrow from the book, however. Some of Hill's additions can be classified as "nice touches": for example, a silly joke never heard in the novel is told by several generations of young males in the film: "Why can't basketball players become fathers? Because they dribble when they shoot." In the most gentle way, this recurring line tells us that there will always be young people, there will always be sexual awakening. And there will always be children, learning to talk: Garp's childhood malapropism, "Long

Ranger," found nowhere in the novel, foreshadows those of his son Walt (Ian MacGregor), which do come from the novel.

The connection between writing and sexual reproduction as human acts of creation is made in the book and strengthened greatly in the film. In both the novel and the film, as the male is traditionally the "active" partner in sex, the female passive, so Garp is a writer, Helen a "reader," as she puts it. Jenny Fields, who violates the customary role by being the active partner in Garp's conception, is also a writer.

It is only in the film, however, that Garp and Helen look in on their sleeping sons, and he says: "I'll never write anything that lovely." And it is only in the film that, when the physical and emotional wounds brought on by the death of Walt begin to heal, two things happen: Garp begins writing again, and Helen gives birth to Jenny. Both are events of creation, and signs of a kind of psychological rebirth within the family. Unlike the film, the novel does not bring the Garp family all the way back from the despair—and, on Garp's part, the paranoia—brought on by the accident. Garp's return to writing, in Irving's novel, is, accordingly, not linked with the birth of Jenny; and what comes out of his typewriter is a dark, paranoid work called *The World According to Bensenhaver.* This clearly would not belong in Hill's version of the story; Hill's Garp returns to writing not with *Bensenhaver* but with *Ellen*, an angry but sane book, which demonstrates not Garp's abandonment of faith in Life but his dedication to the good in it. It is as positive, as constructive, as hopeful an event as the birth of Jenny Garp.

Thus, *in the film*, when Garp returns to writing, it is a *cause célèbre.* Duncan, hearing Garp's typewriter upstairs, smiles: "Is Daddy writing again?" Helen is overjoyed. The script (though not the final print) has her saying: "Can spring be far behind?" (A *perfect* reaction, Helen being an English professor.) Appropriately, the return to writing takes place, in the film, around Christmastime—the sound of Garp's typing, in fact, filters downstairs while the family is trimming the Christmas tree. The suggestion of a seasonal cyclicality in human existence could hardly be more firmly—or powerfully, or beautifully, for that matter—set forth. Nor could the parallel between writing and the act of reproduction, the two ways of achieving immortality, be so solidly established.

The film's insistence on the imperishability of man explains, perhaps, why the film, unlike the book, begins just after Garp's birth and ends just before his death. For, in a sense, in the world of this film, whose boundaries lie just short of the boundaries of his life, *Garp never dies*—he always exists. Throughout the picture, he lives. The novel, on the other hand, begins with Jenny Fields's life before Garp's conception, and ends with a long epilogue about "Life After Garp," detailing the ways by which Garp's survivors meander to their separate ends. Thus, while the film plays down Garp's mortality, the novel emphasizes it; in the novel, Garp is only a fact in time.

Likewise, the film's insistence on the transcendence of human creative powers is expressed unforgettably in one brilliant opening image, that of the baby Garp—who is, like any baby, a manifestation of those powers—flying through the air, smiling. On the soundtrack, the Beatles sing "When I'm Sixty-Four"—a very appropriate choice, because its wedding of a bouncy rhythm and jaunty tone to the twin themes of time and love is shared by the film. ("There Will Never Be Another You," the closing song, also deals with these two themes.) The sequence is arresting and beautiful, simultaneously funny and touching, and at once both establishes the focus—the film is about Garp, his life from infancy to death—and sets the proper tone: a baby-fresh fascination with the sheer wonder of life.

Moreover, the opening shot tells us that the film is about Life, about what it means to be human. For the shot deliberately shows us nothing but baby and sky—no clothes, no cars, no Coke machines or deciduous trees or telephone poles. This baby could be anyone, anytime, anywhere. He could be you, he could be me. To be sure, he is a *boy*, and the proof of that is deliberately not hidden from us: for this film is about the miracle of human life, and sexuality is at the center of that miracle.

It is one of the best beginnings a film has ever had. Rarely has a director managed so quickly to win his audience over, to make it laugh and cry, and to hammer it into the proper frame of mind. Rarely, too, has a director of a film adapted from a novel served notice so stunningly that he has made the material his own. For the scene is aggressively cinematic, and establishes the buoyant tone that identifies Hill's vision as utterly different from Irving's.

The seashore setting of Hill's opening sequence is not accidental. Beaches are traditionally symbolic of the boundaries of life. As in the novel, the water which here heralds the beginning of life will later herald the end of it, when little Walt dies in the automobile accident in the rain. In the film, though not in the novel, yet another form of precipitation presages Walt's death: in bed with Garp, Helen reads a story by Michael Milton (Mark Soper) with the oxymoronically foreboding title "Black Snow." Moreover, the association of precipitation with the accident that kills Walt continues, in the film, after the event itself: in the Christmas-tree decorating scene, Duncan, who lost his right eye in that accident, says he'd like to have a glass eye containing snowflakes. (Thus we have another echo of James Joyce: for the Irishman's story "The Dead" is famous for its closing metaphor of snow as death.)

What happens after the baby Garp stops bouncing in the air? Jenny carries her baby into her family house—a house which, being just above the beach, stands on the border between the known and the unknown. It is the womb, and Jenny is the earth mother, who will one day (in the film, though not in the novel) tell Walt that she is "as old as the hills." Pulling her baby out of the sky, she carries him from the beach into the house, and then out into the world. Later in the film, as in the novel, lost and broken women will come to the house for Jenny's maternal love, comfort, and guidance. ("She was our mother, and now we are motherless," Sally Devlin says—*in the film*—at Jenny's funeral. "She was our home, and now we are homeless.") Garp will return, too, when his love for Helen seems decimated, his life destroyed. Jenny will also—in the film, *toujours le film*—tell young Garp (James McCall) about death here, as the two of them stare out to sea.

As Jenny is the earth mother, so Technical Sergeant Garp, now (as in life) a denizen of the heavens, is the sky father, who has sent his son down to earth and set him into his mother's hands. (In the novel, he appears as a living character, and so can never be the supernal figure he is in the film.) This schema will be pointed up further on in the film, when young Garp pouts: "I don't have a father and I can't fly." Jenny replies: "But you have a mother and you can walk."

The imagery can be read in a Christian as well as a pagan sense. Clearly a naked babe, the son of a heavenly father, sailing slowly and mysteriously through the heavens, and then falling into the arms of his almost-virgin mother, evokes Christ and the Madonna. Garp is certainly godlike in his creative power. In his fiction he makes a world of his own, thus the title *The World According to Garp*. Indeed, as the title indicates, the equation between the characters and gods originates in the novel. But it is a notion that is introduced tenuously, only so that it can be undercut by the book's ultimate negativism. In the film, however, Garp's creative powers *are* seen as godlike: while he is putting the story "Magic Gloves" (original with Hill and Tesich) together in his mind, for instance, we see the action of the story on screen without the usual variation in camera technique, or dissolves at beginning and end, to separate the fictive events of the story from the "real" events of *Garp*. The result of this lack of boundaries between the two levels of action is to suggest that Garp's creations are as "real," in some sense, as the events of the film (which, of course, they are)—and thus, in turn, to strengthen the sense that such creations promise a kind of immortality.

And of course, that is the whole purpose of setting up an identity between the characters of the film and divinities: it gives the characters dimension, substance, eternality. It makes them transcendental heroes to match Irving's existential heroes.

To be sure, the film, like the novel, sets up this identity only to qualify it. We can be like gods, the film says, echoing the novel, but only for a time. We are gods that will die, gods that can get hurt. Physical mutilation, often as a representation of psychological mutilation, is ubiquitous in the film, as it is in the novel. Michael Milton loses his penis; Duncan loses an eye; Roberta has been emasculated; the young Garp loses an earlobe to the Percys' dog Bonkers (and, grown up, bites off Bonkers's ear in revenge); Ellen James and the Ellen Jamesians are missing their tongues. All of this comes right out of the novel. So do Duncan's words as he peers through a telescope at the streets of Manhattan from the office of John Wolf (Peter Michael Goetz). "I see a man with one leg," Duncan says. "I see a man with one eye." Broken human beings are all around. "Everyone here is wounded and maimed," Roberta tells Garp at the seaside house (in the film). But—*in the film*—the possibility of injury and the certainty of death do not mean that life is pointless, or that death is the only ultimate reality. "The thing," Jenny tells young Garp after his grandfather's funeral, "is to have a life before we die. It can be a real adventure . . . having a life." This line appears only in the film; there is nothing resembling it in the book.

To live, in Hill's film, is to fly. To be sure, the flying motif is borrowed from the novel, where it symbolizes the sublime parts of life which are undercut by the Undertoad; it becomes much more prominent in the film, however, in which the sublimeness of life is the essence of life. Whereas the mutilation motif—suggestive of mortality—is the more prominent of the two motifs in the novel, the flying motif—suggestive of immortality—predominates in the film. Hill and

Tesich make the young Garp obsessed with airplanes, and with his dead father. There is no suggestion of either of these preoccupations in the novel. Although Jenny has told Garp that his father was a tail gunner (in the novel, a ball turret gunner), he insists, "My father was a flier," and argues just as defiantly that his father may yet be alive. This is never at issue in the novel. Years later, the manuscript of Garp's first story scatters to the winds—flies!—when he jumps out of the way of a car (a symbol of ungovernable danger throughout the film): a suggestion that art—stories, books, films—preserves the experience of life, symbolized by flight, even in the midst of one's exposure to its harshest perils. (The final freeze-frame of the film would seem to suggest the same thing.) This scene is, of course, original with the film; so is a single line of dialogue near the end of the film, when Helen, in a supremely happy moment, asks Garp what he will do with his time in the near future. His grinning reply: he will take up hang gliding. These occurrences of the flight motif are positive ones; another—a negative one—is, not surprisingly, taken from the novel. Garp and Helen are looking over their future house when a plane smashes into it. The event is so preposterous that we laugh. But it is also a reminder that the sublimeness of life—symbolized by flying—can be interrupted at any time, under the most unusual circumstances. And indeed, Walt, Jenny, and Garp all die unusual deaths.

Yet death, in this film, is no existential horror. It is an integral part of a sublime life. The end of the film, which I have already mentioned, is original with Hill and Tesich. Mortally wounded, Garp flies about the Steering School in a rescue helicopter. "I'm flying—ta-ra! Ta-ra!" he tells Helen, apparently joyfully, remembering his childhood fantasies about his father the flier. Like his character Stephen, in the story "Magic Gloves," Garp "feels life as he flies into the arms of death." (This is what Walt feels too, as he "flies" up the driveway—"Ta-ra, ta-ra!"—toward his fate.) Nowhere in his book does Irving even come close to looking upon death so benignly.

Nowhere in the book, either, does Irving suggest the symbolic events of the "dream"—an animated sequence—that young Garp has in the film. In this dream, Garp's father, in a godlike act, bestows the power of flight upon his son (quite appropriately, since flight equals life, and he certainly did give his son that). Then, machine gun in hand, he shoots down a skeleton symbolizing death (yet another godlike act: the subjugation of death). Later, Duncan will wear a skeleton costume similar to the one in the dream. The animated sequence and the live-action scene preceding it are, interestingly, full of phallic imagery, from Garp's drawings of airplanes and machine guns to his reference to the "Long Ranger." (In addition, the script had death, in the animated sequence, rendered as a snake.) This pattern can at least partly be explained by an Oedipal conflict. For Garp's longing for his late father is to a great extent not a desire for his physical presence as a third member of their small family, but a desire for the adult manhood he represents. Garp does not want *him* so much as he wants to *be* him. He wants to fly as his father flew—to experience life, joy, godhead, that is, as his father experienced it. In short, to sleep with his mother.

The Oedipal theme is explored further in the scenes of Garp's childhood. The boy is attracted to wrestling because the school's wrestlers wear the same kind of helmet he imagines his father to have worn. (In the novel, on the other hand, it is Jenny's idea for Garp to become a wrestler.) One night, playing pilot on the Steering infirmary roof, Garp slips and saves himself by catching hold of a rain gutter. Jenny, hearing him call for her, steps out of a window onto a fire escape, grabs his leg, and tells him to let go of the gutter. He does so, and with a superhuman (godlike?) act of strength she holds onto him and saves his life. The gutter snaps off and falls to the ground—actually on top of Dean Bodger (George Ede). It is hard (especially considering that Garp has been playing the part of his father) to avoid interpreting the loose rain gutter as a phallic symbol, and the rescue by his mother, who hugs him and carries him back into the window of the infirmary (like the seaside house, a womb, a place of refuge) as an Oedipal type-scene. One might argue that Garp's Oedipal fixation is carried out to its logical conclusion: he marries a photostat of his mother. Helen resembles Jenny; when she meets Garp she is dressed as sexlessly as Jenny; her last name is a homonym for "home"—a fact upon which Garp comments more than once (and of which the film makes much more than the book). In marrying Helen, Garp perhaps attempts to return to the womb.

Sex plays a key role in *Garp*. It is what binds man and woman together, as wrestling binds man and man and games on the lawn bind father and child. (Perhaps Garp and Roberta hug so much because their relationship does not fit easily into any one of these categories.) Near the end of the film—never in the novel—Garp says to Helen, "It's really nice, you know. To be able to look back and see the arc of your life . . . that it's all connected . . . and see how you got from there to here . . . to see the line, you know. . . ." In *Garp*, the curve of life is plotted against an axis one end of which points toward joy and the other toward tragedy. The line swoops up, but will eventually swoop down, one never knows when. (The difference between the novel and the film is that in the novel, the line is mostly below the horizontal axis; in the film it is above.) The role of sex in *Garp* is best understood in the context of this flux. Sex is a catalyst, capable of directing the arc of one's life sharply downward or upward. The determining factor is Jenny Field's bugaboo: lust. Sex as a function of lust is dangerous—Helen's lust for Michael Milton leads to the accident that kills one of her sons and gouges out the other's right eye. But sex as a function of love is a good thing, the best possible way of people being close and knowing each other. Sex with love produces life; sex without love destroys it. A sexual motive is behind nearly everything, good and bad, that happens in the movie.

We see the results of sex with love in the scene in which Helen tells Garp that she is pregnant. This sequence, completely original with the film, evokes similar sequences in dozens of vintage American movies. One is reminded in particular of *It's a Wonderful Life*, in which Donna Reed (who, like Helen, is in bed) tells James Stewart (who, like Garp, is not) that she is expecting. But the scenes deviate from there on. "George Bailey lassoes stork!" Donna Reed cries in Capra's film. But in Hill's film, there is no talk of storks, or of the baby being in heaven. Hill shows us where the baby is. Garp pulls the sheets down, and we see Helen's belly in closeup. "He's in there, eh?" Garp says. "Boy, oh boy. It's nice in there. I know." He draws the baby's face on Helen's belly, and kisses it. It is a very effective sentimental sequence, in the manner of a movie of forty years ago, yet at the same time refuses to ignore the clinical aspect of the situation the way an American director of forty years ago would have had to do. The sequence, besides establishing Helen's pregnancy and making an intimate moment of it, draws a strong, clear connection between sex and intimacy and reproduction, and thus dramatizes the fact that sexual contact, when tied to love, can lead to wonderful things.

Lust, however, is a different story. To be sure, the filmmakers go to great pains to establish the notion that, although lust may be destructive, it is also natural. In the first episode set at Steering, some boys are drooling over a girlie magazine (one of them, prefiguring Roberta, says, "I wish I was a girl. If I was a girl I'd take off my clothes and stand in front of a mirror and look at myself for hours").

In the same sequence, Jenny has to help one of the boys, who has been playing with himself, free his penis from his zipper. "Leave it alone for a while," she advises. Finally, one of the Steering boys puts the girlie magazine in Garp's crib. "Sick!" Jenny cries, telling the baby Garp to let go of the magazine (as she will later ask the young Garp to let go of the rain gutter). "Even when they're healthy they're sick with lust!" But she seems to accept the fact of lust years later, when she gives Garp money for a whore (Swoosie Kurtz), telling him to do "what you want to do, or what you *have* to do."

Natural or not, however, loveless intercourse leads only to ruin in *Garp*. Helen's affair with Michael leads to the accident in which Walt dies. Garp's youthful adventures with Cushie lead to his murder by her sister, Pooh. "No glove"—i.e., condom—"no love," says Cushie in the film; but her definition of love is different from the film's. Condoms prevent pregnancy and, like the gloves worn by Stephen in Garp's story "Magic Gloves," blunt sensation. What Cushie gives Garp is not love but sex *sans* love—lust; Garp can only experience real love, real life, real joy, with Helen—gloveless, producing babies. Anything else is lust. And it is because of that lust that Garp's world is (as Donald Spoto says of Hitchcock's world) one "permeated with chaos-at-the-ready."

The film's chief symbol of chaos-at-the-ready is the car. This is appropriate, because the climactic accident of the film involves two cars. I have already mentioned the car (in the script, a hearse) that almost hits Garp when he is chasing after Helen with his first story. There is also the pickup that speeds dangerously through Garp's neighborhood. There is Garp's car, which, pulled over to the side of the road to allow Garp to play around with the babysitter (Sabrina Lee Moore) looms in the darkness like—can it be?—an Undertoad (Walt's malapropism for "undertow," which, as I have explained, signifies that unseen power that draws people suddenly and unexpectedly into the maelstrom of tragedy). Later, Garp, in bed with Helen, suggests that they move away because there are "crazy drivers everywhere." Ironically, the crazy driver who will be partly to blame for his family tragedy is Garp himself, whose unorthodox way of entering a driveway makes possible the accident that kills Walt. Of course, cars make possible Michael's seduction of Helen: he fixes her car so it won't start, then offers her a ride in his. (Perhaps, indeed, the school where Garp will die is called Steering because that word reminds us of cars, the instruments of death.)

Each of these symbolic patterns—the motifs of flight and of cars, of love and of lust—is borrowed from Irving's novel, but in every case Hill and Tesich build an imposing and impressive metaphoric structure to serve their own altered thematic purpose. So expertly do they do this that sometimes a line from the novel, transplanted into the film, is given much greater import by virtue of the filmmakers' having added something of their own to the mix. For instance, when the climactic accident is about to happen, Duncan says, "It's like being underwater." Walt adds: "It's like a dream." Both lines are from the novel. But Duncan's comment is far more significant in the film, which has emphasized the thematic equivalence of water with the Great Beyond. And Walt's line, like Duncan's skeleton costume, seen hanging on the back of the boys' door in an earlier scene, hearkens ironically back to the young Garp's dream, in which Garp's father fights and defeats death. The accident demonstrates, as if any demonstration were necessary, that fathers cannot save their sons from death.

A symbolic pattern that seems to be original with Hill and Tesich involves the American flag. I did not notice this until my fourth viewing of the film, and I would not mention it except that it illustrates the fact that nearly every detail in Hill's film seems to be there for a good reason. There is a flag on the flagpole in front of Jenny's seaside house; there is one on a shelf in the living room of the family quarters at Steering, and in the animated dream that young Garp has in that room; there is one on a mysterious boat which Roberta notices in the harbor, shortly before the assassination of Jenny (the Ship of Death, coming across the waters of the Great Beyond to collect her?); and Duncan, decorating the Christmas tree, even suggests getting a glass eye with a picture of the flag on it. The final occurrence of the flag image is the one that all the other occurrences are leading up to: when Jenny is assassinated on the speakers' platform with the New Hampshire gubernatorial candidate, she is surrounded by flags. And when we first see all these flags, a little voice in our subconscious, which has noticed every detail, tells us that something is going to happen here.

Hill's *Garp* is, in short, that paradox of paradoxes. It is at once an adaptation as faithful as any adaptation from one medium to another can be expected to be, or *should* be, and an impeccably crafted personal vision. It is (one cannot avoid the temptation to say it) an inspired and inspiring film.

"You know," Garp says at one point, in a speech that appears only in the film, and which, perhaps, best summarizes the difference between the novel and the film, "sometimes you can have a whole lifetime in a day and not even notice that this is as beautiful as life gets. I had a beautiful life today." One is tempted to read this line as a coy reference by the director to his film. For, in less than a day, the viewer does live a whole lifetime—Garp's—and, after experiencing that life, may well be inclined to subscribe to a somewhat altered version of that statement: this is as beautiful as film gets.